Philip M. Stahl
Leslie M. Drozd
Editors

Relocation Issues
in Child Custody Cases

Relocation Issues in Child Custody Cases has been co-published simultaneously as *Journal of Child Custody*, Volume 3, Numbers 3/4 2006.

Pre-publication
REVIEWS,
COMMENTARIES,
EVALUATIONS . . .

"A VERY VALUABLE COLLECTION of papers that address the complications of relocation issues. . . . The reader will find the kind of comprehensive multidisciplinary thinking that is necessary to apply the research and consider appropriate factors for child custody assessment and decision-making in these complex cases."

Robin M. Deutsch, PhD
Children and the Law Program
Massachusetts General Hospital
and Harvard Medical School

The Haworth Press, Inc.

Relocation Issues in Child Custody Cases

Relocation Issues in Child Custody Cases has been co-published simultaneously as *Journal of Child Custody*, Volume 3, Numbers 3/4 2006.

Monographic Separates from *Journal of Child Custody™*

For additional information on these and other Haworth Press titles, including descriptions, tables of contents, reviews, and prices, use the QuickSearch catalog at http://www.HaworthPress.com.

Relocation Issues in Child Custody Cases, edited by Philip M. Stahl, PhD, and Leslie M. Drozd, PhD (Vol. 3, No. 3/4, 2006). *"A very valuable collection of papers that address the complications of relocation issues. . . . The reader will find the kind of comprehensive multidisciplinary thinking that is necessary to apply the research and consider appropriate factors for child custody assessment and decision-making in these complex cases." (Robin M. Deutsch, PhD, Children and the Law Program, Massachusetts General Hospital and Harvard Medical School)*

Child Custody Litigation: Allegations of Child Sexual Abuse, edited by Kathryn Kuehnle, PhD, and Leslie Drozd, PhD (Vol. 2, No. 3, 2005). *An invaluable resource for forensic mental health professionals involved with conducting custody evaluations in family court proceedings.*

Psychological Testing in Child Custody Evaluations, edited by James R. Flens, PsyD, and Leslie Drozd, PhD (Vol. 2, No. 1/2, 2005). *"An important new addition to the reference material cited routinely by custody evaluators who recognize the value of staying close to the literature in developing their reports. . . . Provides exciting new empirical findings from Janet Johnston and her colleagues, and gives an insightful view of psychological testing from the perspective of a family law attorney. Newcomers to custody work will be impressed with the breadth of material that this book addresses. . . . Key issues in the emerging science of custody evaluation are discussed." (Daniel J. Rybicki, PsyD, DAPBS, Private Practice, Clinical & Forensic Psychology, Agoura Hills, California)*

Relocation Issues
in Child Custody Cases

Philip M. Stahl
Leslie M. Drozd
Editors

Relocation Issues in Child Custody Cases has been co-published simultaneously as *Journal of Child Custody*, Volume 3, Numbers 3/4 2006.

The Haworth Press, Inc.

New York • London • Victoria (AU)
www.HaworthPress.com

Relocation Issues in Child Custody Cases has been co-published simultaneously as *Journal of Child Custody*, Volume 3, Numbers 3/4 2006.

The development, preparation, and publication of this work has been undertaken with great care. However, the publisher, employees, editors, and agents of The Haworth Press and all imprints of The Haworth Press, Inc., including The Haworth Medical Press® and Pharmaceutical Products Press®, are not responsible for any errors contained herein or for consequences that may ensue from use of materials or information contained in this work. With regard to case studies, identities and circumstances of individuals discussed herein have been changed to protect confidentiality. Any resemblance to actual persons, living or dead, is entirely coincidental.

The Haworth Press is committed to the dissemination of ideas and information according to the highest standards of intellectual freedom and the free exchange of ideas. Statements made and opinions expressed in this publication do not necessarily reflect the views of the Publisher, Directors, management, or staff of The Haworth Press, Inc., or an endorsement by them.

Cover design by Lora Wiggins

Library of Congress Cataloging-in-Publication Data

Relocation issues in child custody cases / Philip M. Stahl, Leslie M. Drozd, editors.
  p. cm.
  "Co-published simultaneously as Journal of Child Custody, Volume 3, Numbers 3/4 2006."
  Includes bibliographical references and index.
  ISBN-13: 978-0-7890-3533-2 (hard cover : alk. paper)
  ISBN-10: 0-7890-3533-2 (hard cover : alk. paper)
  ISBN-13: 978-0-7890-3534-9 (soft cover : alk. paper)
  ISBN-10: 0-7890-3534-0 (soft cover : alk. paper)
  1. Custody of children–United States. 2. Moving, Household–United States. 3. Children of divorced parents–Legal status, laws, etc.–United States. I. Stahl, Philip Michael. II. Drozd, Leslie.
KF547.R45 2006
346.7301'73–dc22
                                                                            2006028648

The HAWORTH PRESS Inc.
Abstracting, Indexing & Outward Linking
PRINT and ELECTRONIC BOOKS & JOURNALS

This section provides you with a list of major indexing & abstracting services and other tools for bibliographic access. That is to say, each service began covering this periodical during the the year noted in the right column. Most Websites which are listed below have indicated that they will either post, disseminate, compile, archive, cite or alert their own Website users with research-based content from this work. (This list is as current as the copyright date of this publication.)

Abstracting, Website/Indexing Coverage . . . . Year When Coverage Began

- *Cambridge Scientific Abstracts (a leading publisher of scientific information in print journals, online databases, CD-ROM and via the Internet) <http://www.csa.com>* 2006

- *Child Welfare Information Gateway (formerly National Adoption Information Clearinghouse Documents Database, and formerly National Adoption Information Clearinghouse on Child Abuse & Neglect Information Documents Database) <http://www.childwelfare.gov>* 2006

- *CINAHL (Cumulative Index to Nursing & Allied Health Literature) (EBSCO) <http://www.cinahl.com>* 2006

- *Contents Pages in Education* 2004

- *EBSCOhost Electronic Journals Service (EJS) <http://ejournals.ebsco.com>* 2004

- *Educational Research Abstracts (ERA) (online database) <http://www.tandf.co.uk/era>* 2004

- *Elsevier Eflow-D <http://www.elsevier.com>* 2006

- *Elsevier Scopus <http://www.info.scopus.com>* 2005

- *Family & Society Studies Worldwide (NISC USA) <http://www.nisc.com>* . . . . *

- *Family Index Database <http://www.familyscholar.com>* 2003

(continued)

Bibliographic Access

(continued)

*Special Bibliographic Notes related to special journal issues
(separates) and indexing/abstracting:*

- indexing/abstracting services in this list will also cover material in any "separate" that is co-published simultaneously with Haworth's special thematic journal issue or DocuSerial. Indexing/abstracting usually covers material at the article/chapter level.
- monographic co-editions are intended for either non-subscribers or libraries which intend to purchase a second copy for their circulating collections.
- monographic co-editions are reported to all jobbers/wholesalers/approval plans. The source journal is listed as the "series" to assist the prevention of duplicate purchasing in the same manner utilized for books-in-series.
- to facilitate user/access services all indexing/abstracting services are encouraged to utilize the co-indexing entry note indicated at the bottom of the first page of each article/chapter/contribution.
- this is intended to assist a library user of any reference tool (whether print, electronic, online, or CD-ROM) to locate the monographic version if the library has purchased this version but not a subscription to the source journal.
- individual articles/chapters in any Haworth publication are also available through the Haworth Document Delivery Service (HDDS).

As part of Haworth's continuing committment to better serve our library patrons, we are proud to be working with the following electronic services:

AGGREGATOR SERVICES

EBSCOhost

Ingenta

J-Gate

Minerva

OCLC FirstSearch

Oxmill

SwetsWise

FirstSearch
Oxmill Publishing
SwetsWise

LINK RESOLVER SERVICES

1Cate (Openly Informatics)

CrossRef

Gold Rush (Coalliance)

LinkOut (PubMed)

LINKplus (Atypon)

LinkSolver (Ovid)

LinkSource with A-to-Z (EBSCO)

Resource Linker (Ulrich)

SerialsSolutions (ProQuest)

SFX (Ex Libris)

Sirsi Resolver (SirsiDynix)

Tour (TDnet)

Vlink (Extensity, *formerly Geac*)

WebBridge (Innovative Interfaces)

LinkOut.

ULRICH'S RESOURCE LINKER
$S \cdot F \cdot X$
SerialsSolutions
SirsiDynix
TOUR
extensity
WebBridge

Relocation Issues in Child Custody Cases

CONTENTS

ABOUT THE EDITORS

Philip M. Stahl, PhD, is a psychologist in private practice. He conducts child custody evaluations and provides consultation and expert witness testimony. He is a provider of continuing education for psychologists and other mental health providers, and attorneys and Family Law Specialists in California. He has conducted trainings throughout the United States and internationally for child custody evaluators and others working with high-conflict families of divorce. He has presented workshops for judges throughout the country and is on the faculty of National Judicial College and the National Council of Juvenile and Family Court Judges. Along with his teaching, Dr. Stahl has written extensively on various issues in high-conflict divorce and custody evaluations. He is the author of *Conducting Child Custody Evaluations: A Comprehensive Guide* (Sage, 1994), *Complex Issues in Custody Evaluations* (Sage, 1999), and *Parenting After Divorce* (Impact Publishers, 2000). The California Supreme Court cited his custody evaluation in its recent landmark decision modifying eight years of relocation case law following Burgess (In re Marriage of LaMusga (2004) 32 Cal.4th 1072, 12 Cal.Rptr.3d 356, 88 P.3d 81).

Leslie M. Drozd, PhD, is a clinical and forensic psychologist. She has an independent practice in Newport Beach, California. She has conducted child custody evaluations for over 15 years and spoken nationally and internationally on issues related to custody, including substance abuse and domestic violence. She is one of the leading experts in the country on domestic violence in child custody cases. Dr. Drozd is author or co-author of many important articles, book chapters, and books including *Domestic Violence: True or False?; Is It Domestic Violence, Alienation and/or Estrangement?; Safety First: Understanding the Impact of Domestic Violence on Children in Child Custody Disputes; What to Do and When to Do It When Children Are Exposed to Domestic Violence; Problems with Attachment in Divorcing*

Families; Child Placement and Custody Decision-Making in Domestic Violence Families; and *Hearing the Child's Voice, Supporting the Child's Needs in Child Custody Evaluations.* She is co-author of *The Missing Piece: Solving the Puzzle of Self,* with Claudia Black.

INTRODUCTION

Introduction to the Volume
on Relocation Issues
in Child Custody Cases

Philip M. Stahl

After the California Supreme Court changed the landscape in relocation cases with its decision in the Marriage of LaMusga (California Supreme Court, 2004), *Journal of Child Custody* editor, Leslie Drozd,

Philip M. Stahl, PhD, is a psychologist in private practice. He conducts child custody
evaluations and provides consultation and expert witness testimony. He is a provider of
continuing education for psychologists and other mental health providers, and attorneys
and Family Law Specialists in California. He has conducted trainings throughout the
United States and internationally for child custody evaluators and others working with
high-conflict families of divorce. He has presented workshops for judges throughout the
country and is on the faculty of National Judicial College and the National Council of Juvenile and Family Court Judges. Along with his teaching, Dr. Stahl has written extensively on various issues in high-conflict divorce and custody evaluations. He is the author
of *Conducting Child Custody Evaluations: A Comprehensive Guide* (Sage, 1994), *Complex Issues in Custody Evaluations* (Sage, 1999), and *Parenting After Divorce* (Impact
Publishers, 2000). The California Supreme Court cited his custody evaluation in its recent landmark decision modifying eight years of relocation case law following Burgess
(In re Marriage of LaMusga (2004) 32 Cal.4th 1072, 12 Cal.Rptr.3d 356, 88 P.3d 81).
Address correspondence to: (E-mail: pstahl@earthlink.net).

[Haworth co-indexing entry note]: "Introduction to the Volume on Relocation Issues in Child Custody
Cases." Stahl, Philip M. Co-published simultaneously in *Journal of Child Custody* (The Haworth Press, Inc.)
Vol. 3, No. 3/4, 2006, pp. 1-5; and: *Relocation Issues in Child Custody Cases* (ed: Philip M. Stahl, and Leslie
M. Drozd) The Haworth Press, Inc., 2006, pp. 1-5. Single or multiple copies of this article are available for a
fee from The Haworth Document Delivery Service [1-800-HAWORTH, 9:00 a.m. - 5:00 p.m. (EST). E-mail
address: docdelivery@haworthpress.com].

Available online at http://jcc.haworthpress.com
doi:10.1300/J190v03n03_01

1

asked if I'd like to guest edit a volume on the topic of relocation. While I was nervous about the task, I was excited about the goal of having an entire book devoted to such an important issue. Given my roots with the Association of Family and Conciliation Courts, I felt it was imperative that this collection have a multi-disciplinary tone for a multi-disciplinary audience. I believe that this has been accomplished with the articles in this publication.

Historically, non-custodial parents have moved whenever and wherever they have wanted, often with no objection. Similarly, it was not uncommon for custodial parents to move with their children with a change in life circumstances, either a return to familial roots or for a re-marriage. When distances were significant, non-custodial parents frequently maintained more limited access with their children, often seeing them at holidays and for an extended time in the summer. There was little conflict and little need for court intervention in such circumstances. Relocation of a parent or the children was rarely problematic for divorced families.

With the growth in shared custody, with more fathers being actively involved in parenting after divorce, and with what appears to be an increase in litigation between conflicted parents, relocation is one of the most difficult issues to resolve. In many jurisdictions, mediation has been quite successful in resolving the disputes between divorcing parents. However, I have observed that the request by one parent to relocate with his/her children is one of the most difficult to resolve through mediation. I have also observed an increase in the extent to which courts refer relocating families to child custody evaluators, especially as courts delineate the factors judges need to consider when making relocation decisions. There is no middle ground in these disputes, as the relocating parent wants to take the children and the non-relocating parent wants the children to remain in their home community. Non-relocating disputes between conflicted parents usually have more options than exist with the relocating families, increasing the risk of a relocation dispute needing an evaluation and/or judicial intervention.

Issues surrounding relocation are very complex. Non-custodial parents can continue to move on a whim, but determining custody and access when the custodial parent wants to move, or when one of two joint custodial parents wants to move, can be very tough. More and more parents come to court representing themselves, making the task for judges even more difficult. As can be seen in the articles in this collection, the psychological literature, case law, and statutory law suggest that various factors need to be considered in order to determine what parenting arrangement is in the child's best interests when one parent wants to move.

In my various roles as a child custody evaluator, as someone who teaches custody evaluations to other mental health professionals and attorneys, and as someone who teaches judges about high conflict parents and the needs of children, I have observed that judges and child custody evaluators often look at relocation cases as the most difficult to solve. Judges have described relocation cases as "gut-wrenching." Child custody evaluators have described these cases as the most difficult to evaluate, often concluding that there is no good solution, while actually suggesting a least detrimental alternative rather than what is in the children's best interests. Finally, with improvements in technologies and the ease of travel, courts and evaluators are also looking to find ways to increase the access between parents and children across long distances so that both parents remain involved in a wide array of their children's life experiences and activities.

Since research should drive public policy and since there was such controversy after publication of Braver, Elman, and Fabricius's study (2003), I asked Dr. Fabricius and his colleagues to update the data and submit a new article addressing the concerns which were raised. While I personally disagreed then and still disagree with their call for courts to consider a "conditional change of custody order" when a parent requests to move, I agree with their conclusion that the research data on relocation and the research data on divorce does not support a presumption that a primary custodial parent should have an automatic right to move for any good-faith reason. I believe that there is not sufficient data to support the belief a move that is in the parent's interests is automatically in the child's best interests. I also believe that it is important to continue gathering research data that helps evaluators, judges, and public policy makers in relocation cases. Their analysis of this additional data is another step in this process.

Another critical task in understanding relocation is to recognize how the law is applied across the country. When I was at a conference sponsored by the American Bar Association in 2000 on the topic of relocation, one of the speakers explained that courts and legislatures around the country essentially had four ways to deal with relocation cases. One was to have a presumption in favor of a custodial parent moving with the child. Another was to have a presumption against the custodial parent moving with the child. A third was to have no presumption, rather each case needed to be decided on its own merits based on relevant factors in the state's Best Interests statute. The fourth group of states had nothing in case law or statutory law to guide the court in its decision in a given case. The speaker then said that about every 10 years, most states revised their approach on relocation so states would often go from one style of dealing with these cases to another. This was evident in California as the case law presumption changed in 1995 with their decision in the *Marriage of Burgess* (which set forth a presumption in favor of a custodial parent moving with the child) and then changed again in 2004 with their decision in the *Marriage of LaMusga* (which still supported that presumption for a primary custodial parent, while simultaneously clarifying how the court needs to address relevant factors if the non-custodial parent can make a showing that the move might be detrimental to the child). (The *LaMusga* court also clarified what to do when parents share physical custody of their child and one parent wants to move.)

To help readers understand current legal thinking, Professor Linda Elrod has done an excellent survey of courts across the country and added her commentary to this important area. Readers of this volume who don't know "Crickett" (as she likes to be called) are in for a treat. Her article helps readers understand the concept of legal presumptions and identify the thinking that led to various decisions across the country.

Since its inception, the *Journal of Child Custody* has been an important source of information for child custody evaluators. Thus, it is important for the views of child custody evaluators to be included in this collection. In 2000, leading child custody evaluator William Austin provided a framework for child custody evaluators to use as they approach cases involving relocation. It made sense to ask him to update his ground-breaking article for this publication. Austin and his co-author Jon Gould, have written many articles for the *Journal of Child Custody* and in this volume, they have done an excellent job helping the reader conceptualize the three functions of an evaluator in these complex cases, i.e., prediction, investigation, and making recommendations. As always, their insights and discussion are very useful both for child custody evaluators as well as attorneys and judges who read this book.

Even before the California decision in the *Marriage of Burgess*, I was concerned about the potential that judges and evaluators might be biased, either in favor of a custodial parent's move with the child or against a custodial parent's move with the child. This concern has grown as I teach judges and evaluators all over the country. This led to my article introducing the concepts of "for the move bias" and "against the move bias." I have always believed that the art of doing child custody evaluations incorporates an understanding of oneself and one's biases, regardless of whether they are based on personal or professional reasons. While I point out that the research in divorce and relocation may cause some to hold a presumption for or against the move, judges and child custody evaluators need to recognize the risk of those biases and set them aside when reaching conclusions about whether or not a specific child in a specific family moves with his or her parent.

Since child custody evaluators prepare reports for the judge, and since judges make the ultimate decisions when parents cannot agree in a relocation dispute, I felt it was important for readers to hear from a judge in this collection. Judge Martha Lott, a family court judge from Florida with whom I have taught, has described the process by which a judge analyzes data before making a decision in a relocation case. Her observations will be quite useful to child custody evaluators who look to the judge for guidance in how to approach their analysis and conclusions when writing their reports.

Finally, with legislatures, courts, and child custody evaluators grappling with the fact that there are many presumptions in family law matters, it is important to have a critical article looking at the concept of presumptions in general. My friends and colleagues Lyn Greenberg, Dianna Gould-Saltman, and Robert Schnider have done a masterful job addressing the benefits and risks when legislatures and the courts institute presumptions in family law matters. Their article explains why well-trained judges need the discretion to make decisions on behalf of children free of mandates, and hence, free of presumptions that may not result in decisions that would be in the best interests of the children to whom they serve.

I am proud of this volume and the contributions of the authors. I hope that the readers will learn as much as I have in the process of putting this collection together. It is also my hope that the task for judges and child custody evaluators, as well as the lives of children caught up in these issues, will be helped by the information in this publication.

REFERENCES

Austin, W. (2000). A Forensic Psychology Model of Risk Assessment for Child Relocation Law. *Family & Conciliation Courts Review*, 38 (2), 192-207.

Braver, S., Elman, I., and Fabricious, W. (2003). Relocation of children after divorce and children's best interests: New evidence and legal considerations. *Journal of Family Psychology*, 2003, 17(2) 206-219.

California Supreme Court (2004). *In re Marriage of LaMusga*. 32 Cal.4th 1072.

Relocation, Parent Conflict, and Domestic Violence: Independent Risk Factors for Children of Divorce

William V. Fabricius
Sanford L. Braver

SUMMARY. We performed several re-analyses of data presented in Braver, Ellman, and Fabricius (2003) to examine whether their findings that parental relocation after divorce was associated with negative long-term outcomes in their grown children could be due to pre-existing levels of parent conflict and domestic violence. Conflict and violence might have caused parents to relocate, and might have caused the negative outcomes. Evidence from analyses of covariance, controlling for levels of conflict and violence (as reported by the grown children), con-

William V. Fabricius is Associate Professor of Psychology, Department of Psychology, Arizona State University. His research on divorce has appeared in the *Journal of Family Psychology, Family Relations, Family Courts Review,* and *Journal of Psychosomatic Research.*

Sanford L. Braver is Professor of Psychology and Co-Principal Investigator, Prevention Research Center, Department of Psychology, Arizona State University. He is author of the monograph "Divorced Dads: Shattering the Myths" (Tarcher/Penguin-Putnam) and over 60 articles and chapters on divorce.

Address correspondence to: William V. Fabricius, Department of Psychology, Arizona State University, Box 871104, Tempe, AZ 85287-1104 (E-mail: William. Fabricius@asu.edu).

[Haworth co-indexing entry note]: "Relocation, Parent Conflict, and Domestic Violence: Independent Risk Factors for Children of Divorce." Fabricius, William V., and Sanford L. Braver. Co-published simultaneously in *Journal of Child Custody* (The Haworth Press, Inc.) Vol. 3, No. 3/4, 2006, pp. 7-27; and: *Relocation Issues in Child Custody Cases* (ed: Philip M. Stahl, and Leslie M. Drozd) The Haworth Press, Inc., 2006, pp. 7-27. Single or multiple copies of this article are available for a fee from The Haworth Document Delivery Service [1-800-HAWORTH, 9:00 a.m. - 5:00 p.m. (EST). E-mail address: docdelivery@haworthpress.com].

Available online at http://jcc.haworthpress.com
doi:10.1300/J190v03n03_02

7

firmed that relocation was associated with negative outcomes over and above the associations of conflict and violence with negative outcomes. These new findings support the original recommendation of Braver et al. that "courts should give greater weight to the child's separate interests in deciding such [relocation] cases" (p. 206). Additionally, there was little indication that moves reduced levels of conflict, but that finding is tentative. doi:10.1300/J190v03n03_02 *[Article copies available for a fee from The Haworth Document Delivery Service: 1-800-HAWORTH. E-mail address: <docdelivery@haworthpress.com> Website: <http://www.HaworthPress.com> © 2006 by The Haworth Press, Inc. All rights reserved.]*

KEYWORDS. Divorce, relocation, custody, parental conflict, domestic violence

A study on relocation after divorce that we recently published (Braver, Ellman & Fabricius, 2003) has attracted considerable attention. Our results disclosed that young adults, one of whose divorced parents had moved more than an hour's drive away from what used to be the family home, scored significantly worse on 11 of 14 variables than those whose parents had not moved. Some of the negative associations were observed if the move separated the child from the father, others were observed if the move separated the child from the mother. Generally, it did not seem to matter how the child was separated from the parent; for example, similar results occurred if the child was separated from the father either by moving away with the mother, or by the father moving away alone. Importantly, these were long-term outcomes because the data came from young adults. In attempting to provide policy makers and courts with some guidance in applying the findings, we concluded:

> courts would be mistaken to assume, in the absence of contrary evidence, that children benefit from moving with their custodial parent to a new location that is distant from their other parent, *whenever* the custodial parent wishes to make the move. Putting the point in legal terminology, the burden of persuasion in relocation disputes, on the question of whether the move is in the child's interests, should probably lie with the custodial parent who seeks to relocate, rather than with the objecting parent. (p. 215)

The timing of the editorial processing and eventual publication of this article increased dramatically the attention paid to it, because the beginning of the process coincided with the California Supreme Court's decision to consider a case, *In re the Marriage of LaMusga*, that could potentially overturn their earlier controversial but influential relocation policy as stated in 1996 (*In re the Marriage of Burgess*, 1996). As ours was the first empirical study to directly explore the effects of relocation on children, it was natural that a link would be made between our findings and this important forthcoming policy declaration with the same focus. Soon after publication, Google reported 129 hits in a search requiring both the keywords "Braver" and "LaMusga," and the study was cited in numerous editorials, media articles, and in Amicus Curia Briefs to the CA Supreme Court on both sides of the *LaMusga* case.[1]

Amici Curiae briefs filed by Dr. Judith Wallerstein et al. (2003), Dr. Carol S. Bruch (2002), and one of the Mother's Briefs (Navarro, 2003) leveled several criticisms of our study. Our goals in this paper are to respond to these criticisms and present new data to test our original findings.[2]

One criticism in all three Briefs focused on the variables on which we did not find differences. Wallerstein et al. stated in their Brief (p. 18) that "on all of the major mental health measures, including personal and emotional adjustment and general life satisfaction, there were *no differences* between those who remained in the same community with both parents and those who moved with the custodial mother." Mother's Brief (p. 18), quoting a newspaper article by Norval Glenn and David Blankenhorn, stated that "In the most crucial areas–friendship and dating behavior, substance abuse, and general life satisfaction–there were no significant differences at all between the two groups." While it is true that we did not find differences on those variables, the authors of the Briefs give no rationale for why those variables are more "crucial" or "major" than the other variables on which we *did* find differences. Specifically, those who moved with their mothers (representing the great majority of child relocations) fared worse than those whose parents did not move in terms of (a) their self-reported global health in young adulthood, (b) lingering inner turmoil and stress from their parents' divorce, (c) current parent conflict, (d) current relationships with fathers, and (e) amount of college financial support received from parents. These are five major and crucial variables. Parent conflict, for example, has well-known negative effects on children, and children who are less close to their fathers have worse behavioral and emotional adjustment, and lower school achievement (Amato & Gilbreth, 1999). We summarized our findings on physical health as follows:

The data also suggest potentially important physical health implications . . . high levels of family conflict have been associated with poorer physical health in adolescents (Mechanic & Hansell, 1989). Other research suggests that childhood stress may have long-lasting influences on the development of physiological stress response systems important in long-term disease susceptibility (DiPietro, 2000). Poor quality parent-child relationships have been associated with higher blood pressure in undergraduate students (Luecken, 1998), and physical health status in middle-age adults (Russek, Schwartz, Bell & Baldwin, 1998). Finally, self-reported global health has been found to be a remarkably consistent predictor of premature mortality, even when controlling for numerous specific health indicators known to predict mortality (Idler & Benyamini, 1997). Combined, it is reasonable to project that even greater and more serious deficits might be found in children of relocating parents the longer the term of the follow-up.

Bruch's Brief is the only one of the three to acknowledge to the California Supreme Court that we found differences on any of these variables, but she mentions only two: "The only important differences identified are those that report distress from the divorce . . . [and] overall physical health" (pp. 3-4). Bruch gives no rationale for why parent conflict, relationship with father, and financial support from parents are not important. She says that we provide no information about how serious these differences are, but the above long quote shows that we took pains to point readers to documentation in the health literature of the long-term implications of most of our findings.

The second criticism was that we "virtually ignored" the fact that "those children in their fathers' custody showed a higher level of distress" (Wallerstein, 2003, pp. 17-18). The implication seems to be that we should have interpreted that to mean that however bad it might be for mothers to move with the child, it would be even worse to deny her permission and instead turn the children over to the father's custody. While it is true that such mean differences were displayed in our Table 1, our data did not permit us to distinguish whether children in these father custody situations had *changed* custody due to courts' denial of the mothers' requests to move with the children, or had simply remained in pre-established father custody when the non-custodial mother moved. These father custody situations are rare (8% for "remaining with dad when mother moved," and 4% for "moving with dad"), and when such a status occurs, it frequently is due to the mother abandoning the child, or the mother being found unfit. These circumstances would commonly cause long-term distress in the child regardless of moving.

Bruch (2002) made the related argument that the proper comparison group should have been those parents who sought permission to move away with the child but were denied permission by the courts. However, even if a study of such contested cases found that outcomes were worse for those in which permission was denied than those in which it was granted, that would not warrant a presumption in favor of permitting moves in all cases (the position argued in these Briefs), just as we did not argue that our finding of negative outcomes would warrant a presumption in favor of denying permission to relocate the child in all cases. Research can only inform courts of potential risks, while it is up to them to assess the likelihood, degree, and type of harm in any particular case. The most likely scenario in which denying permission to move would be harmful to children is when children are being exposed to domestic violence, intense conflict, or other hardship conditions. In these cases courts have to balance the types of negative outcomes our study found were associated with separation from a parent, and the types likely to arise from staying in dangerous or difficult situations.

A third criticism in all three Briefs is that our study lacked *causal evidence* (Wallerstein: ". . . while failing to recognize the equally likely possibility that relocation was a *consequence* of a stressful and unhappy environment rather than *a cause* of it," p. 17; Bruch: "It is just as likely that relocation is a consequence of a stressful and unhappy or dysfunctional living arrangement as a cause of it," p. 4; Mother's Brief: "They did not report . . . the background information on the students that would permit even informed guesses about the reasons for the differences between the two groups" p. 18). We spent a great deal of the Discussion (about 15% of the entire article, far more than is typical) in a section labeled "Limitations", where we discussed at length various causal scenarios. For example, we wrote:

> Although these data are far more on point in evaluating relocation policies than any previously considered by courts, they are of course correlational, not causal. So whereas the data tell us that a variety of poor outcomes are associated with post-divorce parental moves, they cannot establish with anything near certainty that the moves are a contributing cause. It is certainly possible, if not likely, for example, that various pre-existing (or self selection) factors are responsible *both* for the parents' moving and for the child's diminished outcomes. Pre-existing factors that could plau-

sibly play this role include a low level of functioning for one or both parents, the inability of one or both parents to put the child's needs ahead of his or her own, and high levels of pre-move conflict between the parents. . . . (Braver et al., 2003; pp. 214-215)

We regard this "causal direction" question as potentially the most compelling criticism, and it is the one we take up in the remainder of the present paper. In cases where random assignment to condition (i.e., move vs. stay) is impossible, evidence about causal processes that is suggestive but not conclusive may be provided by gathering data about each of the various alternative causal variables, and statistically evaluating each. The Briefs suggest several alternative causal variables. Both Wallerstein's and Mother's Briefs suggest that children whose parents moved were younger at the time of the divorce, and that could be why they were having problems as young adults, although neither cites evidence that divorce has more negative long-term outcomes for younger children. Mother's Brief suggests that parents often move because of remarriage, and that remarriage could lead to less child support which could cause the negative outcomes. In the case of a father's remarriage (and move) the authors suggest that he will be less likely to pay child support, but they offer no rationale for why a mother's remarriage (and move) will result in her receiving less. Wallerstein suggests that parents may move because they have weaker ties to the community and less financial resources, but she offers no rationale for why those circumstances would not have been rectified by the move, and why these pre-move circumstances would result in such long-term outcomes.

Perhaps the most important alternative cause identified by both ourselves and our critics is the relationship between the parents. A poor relationship could predispose parents to relocate and predispose children to long-term negative outcomes. In the present paper, we use the original data presented in Braver et al. (2003) supplemented with eleven variables, not reported in that paper, measuring parental conflict and domestic violence. Two of these variables asked students to report how often they had witnessed either parent "hitting, slapping, or punching" the other *after* the divorce. By coincidence, half of the students answered nine additional questions on parental conflict and domestic violence. These questions were part of another project, and the surveys that contained these questions were randomly distributed to half the students. These questions included frequency and severity of parental conflict at four time periods *before, during* and *after* the divorce, and frequency of domestic violence with *time period left unspecified.*

We addressed the following three questions in these new analyses: First, do the moveaway groups have higher reported levels of parent conflict and domestic violence than the non-moveaway group, which might explain the negative long-term outcomes in the moveaway groups? Second, do the moveaway groups show greater improvement over time in parent conflict than the non-moveaway group, which might indicate that moves were beneficial to both parents and children in reducing conflict? Finally, if we statistically control for conflict and violence, do the negative long-term outcomes persist in the moveaway groups?

In this study we examine only three of the original five groups; namely, the comparison group whose parents did not move ("non-moveaway," 39% of the sample), and the two moveaway groups in which the child was separated from the father, those who moved away with their mothers ("mother moveaway," 25%), and those whose fathers moved away without them ("father moveaway," 26%). The other two groups, in which moves separated the child from the mother, became too small to examine when we included only the half of the sample on which conflict and violence data were available.

METHODS

Respondents and Procedure

As described more fully in Braver et al. (2003), surveys were administered during class periods devoted to research to 602 undergraduate students from divorced families enrolled in a large southwestern state university. Respondents indicated whether either of their parents ever moved more than an hour's drive away from what used to be the family home. Five groups resulted: neither parent moved, the mother moved first and the respondent accompanied her; the father moved first but the respondent stayed with the mother, the father moved first and the respondent accompanied him, and the mother moved first but the respondent stayed with the father. Respondents also indicated their current age, how old they were when their parents permanently separated, and how many years altogether their parents lived more than an hour's drive apart.

Conflict Measures

Four questions asked, "How *frequently* was there conflict between your parents?" in the following time periods: in the year or two years before the final separation, immediately after the final separation, during the first two years after the final separation, and in the next three years after the final separation. The response scale ranged from 0 ("never"), 1 ("rarely"), 2 ("occasionally"), to 8 ("almost always"), with 9 indicating "I don't know or I can't remember." Four questions asked "How *severe* was the conflict between your parents?" during the same time periods, with the response scale from 0 ("not applicable, there was no conflict during this time period"), 1 ("very mild"), 2 ("mild"), 3 ("mild to moderate"), to 8 ("very severe, with violence"), with 9 indicating "I don't know or I can't remember." Note that these four questions about severity of conflict also capture instances of domestic violence (response category 8) before, during, and after the divorce. All eight questions were asked of half of the participants, randomly selected.

Fabricius and Luecken (2007) provided evidence that students' reports of parent conflict were acceptably reliable and valid. In that study, 93 students (different students than the ones assessed here) provided retest data 10 months later on the same four parent conflict frequency questions used here. The test-retest correlations were all significant and between .68 and .75, and the only significant difference in means was a decrease over the 10-month interval in reports of conflict before the divorce. As a check on validity, Fabricius and Luecken compared responses of matched pairs of students and parents (22 fathers and 29 mothers). Students' and parents' reports of overall parent conflict were significantly correlated ($r = .63$, $p < .001$) and not significantly different in terms of mean levels.

Domestic Violence Measures

The same half of the participants answered the following question: "To your knowledge, how often did physical violence occur between your parents?" The time period for this question (e.g., pre- or post-divorce) was left unspecified, thus this question captures instances of witnessed domestic violence that occurred before, during, or after the divorce. The response scale was the same one as above for frequency of conflict. For clarity, this variable will be referred to as the "domestic violence ever" variable.

All participants answered two more domestic violence questions focused on the period after the divorce, "While you were growing up after the divorce, how many times did you witness your [dad/mom] hitting, slapping, or punching your [mother/father]?" These variables will be referred to as the "domestic violence after" variables. The response scale was 0 ("never"), 1 ("once"), 2 ("two or three times"), 3 ("a few times per month"), 4 ("once a week"), 5 ("a few times per week"), 6 ("daily or almost daily"), 7 ("more than I can count"). Pasley and Braver (2004) reported that college students', mothers', and fathers' answers to this question regarding fathers' violence all inter-correlated between .39 and .48, but that mothers reported higher mean levels of father violence than fathers or students, whose mean levels were quite similar.

Outcome Measures

We re-analyzed all 14 of the original outcome measures. In Braver et al. (2003), six of the 14 outcome measures had shown deficits associated with the two moveaway groups that we examine in this paper; namely, those in which the child was separated from the father. These included four deficits associated with both the mother moveaway and father moveaway groups (total parental contributions to college expenses, inner turmoil and distress from the divorce, relationship with father ["dad good supporter"],[3] and how well the parents currently get along with each other). Deficits in students' global health were associated only with the mother moveaway group, and increased worry about college expenses was associated only with the father moveaway group Below we present shortened descriptions of these six outcome measures.

Parental contribution to college expenses was assessed by combining an item for each parent that asked "How much money is your [mother's/ father's] household (including [her/his] new [husband/wife] or live-in partner or [boy/girl]friend, if any) contributing to your total college expenses (tuition, books, room and board, fees, etc.) per year?" The potential responses included 0, 1-8, which represented $1,000 increments and 9, which represented "more than $8,000."

We included four of the original 38 items from the Painful Feelings About Divorce scale (Laumann-Billings & Emery, 2000) to assess inner turmoil and distress from divorce, ("I probably would be a different person if my parents had not gotten divorced," "My parents' divorce still causes struggles for me," "I had a harder childhood than most people" and "My childhood was cut short"). These items were asked with a 0 (strongly disagree) to 4 (strongly agree) response format used in the original.

The student's current relationship with father was assessed with two 0 ("not at all") to 8 ("extremely") items each, devised specially for this purpose, "To what extent is your father really there for you when you need him to be?" and "To what extent do you feel your father is a good role model for you?"

A single item "How well do your parents get along?" on a 0 ("not at all well") to 8 ("extremely well") format, was designed especially for this investigation.

We used a 1-item measure of global health, "Would you say that in general your health is" with responses of 0 = Poor, 1 = Fair, 2 = Good, 3 = Very Good, and 4 = Excellent. Perceived global health, as measured by single items such as this one, has been shown to be related to physical health and premature mortality (e.g., Idler & Benyamini, 1997).

A single item assessed worry about college expenses, "I worry a lot about my college expenses" with a 0 (applies to me very closely) to 8 (doesn't apply to me at all) response format.

RESULTS

At the time of their parents' separation, students in the non-moveaway group were older (mean age = 10.5) than those in the father moveaway group (7.9), who in turn were older than those in the mother moveaway group (5.4; all p's < .01). Relatedly, those in the mother moveaway group spent more years with their parents living an hour's drive apart (10.3 years) than those in the father moveaway group (8.1; p < .01).

Levels of Parent Conflict and Domestic Violence, and Rates of Decline

Students reported on the frequency and severity of parent conflict two years before the final separation, immediately after, during the first two years post-separation, and during the next three years. Those who were older at the time of the separation tended to report higher levels of conflict. Five of the correlations between these eight conflict variables and age at separation were significant (r's = .15 to .24, p's < .05). Number of years spent with their parents living an hour's drive apart did not relate to reports of conflict. Consequently, we controlled for age at separation when testing whether the three groups (non-moveaway, mother moveaway, father moveaway) differed in levels of conflict. A 3 (group) × 4 (time period) repeated measures ANOVA on frequency of conflict with age at separation as a covariate revealed a statistically reliable decrease in conflict over time (F (3, 414) = 7.03, p < .001), a marginally significant difference among the three groups (F (2, 138) = 2.47, p = .09), and no difference in the rates with which the groups improved over time (F (6, 414) = .79). A similar analysis of severity of conflict revealed marginally significant decreases in severity over time (F (3, 417) = 2.27, p = .08) and among the three groups (F (2, 139) = 3.03, p = .052), and no difference in the rates with which the groups improved over time (F (6, 417) = .98). Figures 1 and 2 show the estimated marginal means for frequency and severity of conflict, adjusted for age at separation. These results suggest somewhat higher levels of parent conflict, as experienced and recalled by the students themselves, in the mother moveaway group. The results also suggest that moving away in either group did not lead to any steeper decline in conflict than the "natural" decline in the non-moveaway group.

We explored whether moving might have led to a decline in conflict in a more precise analysis. We first calculated, for each student, when the move occurred in relation to when the parents separated, and catego-

FIGURE 1. Reported Frequency of Parent Conflict During Four Time Periods by Moveaway Status, Controlling for Age at Separation (0 = none, 1 = rarely, 2 = occasionally, 3 = some of the time, 4 = moderate, 5 = substantial, 6 = lot of time)

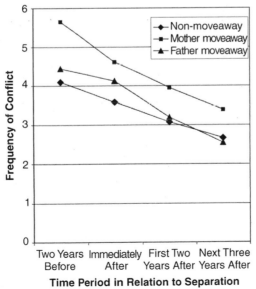

FIGURE 2. Reported Severity of Parent Conflict During Four Time Periods by Moveaway Status, Controlling for Age at Separation (0 = none, 1 = very mild, 2 = mild, 3 = mild to moderate, 4 = moderate, 5 = moderate to severe)

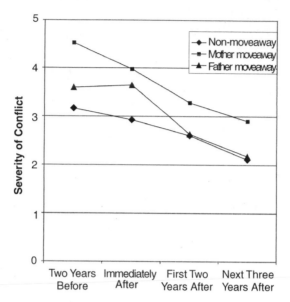

Time Period in Relation to Separation

rized students into four groups depending on whether the move occurred (a) less than six months after the separation, (b) six months to two years after the separation, (c) during the next three years after the separation, or (d) after that. We then calculated conflict frequency and severity scores for each student's time periods before the move versus all time periods after the move. For example, for students in category (a), their frequency score before the move was the variable referring to frequency of conflict in "the two years before the final separation," and their frequency score after the move was the average of the three variables referring to frequency of conflict in the later time periods.[4] In this way we obtained more precise measures of the frequency and severity of conflict before and after the move, and we looked separately at the two moveaway groups, controlling for age at separation. There was no evidence of a decline in either frequency or severity of conflict in either group after the move (p's = .15 to .88).

Regarding domestic violence, Table 1 presents findings on our measures of frequency of physical violence with time period left unspeci-

TABLE 1. Means of the Two Domestic Violence Measures and Proportions of Students Reporting Any Physical Violence Between Parents

Moveaway Status	Domestic Violence Ever		Domestic Violence After	
	Mean*	Proportion	Mean**	Proportion
Non-moveaway	.42[a]	.19[a]	.17	.06[a]
Mother moveaway	1.06[b]	.42[b]	.29	.16[b]
Father moveaway	.78[a,b]	.27[a]	.15	.07[a]

* Scale ranged from 0 = "never," 1 = "rarely," to 8 = "almost always."
** Sum of two scales (father hitting mother and mother hitting father) where each scale ranged from 0 = "never," 1 = "once," to 7 = "more than I can count."
Note: Means with different superscripts are significantly different at p < .05.

fied ("domestic violence ever"), and frequency of witnessing one parent "hitting, slapping or punching" the other after the divorce ("domestic violence after"). Age at separation and years spent with parents residing an hour apart were unrelated to any of these variables. Regarding "domestic violence ever," when mothers moved students reported statistically significantly more frequent physical violence (M = 1.06) than when neither parent moved (.42). When fathers moved, students reported an intermediate level of physical violence (.78). In all three groups the average frequencies were about 1 ("rarely") or less on a scale that ranged from 0 ("never") to 8 ("almost always"). Also shown are the proportions of families in which students reported any occurrence of physical violence. This was defined as any report other than "never." When mothers moved away, significantly more students (42%) reported there had been some occurrence of violence than when fathers moved away (27%) or when neither parent moved (19%).

Regarding "domestic violence after," we summed the responses for dad hitting mom and mom hitting dad to obtain an indication of how often, in total, students had witnessed domestic violence after the divorce. Table 1 shows that although the rate appeared higher when mothers moved (.29) than when neither parent moved (.17) or when father moved (.15), this difference was not statistically significant, F (2, 520) = 1.40, p = .25.[5] All three summed frequencies were substantially less than 1 ("once") on a scale that ranged from 0 ("never"), 1 ("once"), 2 ("two or three times"), to 7 ("more than I can count"). However, the proportion of families in which students reported any occurrence of violence after the divorce (i.e., any report other than "never") from either parent was significantly higher in the mother moveaway group. Table 1 shows that when mothers moved away, 16% of the students reported there had been some occurrence of violence after the divorce (13% reported their father had hit their mother, and 6% reported their mother had hit their father), when fathers moved away 7% reported some violence (5% and 3%, respectively), and when neither parent moved 6% reported some violence (3% and 5%, respectively).

Controlling for Conflict and Violence

In order to statistically control for conflict and violence, we re-analyzed all 14 of the original outcome measures by including as covariates all of the conflict and domestic violence variables (i.e., the mean of the standardized scores for frequency of conflict in whichever time periods the student provided data, the mean of the standardized scores for severity of conflict in whichever time periods the student provided data, frequency of domestic violence ever, frequency of father hitting mother after the divorce, and frequency of mother hitting father after the divorce). We also included students' age at separation and number of years during which parents lived an hour's drive apart as covariates.

Expectedly, none of the eight outcome measures that originally did not show deficits in the mother or father moveaway groups now showed deficits in the re-analyses. We focus below on the remaining six. Table 2 shows the results of the re-analyses of these six variables. In three of the cases (how well the parents currently get along with each other, the students' inner turmoil and distress from the divorce, and their relationships with their fathers), the effect of moveaway status remained significant. Post-hoc tests (two-tailed) showed that in each case students whose mothers had moved away with them, as well as those whose fathers had moved away without them, showed significantly more negative outcomes than those whose parents had not moved. These findings replicate our original findings. In the other three cases (students' global health, parental contributions to college expenses, and students' worry about college expenses), the effect of moveaway status was no longer significant. Also shown in Table 2 are the significant associations that the covariates (conflict, violence, age at separation, years apart) had with each of the outcome measures. Severity of earlier conflict was associated with parents currently not getting along. "Domestic violence ever" was associated with poorer relationships with fathers and lower college contributions. Father hitting mother after the divorce was associated with greater inner turmoil and distress, poorer relationships with fathers, and more worry about college expenses. Mother hitting father

TABLE 2. Results of Analyses of Covariance on Student Outcomes and Estimated Marginal Means by Moveaway Status

	Outcomes					
Factors	Parents get along	Inner turmoil and distress	Relationship with father	Global health	College support	Worry about expenses
Covariates						
Parent conflict						
frequency	ns	ns	ns	ns	ns	ns
severity	** (.044)	ns	ns	ns	ns	ns
Violence ever	ns	ns	** (.050)	ns	* (.032)	ns
Dad hit mom after	ns	* (.035)	* (.030)	ns	ns	+ (.025)
Mom hit dad after	ns	+ (.025)	ns	ns	ns	ns
Age at separation	ns	** (.038)	ns	ns	ns	ns
Years parents apart	ns	ns	ns	ns	ns	ns
Moveaway status	*** (.090)	*** (.083)	* (.045)	ns	ns	ns
Non-moveaway	4.31[a]	1.54[a]	4.68[a]	2.87	$5839	3.65
Mother moveaway	2.95[b]	2.28[b]	3.11[b]	2.74	$4978	4.80
Father moveaway	2.33[b]	2.00[b]	3.32[b]	2.87	$5552	4.24

+ $p < .06$ * $p < .05$ ** $p < .01$
Note: Values in parentheses are measures of effect sizes (partial eta^2).
Note: For college support additional covariates included mother's and father's standard of living, tuition type (in-state versus out-of-state), and legal custody (mother sole versus joint).
Note: Means with different superscripts are significantly different at $p < .05$.

after the divorce was also associated with greater inner turmoil and distress. Finally, the older students were at the time of the separation, the greater inner turmoil and distress they currently experienced over their parents' divorce.

Also shown in Table 2 are measures of effect sizes ("partial eta squared") for each of the significant associations. These measures tell us how much of the total variability is attributable to that factor. Moveaway status accounts for twice as much variability (9%) in parents getting along than does the only other significant factor, severity of conflict (4.4%). The same is true for students' inner turmoil and distress over their parents' divorces, where moveaway status accounts for 8.3% of the variability, and age at separation and each parent hitting the other after the divorce account for less that 4% each. Moveaway status accounts for 4.5% of the variability in students' relationships with their fathers, which is similar to that accounted for by "domestic violence ever" (5%) and father hitting mother after the divorce (3%).

DISCUSSION

What is new in these findings is that over and above the effects associated with parent conflict and domestic violence, parental relocation after divorce itself appears to additionally negatively impact children's long-term relationships with their fathers, their adjustment to their parents' divorce, and their ongoing experience of their parents' relationship. These new findings of course do not prove that moves caused these outcomes, but they do eliminate the alternate possibility, cited by our critics and first raised by ourselves in our original report, that the outcomes were *only* due to higher rates of parent conflict in the moveaway families.

As we found in our original study, when either parent moved away and separated the child from the father, then years later when children had reached young adulthood they experienced poorer relationships with their fathers, they suffered greater inner turmoil and distress about the divorce, and they experienced less amicable and cooperative relations between their parents. Analyses of covariance controlling for conflict and violence showed that these negative long-term outcomes could not be completely accounted for by exposure to parent conflict or domestic violence before, during, or after the divorce. The analyses of covariance did detect effects specifically associated with conflict and violence. These included the following: (a) the parents' ability to present a cooperative relationship to their grown children decreased with severity of conflict between the parents in the period before and up to five years after the divorce, (b) young adults' inner turmoil and distress over the divorce increased with severity of parent conflict, and with domestic violence from either parent toward the other after the divorce, and (c) young adults' relationships with their fathers suffered with domestic violence ever and specifically with violence directed toward the mother after the divorce. These findings on conflict and domestic violence make intuitive sense. But the current findings also make it clear that these same three outcomes are also associated with moves by either parent that separate child from father. In fact, the measures of effect sizes indicate that moves were either stronger indicators of these negative outcomes than parent conflict and domestic violence, or equally strong indicators.

It is notable that the effects associated with moves were strong enough to be detectable even after the sample was cut in half (because most of the conflict and violence data was available for only half the subjects). Another indication that the effects were strong is that we detected them even though we measured the outcomes (relationship with dad, distress, parents getting along) with vastly shortened scales of only one or two items each. Longer, reliable scales generally make effects easier to detect.

Three of the six outcomes (college support, physical health, and worry about college expenses) were not associated with moves in these new analyses. However, the amounts of college support were in the same direction as in our original analyses, with those whose mothers had moved away with them receiving the least support. Our one-item measure of global health no longer related to moves after removing the effect associated with severity of parent conflict. But in a new study (Fabricius & Luecken, 2007), in which we measured health via self-reports of somatic symptoms in addition to global health, we found relationships between health and time with father. We did not assess moves, but instead time spent with father after divorce, which are highly related. The more time students had spent with their fathers, the better their relationships were with their fathers, and better father-child relationships in turn predicted better health in young adulthood. This was over and above any effects associated with parent conflict, because we controlled for conflict (although not violence) as we did here. These new findings suggest that moving away may affect children's health indirectly, by first reducing their time with father, which negatively affects their relationships with their fathers, which in turn negatively affects their health. New findings by Kraft and Luecken (2005) are beginning to reveal the physiological link by which time with father can impact physical health. These researchers found that less time spent with fathers after divorce predicted dysregulated physiological stress responses in young adults. We will test specific indirect pathways between parental relocation and health in future studies.

Implications for Child Custody

Relocation scenarios require policy makers and courts to consider the interests of three stakeholders, the child and the two parents. Our findings suggest that moves are a risk factor for children, over and above the risks associated with parent conflict and domestic violence. In addition, we did not find clear evidence that moves benefited children by reducing the levels of parent conflict from what they would have been had the move not occurred, although more definitive research is needed on this issue. There were no group differences in rates at which frequency or severity of conflict declined over time; instead, on both measures, conflict decreased similarly in all three groups. Using a more precise measure that looked at conflict before and after the move for each individual, we found no decreases associated with the move. Some caution is called for before accepting this latter finding, however, because of the small numbers of families (between 20 and 40) with available data to compare frequency and severity of conflict before and after the move.

Moves that separate fathers and children are a risk factor for fathers also, to the extent that children's relationships with fathers are damaged by the moves. Findings from recent studies (Furstenberg, Hoffman & Shrestha, 1995; Lye, Klepinger, Hyle, & Nelson, 1995) suggest that damaged father-child relationships after divorce persist as fathers grow older, and translate into diminished caring from grown children. Specifically, these studies show that many young to middle-aged adults have substantially weakened relationships with their divorced fathers, as measured by time spent together as adults, quality of the relationship, and support given and received in the form of intergenerational transfers of time and money.

Moving away may benefit mothers in cases of domestic violence, and in fact our data suggest that many moves by mothers may have been motivated by domestic violence concerns (see also Newmark, Harrell, & Salem, 1995). Students reported that domestic violence occurred at some point in 42% of the families in which mothers moved with the child, which broke down to 15% of students saying it occurred "rarely," 11% "occasionally," 9% "some of the time," and 8% "a moderate amount of the time" or higher. Similarly, there was a higher percentage of families (16%) in which students reported some domestic violence after the divorce in the mother moveaway group (13% reported their father had hit their mother, and 6% reported their mother had hit their father). Finally, there were marginally significant trends for frequency and severity of parent conflict to also be higher in the mother moveaway group. While domestic violence and conflict might partially account for mothers' decisions to move, and while the present results show they also partially account for young adults' continued distress over the divorce and worsened relationships with their fathers, they do not account for all of the negative effects associated with moves. The decision to move itself brings added risks, as our data have shown, and in contested cases it appears that courts must try to balance the potential benefits and risks of relocation.

We do not offer this study as a final answer to the issue of whether preexisting conditions in families in which a parent moves away after divorce could explain the long-term negative outcomes of children in those families. Rather, researchers should address these problems more systematically, with larger more representative samples, and with more precisely targeted measures in longitudinal (rather then retrospective) studies. These are the first findings on this important issue, and as such, from a scientific perspective, they serve as a starting point for researchers to attempt to refute them with better methods. From a policy perspective, however, our previous recommendation still stands; namely, that our findings "allow us to say . . . that there is no empirical basis on which to justify a legal presumption that a move by a custodial parent to a destination she plausibly believes will improve her life will necessarily confer benefits on the children she takes with her" (Braver et al., 2003; p. 215), and that "from the perspective of the child's interests, there may be real value in discouraging moves by custodial parents [via strategic use of a conditional change-of-custody orders], at least in cases in which the child enjoys a good relationship with the other parent and the move is not prompted by the need to otherwise remove the child from a detrimental environment' (p. 216). The current findings that there are long-term negative outcomes for children associated with moveaways that are not simply due to higher rates of parent conflict or domestic violence provide no evidence so far to revise that recommendation.

NOTES

1. The Court decided on April 29, 2004, to overturn their holding in *Burgess* and ruled in favor of the father opposing the mother's relocation with the children, declaring "the noncustodial parent bears the initial burden of showing that the proposed relocation of the children's residence would cause detriment to the children, requiring a reevaluation of the children's custody. The likely impact of the proposed move on the noncustodial parent's relationship with the children is a relevant factor in determining whether the move would cause detriment to the children and, when considered in light of all of the relevant factors, may be sufficient to justify a change in custody. If the noncustodial parent makes such an initial showing of detriment, the court must perform the delicate and difficult task of determining whether a change in custody is in the best interests of the children."

2. In the paper we acknowledged an additional, potential criticism: namely, that college students from divorced families may not represent young adults from divorced families in general. We stated, "It may be, for example, that a college sample is likely to include those who were least negatively affected by the relocation" (p. 214). Note that this would have worked *against* the likelihood of finding deficits associated with relocation, and might account for the few variables (i.e., relationship choices and substance

abuse) on which we did not find deficits. We have addressed the representativeness issue at length in a subsequent paper (Fabricius & Braver, 2004) and have found little evidence that college samples are likely to seriously bias the findings. For example, in one of the sources we checked, "McLanahan and Sandefur [1994] examined 5 nationally representative studies and find across all of these that about 50% of children of two-parent families go to college, while about 40% of children of "one-parent families" do so. Even this rather slight 10% discrepancy is an over-estimate of the extent of bias between married and divorced families, because the one-parent families they counted included never-married parents (as well as divorced parents) and McLanahan and Sandefur later show (in Figure 5) that children of never-married parents are about 6% less likely to graduate high school than children of divorced parents. Overall, one could fairly say that, of children from divorced families, those who made it to college appear a very slightly select group" (Fabricius & Braver, 2004, p. 353).

3. The variable "two good role models" in our original report also showed negative outcomes associated with these two groups, but this only reflected the contribution from the "dad good supporter" variable.

4. In calculating these new "before" and "after" variables, we standardized the frequency and severity scores so that the means of different combinations of time periods would not be affected by the overall declines in conflict over time.

5. All of the subjects from our original study were included in this analysis, so we should have been able to detect any real differences among moveaway groups in physical violence directed by either parent toward the other after the divorce.

REFERENCES

Amato, P. R., & Gilbreth, J. G. (1999). Nonresident fathers and children's well-being: A meta-analysis. *Journal of Marriage and the Family, 61,* 557-573.

Braver, S. L., Ellman, I. M., & Fabricius, W. V. (2003). Relocation of children after divorce and children's best interests: New evidence and legal considerations. *Journal of Family Psychology, 17,* 206-219.

Bruch, C. S. (2002). Amica Curiae Brief of Dr. Carol S. Bruch, J.D., Dr. Filed in Case No. S107355, *Marriage of LaMusga,* Supreme Court of the State of California, August, 19, 2002.

DiPietro, J.A. (2000). Baby and the brain: Advances in child development. *Annual Review of Public Health, 21,* 455-471.

Furstenberg, E. F., Jr., Hoffman, S. D., & Shrestha, L. (1995). The effects of divorce on intergenerational transfers: New evidence. *Demography, 32,* 319-333.

Fabricius, W. V., & Braver, S. L. (2004). Expenditures on children and visitation time: A reply to Garfinkel, McLanahan and Wallerstein. *Family Courts Review, 42,* 350-362.

Fabricius, W.V., & Luecken, L.J. (2007). Post-divorce living arrangements, parental conflict, and long-term physical health consequences for children of divorce. *Journal of Family Psychology.*

Idler, F.L., & Benyamini, Y. (1997). Self-rated health and mortality: A review of twenty-seven community studies. *Journal of Health and Social Behavior, 38,* 21-37.

In re the Marriage of Burgess, 913 P.2d 473 (Cal. 1996).

In re the Marriage of LaMusga 32 Cal.4th 1072, 12 CR3d 356, 88 P.3d 81 (Cal. 2004).

Kraft, A., & Luecken, L.J. (April, 2005). Poster presented at the annual meetings of the Society of Behavioral Medicine, Boston, MA.

Laumann-Billings, L., & Emery, R.E. (2000). Distress among young adults from divorced families. *Journal of Family Psychology, 14*(4), 671-687.

Luecken, L.J. (1998). Childhood attachment and loss experiences affect adult cardiovascular and cortisol function. *Psychosomatic Medicine, 60,* 765-772.

Lye, D. N., Klepinger, D. H., Hyle P. D., & Nelson, A. (1995). Childhood living arrangements and adult children's relations with their parents. *Demography, 32,* 261-280.

McLanahan, S., & Sandefur, G. (1994*). Growing up with a single parent.* Cambridge, MA: Harvard University Press.

Mechanic D., & Hansell S. (1989). Divorce, family conflict, and adolescent's well-being. *Journal of Health and Social Behavior, 30,* 106-116.

Newmark, L., Harrell, A., & Salem, P. (1995). Domestic violence and empowerment in custody and visitation cases. *Family and Conciliation Courts Review, 33,* 30-62.

Navarro, S.P. (2003). Appellant's and Dr. Judith Wallerstein's Replies to Amici Briefs Submitted by Leslie E Shear and Richard A. Warshak (2003). Filed in Case No. S107355, *Marriage of LaMusga,* Supreme Court of the State of California, October 17, 2003.

Pasley, K., & Braver, S. L. (2004). Measuring involvement in divorced, nonresident fathers. In R. D. Day & M. E. Lamb (Eds.), *Conceptualizing and measuring father involvement* (pp. 217-240). Mahwah, NJ: Erlbaum.

Russek, L.G., Schwartz, G.E., Bell, I.R., & Baldwin, C.M. (1998). Positive perceptions of parental caring are associated with reduced psychiatric and somatic symptoms. *Psychosomatic Medicine, 60,* 654-657.

Wallerstein, J. S. et al. (2003). Amici Curiae Brief of Dr. Judith S. Wallerstein, Ph.D. et al. Filed in Case No. S107355, *Marriage of LaMusga,* Supreme Court of the State of California, May 12, 2003.

doi:10.1300/J190v03n03_02

A Move in the Right Direction?
Best Interests of the Child Emerging
as the Standard for Relocation Cases

Linda D. Elrod

SUMMARY. Relocation cases have become more common in our increasingly mobile society. After a divorce the parent with primary residential custody of a minor child may seek to move to a new location for a new partner, spouse, job, or family. The nonmoving parent objects and the courts have to decide whether to allow the child to move. This article explores the various legal approaches taken by American courts in trying to solve these difficult custody cases. While some courts presume it is not in the best interests of a child to move, others presume that it is. The majority trend, however, appears to be toward a best interests of the child standard with no presumptions. doi:10.1300/J190v03n03_03 *[Article copies available for a fee from The Haworth Document Delivery Service: 1-800-HAWORTH. E-mail address: <docdelivery@haworthpress.com> Website: <http://www.HaworthPress.com> © 2006 by The Haworth Press, Inc. All rights reserved.]*

Linda D. Elrod is Distinguished Professor of Law and Director, Children and Family Law Center, Washburn University School of Law; Past Chair of American Bar Association Family Law Section and Editor of *Family Law Quarterly* (E-mail: linda.elrod@washburn.edu).

Portions of this article were taken from the author's manuscript for A Lawyer's Guide to Handling Relocation Cases (forthcoming ABA 2007). The chart is updated from Linda D. Elrod, *States Differ on Relocation: A Panorama of Expanding Case Law*, 28 (4) FAM. ADVOC. 8, 10-11 (2006).

[Haworth co-indexing entry note]: "A Move in the Right Direction? Best Interests of the Child Emerging as the Standard for Relocation Cases." Elrod, Linda D. Co-published simultaneously in *Journal of Child Custody* (The Haworth Press, Inc.) Vol. 3, No. 3/4, 2006, pp. 29-61; and: *Relocation Issues in Child Custody Cases* (ed: Philip M. Stahl, and Leslie M. Drozd) The Haworth Press, Inc., 2006, pp. 29-61. Single or multiple copies of this article are available for a fee from The Haworth Document Delivery Service [1-800-HAWORTH, 9:00 a.m. - 5:00 p.m. (EST). E-mail address: docdelivery@haworthpress.com].

29

KEYWORDS. Relocation, change of circumstances, move away, best interests of the child, stability

Across the country, applicable standards remain distressingly disparate.[1]

Relocation cases "present some of knottiest and most disturbing problems."[2] In the past ten years, the number of relocation cases has grown on trial and appellate court dockets as parents try to move themselves and their children across town, the country and even the world. Census data reveals that almost one half of Americans move in a five year period with an estimated one-fourth of custodial[3] mothers moving within four years of a divorce. The reasons for moving are as varied as the people–remarriage, corporate downsizing, job transfers, extended families, educational opportunities, or to put distance between an ex-spouse or partner. As early as 1992, one reporter summarized the problem as follows:

> The pain of divorce wears new guises. . . . The simultaneous rise of the dual-career couple and the divorce rate in recent years has created crises for an unprecedented number of American parents and children. . . . Joint custody or visitation rights, difficult at best, can become a major problem when one parent is transferred or takes a job far away and the other is unable or unwilling to move, too. . . . So people with careers they care about are torn between staying close to their kids and working where the opportunity is. The options all have drawbacks. Children are shuttled hundreds of miles back and forth between parents. A distant parent fades from the children's lives. A parent rejects a move in order to stay near the child and rues the sacrifice of career objectives.[4]

The relocation of the primary residential parent will fundamentally alter the child's existing relationships and environment, including physical residence, school, and community. At the least, the parents or the court will have to adjust the existing parenting schedule. At the most, the nonmoving parent may seek, and sometimes receive, primary residential custody. Legislative and court approaches to parental requests for relocation vary from state to state. Uniformity is woefully lacking. In 1990, the Pennsylvania Supreme Court observed, "Our research has failed to reveal a consistent, universally accepted approach to the question of when a custodial parent may relocate out-of-state over the objection of the non-custodial parent. . . ."[5]

Sixteen years, and hundreds of cases later, confusion and controversy remain over what are, and what should be, the legal standards to apply when a parent seeks to move away with a minor child. As the New Jersey Supreme Court observed in a relocation case:

> . . . there is a clash between the custodial parent's interest in self-determination and the noncustodial parent's interest in the companionship of the child. There is rarely an easy answer or even an entirely satisfactory one . . . If the removal is denied, the custodial parent may be embittered by the assault on his or her autonomy. If it is granted, the noncustodial parent may live with the abiding belief that his or her connection to the child has been lost forever.[6]

Among the complex issues that need to be faced are the constitutional rights of both parents and children and whether the same standards used to modify existing custodial and residency arrangements should be applied in relocation cases. Courts and legislatures have experimented with burdens of proof, presumptions for and against relocation, and have developed lists of factors. The American Law Institute has developed principles which include a relocation provision[7] and the American Academy of Matrimonial Lawyers has developed standards for relocation cases.[8]

This article explores the constitutional issues raised by relocation cases; the use of geographical restrictions in initial custody orders; and provides an overview of the patchwork of statutory and court-made standards, presumptions and burdens applicable throughout the country. The article concludes that the current movement appears to be away from presumptions and towards applying a best-interests-of-the-child analysis using a variety of factors in relocation cases.

THE CONSTITUTION AND RELOCATION

The United States Supreme Court has recognized at least two fundamental rights that may compete in a relocation case. First, parents have a fundamental right to the care, custody and control of their children.[9] As between fit parents who are divorcing or do not live together, courts award custody and make residential provisions based on the "best interest" of the child.[10] The second fundamental right is the right of citizens of the United States to travel freely between the states.[11] A citizen's right to travel encompasses the right to migrate, resettle, find a new job and start a new life. The right to travel can be infringed upon only if there exists a compelling state interest.[12] Changing a child's custody solely because the residential parent attempts to relocate would appear to infringe on the parent's right to travel. The Wyoming Supreme Court stated:

> . . .[T]he right to travel enjoyed by a citizen carries with it the right of a custodial parent to have the children move with that parent. This right is not to be denied, impaired, or disparaged unless clear evidence before the court demonstrates another substantial and material change of circumstance and establishes the detrimental effect of the move upon the children.[13]

Finding that neither the rights of a parent nor the duty of state courts to adjudicate custody justified restricting the right to travel under the United States and Wyoming Constitutions, the Wyoming Supreme Court found that a proposed relocation could not be a change of circumstances by itself to allow a court to reconsider a custodial placement.[14] The necessity for the nonmoving parent to prove a substantial change or circumstances *and* to prove that the move will have a detrimental effect on the child makes it easier for a custodial parent to move.

A couple of courts have avoided the constitutional argument by disingenuously finding that the parent is free to travel, but without the child.[15] The reality is that the "threat of losing custody makes the right to travel meaningless for many custodial parents who will not leave even in the face of few job prospects or a spouse living elsewhere."[16] The nonresidential parent's right to travel remains as no court approval is needed. One court found that a parent voluntarily waives the constitutional right to travel by agreeing to a geographical restriction.[17]

Minnesota elevates the child's welfare to a compelling state interest, thereby eliminating the need to balance the parents' competing constitutional rights. Therefore, the best interests of the child will trump the parents' right to travel.[18] However, the Colorado Supreme Court explicitly rejected this view, finding that "in the absence of demonstrated harm to the child, the best interests of the child standard is insufficient to serve as a compelling state interest overruling the parents' fundamental rights."[19] The Court noted:

... from a practical standpoint, adopting the best interests of the child as a compelling state interest to the exclusion of balancing the parents' rights could potentially make divorced parents captives of Colorado. This is because a parent's ability to relocate would become subject to the changing views of social scientists and other experts who hold strong, but conflicting, philosophical positions as to the theoretical "best interests of the child."[20]

The Colorado Supreme Court chose to adopt the view of the courts in Maryland[21] and New Mexico[22] that places the burden equally on both parents to demonstrate under the state's statutory factors what is in the child's best interest.[23] The court must promote the best interests of the child while affording protection equally between the majority time parent's right to travel and the minority time parent's right to parent.[24]

INITIAL ORDERS AND GEOGRAPHICAL RESTRICTIONS

If a parent wishes to move at the time of the initial custody proceeding, most courts use the same best interest of the child standard used in any custody dispute between fit parents.[25] The proposed relocation will be viewed as part of the best interests analysis with one parent living in another jurisdiction.[26]

Even if a move is not contemplated, some courts have inserted geographical restrictions in either the initial or a modified custody order.[27] Most parents determine their own parenting plan by a mediated or negotiated agreement, many of which contain geographical restrictions. Several states presume that the parents' agreement is in the best interests of the child.[28] The Arizona statute illustrates this:

> The court shall not deviate from a provision of any parenting plan or other written agreement by which the parents specifically have agreed to allow or prohibit relocation of the child unless the court finds that the provision is no longer in the child's best interests. There is a rebuttable presumption that a provision from any parenting plan or other written agreement is in the child's best interests.[29]

Based on the circumstances, however, a court may find that an agreement containing a provision to remain in one community is contrary to the best interest of a particular child.[30] Several appellate courts have disapproved of self-executing geographical restrictions, i.e., those that provide for an automatic change of custody to the nonmoving parent if the restriction is violated.[31] These self-executing provisions amount to improper speculation concerning the possibility of future changed circumstances and are unenforceable.[32] As in other instances, the judge has the power to act to protect the best interests of the child, irrespective of the parties' stipulations.

POST-DECREE RELOCATION

The vast majority of relocation cases occur following an initial custody order. Before the enactment of the Uniform Child Custody Jurisdiction Act (UCCJA), the fear of losing jurisdiction caused many courts to deny relocations without the noncustodial parent's consent or without a showing of extraordinary circumstances.[33] The Parental Kidnapping Prevention Act, and the Uniform Child Custody Jurisdiction and Enforcement Act, now in 45 jurisdictions, use the concept of continuing exclusive jurisdiction which clarifies that jurisdiction remains in the decree state as long as one parent remains in the state and there is a basis for jurisdiction under the state's law. Therefore, the fear of loss of jurisdiction is no longer a factor in most relocation cases.

The typical case begins with the residential parent filing a motion for permission to relocate. Some cases, however, start when the nonmoving parent learns of the move, either by letter or official notice required by statute, and files a motion to modify the existing order. States vary as to the requirements that a moving parent must take and as to which parent bears the burden of proof. Some courts use the same standards for an intrastate and interstate move.[34]

Notice Requirements

Since 1990, several states have enacted statutes requiring notice of an intent to move if the nonresidential parent does not consent. These statutes vary on when notice must be given, who is entitled to notice, the effect of notice and the penalties for noncompliance. In some states, notice is to be given not only to parents but also to others with court-ordered access, such as grandparents. Notice may not be required if the nonmoving parent has been convicted of any crime in which the child is the victim or if the reason for the move is fear of domestic violence. Times vary from "reasonable" to a specific number of days.[35] The

AAML Standards and *ALI Principles*, as well as several state statutes, require 60 days notice.[36] Some states require notice for any move.[37] In other states, parents need only give notice if the parent is moving out of state or a certain geographical distance.[38]

Many statutes leave the contents of the notice to local practice. The *ALI Principles* require the notice to include:

    a. the intended date of the relocation;
    b. the address of the intended new residence;
    c. the specific reasons for the intended relocation; and
    d. a proposal for how custodial responsibility should be modified, if necessary, in light of the intended move.[39]

The requirement for notice does not necessarily mean that the move is a change of circumstances.[40] It may, however, mean that the court will allow a hearing if the nonrelocating parent objects to the move. The failure to give notice may be relevant.[41] Generally, if the nonrelocating parent does not object within a certain time after receiving notice, the statute may allow the relocation without a return to the court.

Presumptions and Burdens of Proof

Most relocation cases require modifications to an original order. In most states, to encourage stability for the child, there is a presumption that the original order should stay in effect. A parent wishing to modify an existing custody order has the initial burden of showing that a material or substantial change of circumstances has occurred since the original decree that justifies a hearing on whether the child's custody should be changed.[42] If a hearing is granted, the person seeking modification must show that a change of the current arrangements is in the child's best interest. A few states use a variation of the Uniform Marriage and Divorce Act "endangerment" standard which requires a showing that "the child's present environment may endanger seriously his physical, mental, moral, or emotional health" before custody may be modified.[43]

Relocation cases in some states are handled as are other modification cases. In other states, there are either different or additional standards for relocation cases. There are basically three approaches:

    1. a move alone is not a change in circumstances, resulting in a presumption in favor of relocation by the custodial or residential parent;

2. a move may be change of circumstances and the court may use shifting presumptions so the custodial or residential parent has the initial burden to show good faith and the move is in the child's best interest, then the burden shifts to the nonresidential parent to show the move is not in the child's best interests; and
3. no presumptions, where each party bears the burden of showing why the child's best interests is to be with one of them.

Jurisdictions are split as to whether the custodial parent's proposal to relocate is sufficient by itself to constitute a material change in circumstances that warrants a hearing on the best interests of the child. Whether the proposed move is a change of circumstances affects the burden of proof. If the relocation is not a change in circumstances, then the presumption is that the custodial parent can move. If the move is a change of circumstances, then both parents must put on evidence showing why the move is, or is not, in the child's best interests.

Not a Change of Circumstances–Presumption for Relocation

Several courts have found that the relocation of the primary residential parent does not necessarily constitute a change in circumstances.[44] These jurisdictions favor the child's stability (emotional as opposed to geographical) in the primary custodial relationship.[45] For example, the Oklahoma Supreme Court stated:

> In a relocation case the noncustodial parent seeking to restrain the custodial parent from moving must meet the heavy burden to show that circumstances justify reopening the question of "custody."[46]

Some states find there no change of circumstances if the move is within the same state.[47] Most courts that do not find the proposed relocation itself to be a change of circumstances create a presumption which favors the moving parent. These courts give the residential parent the right to make decisions as to residence and put the burden on the nonmoving parent to show harm.[48] For example, the Arkansas Supreme Court stated:

> . . . [T]oday, we hold that relocation alone is not a material change in circumstance. We pronounce a presumption in favor of relocation for custodial parents with primary custody. The noncustodial parent should have the burden to rebut the relocation presumption.

The custodial parent no longer has the obligation to prove a real advantage to herself or himself and to the children in relocating.[49]

Other states appear to have a presumption in favor of allowing a custodial parent to move either by statute[50] or by case law.[51] Such a presumption reduces litigation because it makes contesting a move more difficult. Only those nonresidential parents who are actively involved in the child's day to day life or have shared custody may feel they have enough evidence to overcome the presumption.

The *ALI Principles* favor relocation. The relocation of a parent constitutes a substantial change in circumstances only when the relocation significantly impairs either parent's ability to exercise responsibilities the parent has been exercising or attempting to exercise under the parenting plan. Even if the relocation constitutes a change of circumstances, the ALI would allow the parent who has been exercising the clear majority of custodial responsibility to relocate with the child if that parent shows that the relocation is for a valid purpose, in good faith, and to a location that is reasonable in light of the purpose.[52]

In the much publicized *Burgess* case,[53] the California Supreme Court allowed a mother to move forty miles away so she would not have to commute to her job and found that the statute stressing the importance of frequent contact with both parents did not require the court to impose a burden of proof on those wishing to relocate or alter its best interest analysis. In the more recent *LaMusga* case, the California Supreme Court reiterated that if there is an existing order, "a change of custody is not justified simply because the custodial parent has chosen, for any sound good faith reason, to reside in a different location, but only if, as a result of relocation . . . the child will suffer detriment. . . ."[54] The Court, however, went on to note:

> . . . the noncustodial parent bears the initial burden of showing that the proposed relocation of the children's residence would cause detriment to the children, requiring a reevaluation of the children's custody. The likely impact of the proposed move on the noncustodial parent's relationship with the children is a relevant factor in determining whether the move would cause detriment to the children and, when considered in light of all of the relevant factors, may be sufficient to justify a change in custody. If the noncustodial parent makes such an initial showing of detriment, the court must perform the delicate and difficult task of determining whether a change in custody is in the best interests of the children.[55]

Therefore, while the relocation alone may not be a sufficient change of circumstances, a showing of harm to the children's relationship with the nonmoving parent may be a sufficient change in circumstances to allow a review of the children's best interests.[56] The California Supreme Court in *LaMusga* indicated that there may be additional factors which will make the proposed relocation a sufficient change to conduct an evidentiary hearing:

> . . . [T]he likely consequences of a proposed change in the residence of a child, when considered in the light of all the relevant factors, may constitute a change of circumstances that warrants a change in custody, and the detriment to the child's relationship with the noncustodial parent that will be caused by the proposed move, when considered in light of all the relevant factors, may warrant denying a request to change the child's residence or changing custody.[57]

Relocation Alone a Change in Circumstances

In some states, either statutes[58] or judges require that the relocation of the custodial parent constitutes a material change in circumstances which requires a full evidentiary hearing.[59] If a hearing is held, most states require the relocating parent to initially bear the burden of proving that the proposed relocation is made in good faith (there is a legitimate reason for the move) and that it is in the child's best interests to continue living with him or her.[60] The burden then shifts to the nonmoving parent to show that the proposed relocation is not in the best interest of the child.[61] The New Hampshire statute illustrates this approach:

> V. The parent seeking permission to relocate bears the initial burden of demonstrating, by a preponderance of the evidence, that:
> (a) The relocation is for a legitimate purpose; and
> (b) The proposed location is reasonable in light of that purpose.
> VI. If the burden of proof . . . is met, the burden shifts to the other parent to prove, by a preponderance of the evidence, that the proposed relocation is not in the best interest of the child.[62]

The shifting burden of proof looks at the reality that the court has already entrusted the care of the child to one of the parents who makes the day to day decisions. If the relocating parent can show a good faith reason for the move, the non-custodial parent then has the burden of showing (with concrete, material reasons) why relocation is not in the child's best interest.[63]

Courts are more likely to find that a proposed relocation is a material change of circumstances in a true shared physical custody situation. If both parents are involved in the day to day care of the child, either the parents or the court will need to fashion a new parenting schedule.[64] The label attached to the custody/residency arrangement is less important than the actual parenting that is happening. Where the parents truly share both legal and physical custody, an application by one parent to relocate with the child to an out-of-state location is analyzed as an application for a change of custody.[65] Among the things that courts look at to determine if parents are sharing "primary custodial responsibilities" are (1) transporting the child to and from school; (2) attending the child's school activities and sporting events; (3) helping the child with homework; (4) preparing the child's meals; (5) caring for the child overnight; and (6) attending to the child's medical needs.[66]

No Presumption Either Way

The trend, however, is away from presumptions and toward using a best interests test.[67] Some courts handle relocation cases in cases in which the parents share custody, discussed *supra*, as initial custody orders, using the best interests rules, rather than requiring a change of circumstances.[68] In overturning the stringent standard requiring a custodial parent to show "exceptional circumstances" for a move, the New York Court of Appeals stated:

> It serves neither the interest of the children nor the needs of justice to view relocation cases through the prisms of presumptions and threshold tests that artificially skew the analysis in favor of one outcome or the other.[69]

In Georgia, the Supreme Court, in changing from a presumption in favor of relocation to the best interest standard, stated:

> [T]he primary consideration of the trial court in deciding custody matters must be directed to the best interests of the child involved

> . . . any determination of the best interests of the child must be made on a case-by-case basis. This analysis forbids the presumption that a relocating custodial parent will always lose custody and, conversely, forbids any presumption in favor of relocation.[70]

Recently, the Colorado Supreme Court stated:

> . . . each parent has the burden to persuade the court that the relocation of the child will be in or contrary to the child's best interests, or that the parenting plan he or she proposes should be adopted by the court. The focus of the court, however, should be the best interests of the child. The court may decide that it is not in the best interests of the child to relocate with the majority time parent. Then, if the majority time parent still wishes to relocate, a new parenting time plan will be necessary.
>
> Alternatively, the court may decide that it is in the best interests of the child to relocate with the majority time parent. In that situation, the court must fashion a parenting time plan which protects the constitutional right of the minority time parent to care for and control the child. In either event, the court must thoroughly disclose the reasons for its decision and make specific findings with respect to each of the statutory factors.[71]

These cases, and others represent a clear trend toward using a case specific, fact sensitive, best interest analysis in every case.

FACTORS IN EVALUATING
MOVE IN CHILD'S BEST INTEREST

> . . . *Sensitive case-by-case balancing is required to ensure that all interests–both parents' and children's are treated as equitably as possible.*[72]

As in other custody determinations between fit parents, the best interest of the child is not always clear.[73] Some state legislatures and courts have developed lists of factors for the court to consider in evaluating the child's best interests in custody cases; others have lists specific to relocation. Unfortunately, most statutes have no weight assigned to the importance of the factors. If the best interest of the child is truly the standard, then the focus should be on the individual child's age and developmental, physical, emotional, spiritual and educational needs. The judge then must evaluate if the child's needs are being met by an individual, such as the primary caregiver, by both parents, or by the larger community. However, many of the factors stress "parent" considerations such as the distance, cost and difficulty of visitation.

Statutory Factors

Statutory factors vary from state to state but contain many similarities. Louisiana enacted the factors developed by the American Academy of Matrimonial Lawyers which are among the most child-focused. These factors require consideration of:

A. (1) The nature, quality, extent of involvement, and duration of the child's relationship with the person proposing to relocate and with the nonrelocating person, siblings, and other significant persons in the child's life;

(2) The age, developmental stage, needs of the child, and likely impact of relocation on the child's physical, educational, and emotional development, taking into consideration any special needs of the child;

(3) The feasibility of preserving the relationship between the nonrelocating person and the child through suitable visitation arrangements, considering the logistics and financial circumstances of the parties;

(4) The child's preference, taking into consideration the age and maturity of the child;

(5) Whether the person seeking relocation has an established pattern of conduct promoting or thwarting the nonrelocating person's relationship with the child;

(6) Whether the relocation will enhance the general quality of life for both the custodial party seeking relocation and the child, including but not limited to financial or emotional benefit or educational opportunity;

(7) The reasons each person seeks or opposes relocation; and

(8) Any other factor affecting the best interest of the child.

B. The court may not consider whether or not the person seeking relocation of the child will relocate without the child if relocation is denied or whether or not the person opposing relocation will also relocate if relocation is allowed.[74]

Colorado amended its statute in 2001 to require a court to consider twenty-one factors: those used to make the initial best interests determination, plus nine additional factors particularly relevant to relocation.[75] Several other states have lists of factors.[76]

Court Enumerated Factors

In the absence of a statute specifically tailored to relocation, appellate courts have set out factors to help trial judges evaluate the child's best interest in move away cases. A summary laundry list of the various factors that courts consider are:

1. The prospective advantages of the move in improving the moving parent's and the child's quality of life;
2. The integrity of the moving parent's motive for relocation, considering whether it is to defeat or deter visitation by the non-moving parent;
3. The integrity of the nonmoving parent's motives for opposing the move;
4. Whether there is a realistic opportunity for visitation which can provide an adequate basis for preserving and fostering the nonmoving parent's relationship with the child, and the likelihood that each parent will comply with such alternate visitation;
5. What was contemplated by the parties and the court at the time the original orders were entered;
6. The history of the relationship of the child and each party;
7. The input from the attorney for the minor child;
8. The family relations report;
9. The cost of visitation, considering the distance between the two cities, the cost of travel, and the ease of travel;
10. The impact of relocation on the child and the chance for improving the child's quality of life:
    a. Emotional, physical and developmental needs of the children;
    b. the children's opinion or preference as to where to live;
    c. the extent to which the moving parent's income or employment will be enhanced;
    d. the degree to which housing or living conditions would be improved;
    e. the existence of educational, health and leisure opportunities at least equivalent to existing ones;

f. the quality of the relationship between the children and each parent;

g. the strength of the children's ties to the present community and extended family there;

h. the likelihood that allowing or denying the move would antagonize hostilities between the two parties;

i. any special needs or talents of the child that require accommodation and whether it is available in the new location;

j. whether the child is a senior year in high school and should not which be moved until graduation without his or her consent; and

k. any other factor bearing on the child's interest.[77]

Using the Factors to Find the Best Interests of the Child

. . . Usually, in relocation cases, there is no good or right answer, especially for the child.[78]

Although numerous factors are found in the statutes and cases, trial judges seem to concentrate on three major factors: the reasons for and against the move; whether the move will enhance the child's quality of life; and the availability of realistic substitute visitation schedule to maintain a relationship with the nonmoving parent. Several states have noted that when analyzing a situation in which one parent seeks to relocate with the minor children, the paramount need for continuity and stability in custody arrangements, and the harm that may result from disruption of established patterns of care and emotional bonds with the primary caretaker, weigh heavily in favor of maintaining ongoing custody arrangements. On the other hand, the attachment between the child and the non-relocating parent also will be an important consideration.[79]

Motives Matter

Courts have approved a number of reasons as valid for moving, with most relating to starting a new life and improving the overall economic condition of the custodial parent and the child.[80] The *ALI Principles* set out the following as valid reasons for a move:

(1) to be close to significant family or other sources of support, (2) to address significant health problems, (3) to protect the safety of the child or another member of the child's household from a signifi-

cant risk of harm, (4) to pursue a significant employment or educational opportunity, (5) to be with one's spouse or domestic partner
who lives in, or is pursuing a significant employment or educational opportunity in, the new location, (6) to significantly improve the family's quality of life. The relocating parent should
have the burden of proving the validity of any other purpose. . . .
The court should find that a move for a valid purpose is reasonable
unless its purpose is shown to be substantially achievable without
moving, or by moving to a location that is substantially less disrup-
tive of the other parent's relationship to the child.[81]

These ALI reasons have been cited with approval in Rhode Island,[82]
Vermont,[83] and West Virginia.[84]

Most courts have been sympathetic to a residential parent who wants
to move because either the parent or a new spouse is being transferred,
is getting a promotion or has better job opportunities.[85] A parent who is
moving to take a new job may be required to show that he or she at the
very least applied for a job or seriously looked for one in the area.[86] On
the other hand, the parent is not required to apply for every job that
might be available in the state if the parent has made a reasonable
search.[87] Just because a parent has remarried or has a higher paying job
offer does not ensure that the request to move will be allowed.[88]

Most often, there is not just one motive for the move, but several. For
example, one mother wanted to move with a three year old because she
was going to remarry, the new location had a lower cost of living than
California, she would be able to stay home to care for the child, and she
had family there.[89] Some courts have found a valid reason in the custodial
parent's desire to move to an area in closer proximity to relatives[90] or to
advance one's education.[91] However, a Nevada court denied a mother's
request to move where she could obtain the same degree from the same
college without relocating through either Internet classes, audio and
video classes, or live classes through the college's extension campus.[92]

Courts have found the custodial parent's reasons inadequate when
they seem to be not concrete or to frustrate the nonresidential parent's
visitation. In the absence of abuse, the desire of one parent to distance
the child from the other parent certainly will not be a sufficient reason.[93]
For example, when a mother wanted to move from California to Florida
to explore the possibility of a job as a parapsychologist, the court found
the reason really to be to thwart the father's visitation.[94] A parent who
"thinks" that the environment in another location may be better for their
health may find the court rejecting the relocation for that reason.[95]

Courts have not been sympathetic to parents who unilaterally act in taking the children from the jurisdiction without the court or the other parent's permission. The court may change custody to the nonmoving parent.[96] If there is concern about parental alienation, a court may be reluctant to allow the parent and child to relocate.[97]

The motives of the nonresidential parent are important also. A parent who has not exercised visitation but just wants to keep the other parent from moving is not in a strong position. In one case, the court allowed the move where the father had been manipulative and controlling.[98] The court can look at the likelihood that allowing or denying the move would antagonize the hostilities between the two parties.[99]

Child's Quality of Life Issues

The proposed relocation may justify a change in custody only if such a change is in the child's best interests. If the judge changes the child's custody to the noncustodial parent, even if staying in the same city, the child will experience a change. Therefore, the judge has to weigh carefully the two living arrangements, keeping in mind that it is the child, not the warring parents, whose interests need to be protected. As one judge noted:

> . . . a child's development is not something with which courts should experiment and risk disruption. Although ideally a child would develop a close relationship with his loving and caring parents through an equal division of parenting time, the ideal is difficult to achieve when, as in this case, the child's parents elect to establish their homes in different communities. This problem is further compounded by the friction that often develops between ex-spouses as they move on with their lives after their divorce. . . . In ordering this change in custody the *trial court forgot that the paramount consideration in a child custody decision is the child's best interests, not those of his parents.*[100]

The child's quality of life may be tied to a large extent to the custodial/residential parent's quality of life. A child theoretically benefits from a custodial parent who has a stable relationship, more money, more time, and less conflict.[101] Where the proposed relocation provides education, emotional and economic benefits for the child, many courts feel the relocation should be granted.[102]

Courts have changed custody to the nonmoving parent where the reasons for the move and the quality of the new environment do not outweigh the adverse impact.[103] For example, when a mother who had sole custody moved to North Carolina before the court hearing, the court changed custody to the father. The court found that a relocation was not in child's best interest because both sets of child's grandparents lived where father resided, the child was familiar and happy in father's home and had lived there almost nine months at the time of the modification hearing and expressed a preference to live with the father.[104] A Missouri court found that it was not in the children's best interests to move 1,200 miles because the father lived only seven houses away and was an active participant in their daily lives.[105] In another case, where children had moved and were experiencing academic and attendance difficulties in addition to separation from their father, the court changed custody to the father during the school year.[106]

There is little valid research on whether it is in the best interests of a child to remain near to both parents.[107] Research does show that children suffer the most harm in high conflict cases.[108] To the extent that a relocation reduces the conflict between the parents, it could enhance the child's quality of life. Studies have shown that contact with both parents is best when the parents can cooperate.[109] Although one study purports to show that children of divorced parents who are separated from one parent due to either parent moving beyond an hour's drive are significantly less well off on many child mental and physical health measures compared to those children whose parents do not relocate,[110] this study has been severely criticized both for its methodology and for its conclusions.[111] More research needs to be done on the effects of relocation on children of different ages.

Alternative Parenting Plans

Almost every move to a distant relocation is going to adversely affect the nonmoving parent's visitation rights or parenting time.[112] That new arrangements have to be made that are more difficult or less convenient is not sufficient reason to deny the move.[113] The New York Court of Appeals stated:

> Like Humpty Dumpty, a family, once broken by divorce, cannot be put back together in precisely the same way. The relationship between the parents and children is necessarily different after a divorce and, accordingly, it may be unrealistic in some cases to try to

preserve the noncustodial parent's accustomed close involvement in the children's everyday life at the expense of the custodial parent's efforts to start a new life or to form a new family unit.[114]

The key is to craft an alternate visitation schedule that continues and preserves the relationship between the child and the non-custodial parent without imposing all of the burdens of relocation on the child. The cases which are most successful in allowing a move have been those in which the moving parent has carefully considered and drafted plans that will minimize the adverse effect that the move will have on the parent-child relationship with the nonmoving parent.

Among the factors the court will consider are the distance between the two cities, the costs of travel, and the ease of travel. Restructuring visitation often means scheduling physical visitation for more time during the summer and school holidays. The result may be more actual days, but less frequency than the original order.

With today's modern methods of communication, there are more opportunities for maintaining contact with parents and others who do not live close to the child. Virtual visitation offers alternate ways for parents to have contact.[115] One court noted that "increased use of alternatives to normal physical visitation, such as phone calls, letters and even e-mail . . . are feasible."[116] Several other courts have recognized the advances in technology that have made possible contacts that would have been unheard of twenty years ago.[117] While the new technology will not substitute for personal contact, it can help maintain the parent-child connection.

INTERNATIONAL MOVES

A handful of states that has considered the issue have used the same standard for a contemplated international move as for an interstate move.[118] Relocation to a foreign country, however, may involve additional considerations. For example, there may be the introduction of cultural conditions far different from those experienced in the United States. The greater distance may make the additional costs of visitation prohibitive in many cases, although virtual visitation alternatives may exist.[119] In addition, there may be some concerns about enforcement of custody and visitation orders in another country. Alabama has a statute which considers as a factor whether the proposed relocation is to a foreign country which does not normally enforce the rights of noncustodial parents.[120]

CONCLUSION

Statutes and court decisions on relocation have created a true hodge- podge of presumptions, burdens, factors and lists. There remains no universal standard. Within the past four years, it does appear clear that the emerging standard is the case-by-case best interests of the child approach. While it is hard to argue with a judge trying to do what is in a child's best interests, as we have seen in other areas, the child's best interests are hard to predict and the decision can be highly subjective. In addition, if the concern is for the child to maintain contact with both parents, there needs to be an avenue for a custodial parent to challenge a noncustodial parent's relocation which may not be in the child's best interests. The uncertainty inherent in a best interest test leads to often painful, expensive, and time-consuming litigation with inconsistent results. As one dissenting judge noted:

> [R]eplacement of concrete standards with an amorphous best-interest-of-the-child standard will leave the trial courts free to consider any circumstance in a child's life as a potential reason to uproot the child . . . Without any guidance [in the form of presumptions] . . . every dissatisfaction a noncustodial parent has with the parenting of the custodial parent becomes a proper basis for re-litigating custody.[121]

Relocation cases are hard on the parents, the children, the lawyers and the judge. While a parent may think he or she has won a relocation case, if the child suffers loss of a strong parent-child relationship or has to fly across the country during every break, the child has lost something significant. On the other hand, if the courts truly focus on the needs of the child, rather than the demands and wishes of the parents, the best interest test may be the most equitable way to decide these troublesome cases. The outcome of any given case will depend upon the existence of a statute or case precedent making it easy or difficult for a parent to relocate with a child, the type of parenting arrangement or order that currently exists, and the attitudes of the judge who will be hearing the motion as to the best interests of any given child.[122]

NOTES

1. Gruber v. Gruber, 583 A.2d 434, 437 (Pa. Super. Ct. 1990).

2. Tropea v. Tropea, 665 N.E.2d 145, 148 (N.Y. 1996).

3. While the majority of states still use the term "custodial" parent to designate the parent who has physical residency of the child, some states distinguish residency from custody; other states use "majority time" or "residential parent."

4. JoAnne S. Lublin, *Cast Asunder: After Couples Divorce, Long-Distance Moves are Often Wrenching*, WALL STREET J., Nov. 20, 1992.

5. Gruber, 583 A.2d at 437.

6. Bauers v. Lewis, 770 A.2d 214, 217 (N.J. 2001).

7. ALI PRINCIPLES OF THE LAW OF FAMILY DISSOLUTION § 2.17 (2002) [hereinafter ALI PRINCIPLES].

8. *American Academy of Matrimonial Lawyers Proposed Model Relocation Act*, 15 J. AM. ACAD. MATRIMONIAL LAWYERS 1 (1998) [hereinafter AAML Standards].

9. Troxel v. Granville, 530 U.S. 57 (2000); Santosky v. Kramer, 455 U.S. 745 (1982).

10. *See generally* LINDA D. ELROD, CHILD CUSTODY PRACTICE AND PROCEDURE, ch. 4 (West/Thomson 2004 and Supp. 2005).

11. *Id.* at § 17:26. *See* United States v. Guest, 383 U.S. 745 (1966); Shapiro v. Thompson, 394 U.S. 618 (1969); Jones v. Helms, 452 U.S. 412 (1981); Saenz v. Roe, 526 U.S. 489 (1999). *See* Arthur B. La France, *Child Custody and Relocation: A Constitutional Perspective*, 34 U. LOUISVILLE J. FAM. L. 1 (1996); Paula M. Raines, *Joint Custody and the Right to Travel: Legal and Psychological Implications*, 24 J. FAM. L. 625 (1985); Anne L. Spitzer, *Moving and Storage of Post-Divorce Children: Relocation, the Constitution and the Courts*, 1985 ARIZ. ST. L. J. 1 (1985).

12. Jones v. Helms, 452 U.S. at 415-16.

13. Watt v. Watt, 971 P.2d 608, 615-16 (Wyo. 1999).

14. *Id.*

15. *See In re* Marriage of Johnson, 660 N.E.2d 1370 (Ill. App. Ct. 1996); *In re* C.R.O., 96 S.W.3d 442 (Tex. Ct. App. 2002). *See* Roger M. Baron, *Custody Relocation Restrictions: A Tool for Preventing Conflicts*, 17 FAIR$HARE 5-6 (Apr. 1997)(arguing that parents' constitutional rights to travel do "not include the freedom to 'travel with the child.'").

16. *See* Leslie Eaton, *Divorced Parents Move, and Custody Gets Trickier*, LAW WISE 5 (Feb. 2005)(discussing Colorado case in which judge denied mother's move to Arizona for a job and another case of a mother who shuttles between her husband and son in California and her daughter from a first marriage who judge made stay in New York).

17. Tomasko v. DuBuc, 761 A.2d 407 (N.H. 2000).

18. *See* LaChappelle v. Mitten, 607 N.W.2d 151, 163 (Minn. Ct. App.), *cert. denied* Mitten v. LaChapelle, 531 U.S. 1011 (2000); Weiland v. Ruppel, 75 P.3d 176 (Idaho 2003). *See also* David M. Cotter, *Oh, The Place You'll (Possibly) Go! Recent Case Law on Relocation of the Custodial Parent*, 16(9) DIVORCE LITIG. (Sept. 2004).

19. *In re* Marriage of Ciesluk, 113 P.3d 135, 145 (Colo. 2005).

20. *Id.*

21. *See* Braun v. Headley, 750 A.2d 624, 635 (Md. Ct. Spec. App. 2000), *cert. denied*, 755 A.2d 1139 (Md. 2000), *cert. denied*, 531 U.S. 1191 (2001) (finding no constitutional infirmity in giving *equal* status to the custodial parent's right to travel, and the benefit to be given the child from remaining with the custodial parent and the benefit from the non-custodial parent's exercise of his right to maintain close association and frequent contact with the child). *See also In re* D.M.G., 951 P.2d 1377 (Mont. 1998).

22. *See* Jaramillo v. Jaramillo, 823 P.2d 299, 307-09 (N.M. 1991).

23. *In re* Marriage of Ciesluk, 113 P.3d 135 (Colo. 2005).

24. Ciesluk, 113 P.3d at 142.

25. ELROD, CHILD CUSTODY, *supra* note 10, at § 4:35. *See* Spahmer v. Gullette, 113 P.3d 158 (Colo. 2005); Ford v. Ford, 789 A.2d 1104, *cert. denied* 796 A.2d 556 (Conn. 2002); Stangel v. Stangel, 355 N.W.2d 489, 490 (Minn. Ct. App .1984), *rev. denied*; Barney v. Barney, 754 N.Y.S.2d 108 (App. Div. 2003); Landis v. Landis, 869 A.2d 1003 (Pa. Super. Ct. 2005); Resor v. Resor, 987 P.2d 146 (Wyo. 1999).

26. *See* Ragghanti v. Reyes, 20 Cal. Rptr. 3d 522 (Ct. App. 2004); Davis v. Davis, 588 S.E.2d 102 (S.C. 2003); Pahl v. Pahl, 87 P.3d 1250 (Wyo. 2004).

27. *See* Leeds v. Adamse, 832 So. 2d 125 (Fla. Dist. Ct. App. 2002); Ziegler v. Ziegler, 691 P.2d 773 (Idaho 1985); Carlson v. Carlson, 661 P.2d 833 (Kan. Ct. App. 1983).

28. *See* KAN. STAT. ANN. § 60-1610(a) (2005); MICH. COMP. L. ANN. § 722.31(5) (2004). *See* Pointer v. Bell, 719 So. 2d 222 (Ala. Civ. App. 1998). *See also* ELROD, *supra* note 10, at § 4.07.

29. ARIZ. REV. STAT. ANN. § 25-408 (2004).

30. *See* Godwin v. Balderamos, 876 So. 2d 1169 (Ala. Civ. App. 2003); Bell v. Bell, 572 So. 2d 841 (Miss. 1990); Zeller v. Zeller, 640 N.W.2d 53 (N.D. 2002); *In re* Duckett, 905 P.2d 1170 (Or. Ct. App. 1995).

31. *See* Scott v. Scott, 578 S.E.2d 876, 879 (Ga. 2003); Hovater v. Hovater, 577 So. 2d 461 (Ala. Ct. App. 1990); *In re* Marriage of Seitzinger, 77 N.E.2d 282 (Ill. App. Ct. 2002); *In re* Marriage of Thielges, 623 N.W.2d 232 (Iowa Ct. App. 2000); Wilson v. Wilson, 408 S.E.2d 578 (Va. Ct. App. 1991); Watt v. Watt, 971 P.2d 608 (Wyo. 1999).

32. *See In re* Marriage of Pape, 989 P.2d 1120 (Wash. 2000); Savage v. Morrison, 691 N.Y.S.2d 842 (App. Div. 1999); Grathwol v. Grathwol, 727 N.Y.S.2d 825 (App. Div. 2001).

33. *See generally* Connie Peterson, *Relocation of Children by the Custodial Parent*, 65 AM. JUR. TRIALS 127 (2004); Nadine E. Roddy, *Stabilizing Families in a Mobile Society: Recent Case Law on Relocation of the Custodial Parent*, 8 DIVORCE LITIG. 141 (Aug. 1996).

34. *See, e.g.*, Van Asten v. Costa, 874 So. 2d 1244 (Fla. Dist. Ct. App. 2004); Schulze v. Morris, 825 A.2d 1173 (N.J. Super. Ct. App. Div. 2003).

35. For example, Indiana requires no specific time; other states require thirty or forty-five days notice. *See* Chart in Appendix.

36. ALI PRINCIPLES, *supra* note 7; AAML STANDARDS, *supra* note 8. *See* Chart in Appendix.

37. KAN. STAT. ANN. § 60-1620(a)(Supp. 2004). *See also* AAML STANDARDS, *supra* note 8.

38. *See, e.g.*, ARIZ. REV. STAT. ANN. § 25-408 (2004) (100 miles intrastate); MICH. COMP. LAWS ANN. § 722.31 (2004) (100 miles); OR. REV. STAT. § 107.159 (2004) (60 miles); UTAH CODE ANN. § 30-3-37 (2004) (150 miles).

39. ALI PRINCIPLES, *supra* note 7.

40. *See* LA. REV. STAT. 9:355.11 (providing notice of a proposed relocation of a child shall not constitute a change of circumstance warranting a change of custody); Lamb v. Wenning, 583 N.E.2d 745 (Ind. Ct. App. 1991).

41. *See* LA. REV. STAT. 9:355.11 (2004) (moving without prior notice or moving in violation of a court order may constitute a change of circumstances warranting a modification of custody); Wright ex rel McBath v. Wright, 129 S.W.3d 882 (Mo. Ct. App. 2004).

42. ELROD, *supra* note 10, at § § 17:01, 17:29; JEFF ATKINSON, MODERN CHILD CUSTODY PRACTICE § 10-5 (2d ed. 2004).

43. *See* Fenwick v. Fenwick, 114 S.W.3d 767 (Ky. 2003); Silbaugh v. Silbaugh, 543 N.W.2d 639 (Minn. 1996); Dehring v. Dehring, 559 N.W.2d 59 (Mich. Ct. App. 1996); Cook v. Cook, 898 P.2d 702 (Nev. 1995); Perry v. Perry, 943 S.W.2d 884 (Tenn. Ct. App. 1996).

44. *See* Hollandsworth v. Knyzewski, 109 S.W.3d 653, 657 (Ark. 2003); Botterbusch v. Botterbusch, 851 So. 2d 903 (Fla. Dist. Ct. App. 2003); Evans v. Evans, 530 S.E.2d 576 (N.C. 2000); Latimer v. Farmer, 602 S.E.2d 32 (S.C. 2004); Watt v. Watt, 971 P.2d 608, 616 (Wyo. 1999). *See also* KAN. STAT. ANN. §60-1620(c) (2005) (stating a proposed move *may* be change).

45. *See In re* Marriage of Burgess, 913 P.2d 473 (Cal. 1996); Ireland v. Ireland, 717 A.2d 676 (Conn. 1998); *Ex Parte* Murphy, 670 So. 2d 51 (Ala. 1995); Pollock v. Pollock, 889 P.2d 633 (Ariz. Ct. App. 1995); *In re* Duckett, 905 P.2d 1170 (Or. Ct. App. 1995), *rev. denied* 912 P.2d 375 (1996); Aaby v. Strange, 924 S.W.2d 623 (Tenn. 1996). For a discussion of legal issues and social science considerations *see* Carol S. Bruch & Janet M. Bowermaster, *The Relocation of Children and Custodial Parents: Public Policy, Past and Present,* 30 FAM. L.Q. 245 (1996); Judith S. Wallerstein & Tony J. Tanke, *To Move or Not to Move–Psychological and Legal Considerations in the Relocation of Children Following Divorce,* 30 FAM. L.Q. 305 (1996); Richard Warshak, *Social Science and Children's Interest in Relocation Cases: Burgess Revisited,* 34 FAM. L.Q. 83 (2000).

46. Kaiser v. Kaiser, 23 P.3d 278, 286-87 (Okla. 2001).

47. *See* Bednarek v. Velazquez, 830 A.2d 1267 (Pa. Super. Ct. 2003); *In re* Marriage of Seitzinger, 775 N.E.2d 282 (Ill. App. Ct. 2002); Watt v. Watt, 971 P.2d 608 (Wyo. 1999). *But see* ME. REV. STAT. 19A § 1657.2.A-1 (moving more than 60 miles is presumed to disrupt the parent-child contact of nonmoving parent);

48. Godwin v. Balderamos, 876 So. 2d 1169 (Ala. Civ. App. 2003); Casey v Casey, 58 P.3d 763, 771 (Okla. 2002); Watt v. Watt, 971 P.2d 608 (Wyo. 1999).

49. Hollandsworth v. Knyzewski, 109 S.W.3d 653, 663 (Ark. 2003).

50. *See* CAL. FAM. CODE § 7501(a) (2004); KY. REV. STAT. § 403.340 (2)(2004); TENN. CODE ANN. § 36-6-108 (2004); WASH. REV. CODE ANN. § 26.09.520 (2004); WIS. STAT. ANN. § 767.327(3) (2004).

51. *See, e.g.*, Klotz v. Klotz, 747 N.E.2d 1187 (Ind. Ct. App. 2001); Rutz v. Rutz, 644 N.W.2d 489 (Minn. Ct. App. 2002); Casey v. Casey, 58 P.3d 763 (Okla. 2002);

Miller v. Miller, 2004 WL 1049158 (Ohio App. Ct. 2004); Fossum v. Fossum, 545 N.W.2d 828 (S.D. 1996); Habecker v. Giard, 820 A.2d 215 (Vt. 2003); *In re* Marriage of Horner, 93 P.3d 124 (Wash. 2004).

52 ALI PRINCIPLES, *supra* note 7.

53. *In re* Marriage of Burgess, 913 P.2d 473 (Cal. 1996). *See also* CAL. FAM. CODE § 7501(a) (2004)(codifying *Burgess*).

54. *In re* Marriage of LaMusga, 88 P.3d 81 (Cal. 2004)(citing *Burgess*).

55. *Id.* at 84-85.

56. *Id.* (clarifying that the best interest test was to be used when noncustodial parent shows harm to the parent-child relationship).

57. *Id. But see In re* Marriage of Brown & Yana, 127 P.3d 28 (Cal. 2006) (finding that while noncustodial parent could seek modification of custody order based on changed circumstances if custodial parent relocates, trial court had discretion to deny the modification request without holding an evidentiary hearing if the noncustodial parent fails to make a legally sufficient showing of detriment).

58. *See* COLO. REV. STAT. § 14-10-129(2) (2004); IOWA CODE ANN. § 598.21 (8A) (2004); ME. REV. STAT. ANN. tit. 19-A, § 1657 (2004); MO. REV. STAT. § 452.411 (2004).

59. *See* Hamilton v. Hamilton, 42 P.3d 1107, 1115 (Alaska 2002); Fowler v. Sowers, 151 S.W.3d 357 (Ky. Ct. App. 2004) (finding mother's proposed move to Alaska to be a change of circumstances); *In re* Marriage of Syverson, 931 P.2d 691 (Mont. 1997); Gietzen v. Gietzen, 575 N.W.2d 924 (N.D.1998).

60. *See* ARIZ. REV. STAT. ANN. § 25–408 (2004); 750 ILL. COMP. STAT. ANN. 5/609 (2004); MO. ANN. STAT. § 452.377 (2004). *See also* Moeller-Prokosch v. Prokosch, 27 P.3d 314 (Alaska 2001); Roberts v. Roberts, 64 P.3d 327 (Idaho 2003); Brown v. Loveman, 680 N.W.2d 432 (Mich. Ct. App.), *appeal denied*, 682 N.W.2d 86 (Mich. 2004); Devore v. Devore, 62 S.W.3d 59 (Mo. Ct. App. 2001); McLaughlin v. McLaughlin, 647 N.W.2d 577, 586 (Neb. 2002); Schmidt v. Bakke, 691 N.W.2d 239 (N.D. 2005).

61. Ireland v. Ireland, 717 A.2d 676, 682 (Conn. 1998); Bauers v. Lewis, 770 A.2d 214 (N.J. 2001); Wild v. Wild, 696 N.W.2d 886 (Neb. Ct. App. 2005).

62. N.H. REV. STAT. ANN. § 461-A:12 (2005); *In re* Pfeuffer, 837 A.2d 311 (N.H. 2003).

63. NEV. REV. STAT. ANN. § 125C.200.3 (2004). Flynn v. Flynn, 92 P.3d 1224 (Nev. 2004). *See also* Ireland v. Ireland, 717 A.2d at 682-83; Weaver v. Kelling, 53 S.W.3d 610 (Mo. Ct. App. 2001) (allowing mother's relocation because father failed to show how children's best interest would be served by transfer of custody). *But see* Classick v. Classick, 155 S.W.3d 842 (Mo. Ct. App. 2005); *In re* Marriage of Colson, 51 P.3d 607 (Or. App. Ct. 2002).

64. O'Connor v. O'Connor, 793 A.2d 810 (N.J. Super. Ct. App. Div. 2002). *See also* Brody v. Kroll, 53 Cal. Rptr. 2d 280 (Ct. App. 1996), *rev. denied*; Ayers v. Ayers, 508 N.W.2d 515 (Minn. 1993). *See also* ELROD, *supra* note 10, at §17:35.

65. O'Connor, 793 A.2d at 821-22.

66. *Id.* at 824 (finding shared custody a father who picked the child up from school several days a week, kept child evenings and overnights and during times mother traveled).

67. *See* FLA. STAT. § 61.13 (2)(d)(2004) (no presumption shall arise in favor or against a relocation by primary residential parent); *In re* Marriage of Ciesluk, 113 P.3d 135 (Colo. 2005); Fohey v. Knickerbocker, 130 S.W.3d 730 (Mo. App. 2004).

68. *See* Lewellyn v. Lewellyn, 93 S.W.3d 681 (Ark. 2002); Farag v. DeLawter, 743 N.E.2d 366 (Ind. Ct. App. 2001); Landis v. Landis, 869 A.2d 1003 (Pa. Super. Ct. 2005); Graham v. Graham, 2005 WL 1467878 (Tenn. Ct. App. June 22, 2005) (unpublished); Hoover (Letourneau) v. Hoover, 764 A.2d 1192 (Vt. 2000). *See also* TENN. CODE ANN. § 36-6-108 (2004) (where parents are spending substantially equal amounts of time with child, no presumption in favor of either parent arises when one parent seeks to relocate).

69. Tropea v. Tropea, 145, 151-52 (N.Y. 1996) (stating that ". . . bright line rules in this area are inappropriate; each case must be evaluated on its own merits.").

70. Bodne v. Bodne, 588 S.E.2d 728 (Ga. 2003) (finding that physician father's proposed move to Alabama to "leave behind" his predivorce life was putting his interests above his children and changing custody to the mother).

71. *In re* Marriage of Ciesluk, 113 P.3d 135 (Colo. 2005).

72. Gruber v. Gruber, 583 A.2d 434, 437 (Pa. Super. Ct. 1990). *See also In re* Marriage of Stahl, 810 N.E.2d 259 (Ill. App. Ct. 2004) (finding that a determination of the child's best interests cannot be reduced to a "bright line rule" but requires a case by case analysis).

73. For criticisms of the best interests test, *see* Robert H. Mnookin & Lewis Kornhauser, *Bargaining in the Shadow of the Law: The Case of Divorce,* 88 YALE L.J. 950 (1979); Robert H. Mnookin, *Child-Custody Adjudication: Judicial Functions in the Face of Indeterminacy,* 39 LAW & CONTEMP. PROBS. 226 (1975); Jon Elster, *Solomonic Judgments: Against the Best Interest of the Child,* 54 U. CHI. L. REV. 1 (1987); Martha Fineman, *Dominant Discourse, Professional Language, and Legal Change in Child Custody Decisionmaking,* 101 HARV. L. REV. 727 (1988); Mary Ann Glendon, *Fixed Rules and Discretion in Contemporary Family Law and Succession Law,* 60 TULANE L. REV. 1365 (1986).

74. LA. REV. STAT. § 9:355.12 (2003). *See also* Gary A. Debele, *A Children's Rights Approach to Relocation: A Meaningful Best Interests Standard,* 15 AM. ACAD. MATRIMONIAL L. J. 75 (1998).

75. COLO. REV. STAT. ANN. § 14-10-124(1.5)(a)(I)-(XI) (2004); COLO. REV. STAT. ANN. § 14-10-129 (I)–(IX) (2004).

76. *See* ARIZ. REV. STAT. ANN. § 25-408 (2004); FLA. STAT. ANN. § 61.13 (2004); KAN. STAT. ANN. § 60-1620(c) (2005); MICH. COMP. LAWS ANN. § 722.31 (2004); TENN. CODE ANN. § 36-6-108 (2004); UTAH CODE ANN. § 30-3-37 (2004); and WASH. REV. CODE ANN. § 26.09.520 (2004).

77. *See In re* Marriage of Hamilton-Waller, 2005 WL 294687 (Or. App. Nov. 9, 2005)(dissent) (citing Linda D. Elrod, *Current Trends in Custody Relocation* 10-11) (written materials from ABA Council of Appellate Staff Attorneys Seminar, July 30, 2005)(summarizing factors). *See also* Baures v. Lewis, 770 A.2d 214, 229-30 (N.J. 2001); Hollandsworth v. Knyzewski, 109 S.W.3d 653 (Ark. 2003); *In re* Marriage of LaMusga, 88 P.3d 81 (Cal. 2004); Auge v. Auge, 665 N.E.2d 145 (Minn. 1983); McLaughlin v. McLaughlin, 647 N.W.2d 577 (Neb. 2002); Schwartz v. Schwartz, 812

P.2d 1268 (Nev. 1991); Stout v. Stout, 560 N.W.2d 903 (N.D. 1997); Gruber v. Gruber, 583 A.2d 434 (Pa. Super. Ct. 1990).

78. Bretherton v. Bretherton, 805 A.2d 766, 770 (Conn. App. Ct. 2002).

79. *In re* Marriage of LaMusga, 88 P.3d 81 (Cal. 2004); Dupre v. Dupre, 857 A.2d 242 (R.I. 2004); *In re* Marriage of Pape, 989 P.2d 1120 (Wash. 2000).

80. Bauers v. Lewis, 770 A.2d 214, 217 (N.J. 2001) (noting that ". . . In our global economy, relocation for employment purposes is common. On a personal level, people remarry and move away . . .").

81. ALI PRINCIPLES, *supra* note 7, at § 2.17(4)(a)(ii).

82. Dupre v. Dupre, 857 A.2d 242 (R.I. 2004).

83. Hawkes v. Spence, 878 A.2d 273 (Vt. 2005).

84. W. VA. CODE § 48-9–403(d)(1) (2004).

85. *See* Hass v. Hass, 44 S.W.3d 773 (Ark. Ct. App. 2001); Botterbusch v. Botterbusch, 851 So. 2d 903, 905 (Fla. Dist. Ct. App. 2003); *In re* Marriage of Parr, 802 N.E.2d 393 (Ill. App. Ct. 2003); *In re* S.E.P., 35 S.W.3d 862 (Mo. Ct. App. 2001); McLaughlin v. McLaughlin, 647 N.W.2d 577 (Neb. 2002); Long v. Long, 675 N.Y.S.2d 673 (1998); Tibor v. Tibor, 598 N.W.2d 480 (N.D. 1999); Keller v. Keller, 584 N.W.2d 509 (N.D.1998); Perrott v. Perrott, 713 A.2d 666 (Pa. Super. Ct. 1998).

86. *See* Leach v. Santiago, 798 N.Y.S.2d 242 (App. Div. 2005); Levine v. Bacon, 687 A.2d. 1057 (N.J. Super. App. Div. 1997) (denying move where the father failed to look for a job in the current location); Baldwin v. Baldwin, 710 A.2d 610 (Pa. Super. Ct. 1998); Sullivan v. Knick, 568 S.E.2d 430 (Va. Ct. App. 2002).

87. Dickson v. Dickson, 634 N.W.2d 76 (N.D. 2001).

88. *See In re* Marriage of Sale, 808 N.E.2d 1125 (Ill. App. Ct. 2004); Tremain v. Tremain, 646 N.W.2d 661 (Neb. 2002); Fohey v. Knickerbocker, 130 S.W.3d 730 (Mo. Ct. App. 2004).

89. *See* Hales v. Edlund, 78 Cal. Rptr. 2d 671 (Ct. App. 1998); Oliver v. Oliver, 855 A.2d 1022 (Conn. App. Ct. 2004); *In re* Marriage of Collingbourne, 791 N.E.2d 532 (Ill. 2003); Rosenthal v. Maney, 745 N.E.2d 350 (Mass. App. Ct. 2001); Caudill v. Foley, 21 S.W.3d 203 (Tenn. Ct. App. 1999).

90. *See* Reel v. Harrison, 60 P.3d 480 (Nev. 2002); Aziz v. Aziz, 779 N.Y.S.2d 539 (App. Div. 2004); Paulson v. Bauske, 574 N.W.2d 801 (N.D. 1998).

91. Geiger v. Yaeger, 846 A.2d 691 (Pa. Super. Ct. 2004).

92. Flynn v. Flynn, 92 P.3d 1224 (Nev. 2004) (denying mother's relocation to enroll in a Theology program when degree would not enhance earning ability, educational opportunities existed in area and child's lifestyle would not be enhanced by the move).

93. *See* Bodne v. Bodne, 588 S.E.2d 728 (Ga. 2003); Jones v. Jones, 903 S.W.2d 277 (Mo. App. Ct. 1995); Tishmack v. Tishmack, 611 N.W.2d 204 (N.D. 2000).

94. Cassady v. Signorelli, 56 Cal. Rptr. 2d 545 (Ct. App. 1996).

95. *See* Delgado v. Nazario, 677 N.Y.S.2d 336 (App. Div. 1998).

96. *See* Dymitro v. Dymitro, 927 P.2d 917 (Idaho Ct. App. 1996); Shunk v. Walker, 589 A.2d 1303 (Md. Spec. Ct. App. 1991); *In re* Marriage of Cook, 725 P.2d 562 (Mont. 1986); Leach v. Santiago, 798 N.Y.S.2d 242 (App. Div. 2005) (changing custody to father partly because of mother's actions in leaving child with grandmother while she moved and not telling father).

97. *In re* T.M., 831 N.E.2d 526 (Ohio App. 2005). For further discussion of parental alienation, see Janet R. Johnston, *Children of Divorce Who Reject a Parent and Refuse Visitation: Recent Research and Social Policy Implications for the Alienated Child*, 38 FAM. L. Q. 757 (2005; Carol S. Bruch, *Parental Alienation Syndrome and Parental Alienation: Getting It Wrong in Child Custody Cases*, 35 FAM. L.Q. 527 (2001).

98. Tibor v. Tibor, 598 N.W.2d 480 (N.D. 1999) (father had entered house to check messages and rummage through trash).

99. Jack v. Clinton, 609 N.W.2d 328 (Neb. 2000).

100. Winn v. Winn, 593 N.W.2d 662, 669 (Mich. Ct. App. 2000)(emphasis added).

101. Frieze v. Frieze, 692 N.W.2d 912 (N.D. 2005); Winn v. Winn, 593 N.W.2d 662, 669 (Mich. Ct. App. 2000).

102. *See* Schmidt v. Bakke, 691 N.W.2d 239 (N.D. 2005); Aziz v. Aziz, 779 N.Y.2d 539 (2nd Dep't 2004).

103. *See* Hanks v. Arnold, 674 N.E.2d 1005 (Ind. Ct. App. 1996); Dale v. Pearson, 555 N.W.2d 243 (Iowa Ct. App. 1996); *In re* Marriage of Tade, 938 P.2d 673 (Mont. 1997). *See* Jay M. Zitter, Annotation, *Custodial Parent's Relocation as Grounds for Change of Custody*, 70 A.L.R.5th 377 (1999).

104. Brennan v. Brennan, 857 A.2d 927 (Conn. App. Ct. 2004).

105. Classick v. Classick, 155 S.W.3d 842 (Mo. Ct. App. 2005).

106. Hardin v. Hardin, 618 S.E.2d 169 (Ga. Ct. App. 2005).

107. *See* Joan B. Kelly & Michael E. Lamb, *Using Child Development Research to Make Appropriate Custody and Access Decisions For Young Children*, 38 FAM. & CONCILIATION CTS. REV. 297, 309 (2000)(concluding that "[r]egardless of who has been the primary caretaker . . . children benefit from the extensive contact with both parents that fosters meaningful father-child and mother-child relationships"); Judith S. Wallerstein & Tony J. Tanke, *To Move or Not to Move: Psychological and Legal Considerations in the Relocation of Children Following Divorce*, 30 FAM. L.Q. 305, 318 (1996) (concluding that "[w]hen a child is de facto in the primary residential or physical custody of one parent, that parent should be able to relocate with the child, except in unusual circumstances").

108. *See High Conflict Custody Cases: Reforming the System for Children–Conference Report and Action Plan*, 34 FAM. L.Q. 589 (2001); Linda D. Elrod, *Reforming the System to Protect Children in High Conflict Custody Cases*, 28 WM. MITCHELL L. REV. 495, 515 (2001).

109. Paul Amato & Joan Gilbreth, *Non-resident Father's and Children's Well-Being: A Meta Analysis*, 61 J. MARRIAGE & FAMILY 557, 560 (1999) (". . . contact with nonresident fathers following divorce is associated with positive outcomes among children when parents have a cooperative relationship but is associated with negative outcomes when parents have a conflicted relationship").

110. Sanford L. Braver, et al., *Relocation of Children After Divorce and Children's Best Interests: New Evidence and Legal Considerations*, 17 J. FAM. PSYCHOLOGY 206 (2003).

111. *See In re* Marriage of Ciesluk, 113 P.3d 135, 149 (Colo. 2005)(criticizing trial court reliance on Braver article); Brief of Dr. Judith Wallerstein in *In re* Marriage of LaMusga, 16-18 (. . . the youngsters in the custody of their fathers when the mother moved or who moved with the father were the only young people who showed trou-

bled behavior). Trish Wilson, *Post-Divorce Relocating with Mothers Do Best: So Why Does the Braver Study Hide Its Own Results*, Pt. I, 9(1) DOM. VIOL. REP'T (2003); Pt. II, 9(2) DOM. VIOL. REP'T 19 (2004); Pt. III, 9(3) DOM. VIOL. REP'T 37 (2004) (showing that study shows that the children who fared best overall were those whose noncustodial fathers moved). Norval Glenn & David Blankenhorn, Institute for American Values, Sept. 11, 2003 (stating the "Braver study is a weak one that provides no credible evidence on the effects on children of moving away after divorce"). *See also* Carol S. Burch, Sound Research or Wishful Thinking in Child Custody Cases? Lessons from Relocation Law, 40 Fam. L.Q. (2006), 285.

112. Landis v. Landis, 869 A.2d 1003 (Pa. Super. Ct. 2005) (reversing trial judge who denied relocation because the existing shared custody arrangement could not stay in place but ignored the father's indirect criminal contempt conviction, the Protection from Abuse Order that was in place, and the criminal charges against father for weapons violations).

113. Moeller-Prokosch v. Prokosch, 27 P.3d 314 (Alaska 2001); McCoy v. McCoy, 764 A.2d 449 (N.J. Super. Ct. App. Div. 2001); Billhime v. Billhime, 869 A.2d 1031 (Pa. Super. Ct. 2005).

114. Tropea v. Tropea, 665 N.E.2d 145 (N.Y. 1996).

115. Kimberly R. Shefts, *Virtual Visitation: The Next Generation of Options for Parent-Child Communication*, 36 FAM. L.Q. 303 (2002); Sarah Gottfried, *Virtual Visitation: The Wave of the Future in Communication Between Children and Non-Custodial Parents in Relocation Cases*, 36 FAM. L.Q. 475 (2002). *See also* William C. Smith, *Just Wait Until Your Dad Logs On!*, 87 A.B.A. J. 24 (Sept. 2001).

116. Rice v. Rice, 517 S.E.2d 220, 227-28 (S.C. Ct. App. 1999).

117. *See In re* Marriage of Thielges, 623 N.W.2d 232 (Iowa Ct. App. 2000); McGuinness v. McGuinness, 970 P.2d 1074 (Nev. 1998); Chen v. Heller, 759 A.2d 873 (N.J. Super. Ct. App. Div. 2000); Surma v. Surma, 561 N.W.2d 290 (N.D. 1997).

118. Arnold v. Arnold, 847 A.2d 674 (Pa. Super. Ct. 2004). *See In re* Marriage of Condon, 62 Cal. Rptr. 2d 33 (Ct. App. 1998)(Australia); Hayes v. Gallacher, 972 P.2d 1138 (Nev. 1999)(Japan); Goldfarb v. Goldfarb, 861 A.2d 340 (Pa. Super. Ct. 2004).

119. Lazarevic v. Fogelquist, 668 N.Y.S.2d 320 (App. Div. 1997).

120. ALA. CODE 30-3-169.3 (2004).

121. Bodne v. Bodne, 588 S.E.2d 728 (Ga. 2003)(J. Benham, dissenting). *See also* Kimberly K. Holtz, *Note: Move Away Custody Disputes: The Implications of Case by Case Analysis and the Need for Legislation*, 45 SANTA CLARA L. REV. 319 (1994).

122. *See In re* Marriage of Ciesluk, 113 P.3d 135 (Colo. 2005); Landis v. Landis, 869 A.2d 1003 (Pa. Super. Ct. 2005); Fowler v. Sowers, 151 S.W.3d 357 (Ky. Ct. App. 2004); Hawkes v. Spence, 878 A.2d 273 (Vt. 2005).

doi:10.1300/J190v03n03_03

APPENDIX
State Statutes on Relocation**

STATE	Notice	Presumption For/Against or Burdens	Best Interests of Child Paramount	Recent or Significant Case
Alabama ALA. CODE § 30-3-160 -30-3-169.10	45 days	Against	X	Clements v. Clements, 906 So. 2d 952 (Ala. Civ. App. 2005)
Alaska ALASKA STAT. § 25.24.150			X	Chesser-Witmer v. Chesser, 117 P.3d 711 (Alaska 2005) Moeller-Prokosch v. Prokosch, 53 P.3d 152 (Alaska 2002)
Arizona ARIZ. REV. STAT. § 25-408	60 days	Burden on moving party	X	Woodworth v. Woodworth, 42 P.3d 610 (Ariz. App. 2002)
Arkansas* ARK. CODE ANN. § 9-13-101		For	X	Hollandsworth v. Knyzewski, 109 S.W.3d 653 (Ark. 2003)
California CAL. FAM. CODE § 3406		For	X	*In re* Marriage of LaMusga, 88 P.3d 81 (Cal. 2004)
Colorado COLO. REV. STAT. Ann. § 14-10-129 & 14-10-124		Both parents must show BIOC	X	*In re* Marriage of Ciesluk, 113 P.3d 135 (Colo. 2005)
Connecticut* CONN. GEN. STAT. ANN. § 46b-56		Initial burden on moving party	X	Brennan v. Brennan, 857 A.2d 927 (Conn. App. 2004)
Delaware* 13 DEL. CODE §§ 728 & 729			X	Karen J.M. v. James W., 792 A.2d 1036 (Del. Fam. Ct. 2002)
District of Columbia				
Florida FLA. STAT. ANN. § 61.13(2)(d)			X	Jenson v. Jenson, 904 So. 2d 635 (Fla. Dist. Ct. App. 2005)

APPENDIX (continued)

STATE	Notice	Presumption For/Against or Burdens	Best Interests of Child Paramount	Recent or Significant Case
Georgia GA. CODE ANN. § 19-9-1	30 days		X	Hardin v. Hardin, 618 S.E.2d 169 (Ga. Ct. App. 2005)
Hawaii* HAW. REV. STAT. § 571-46			X	Tetreault v. Tetreault, 55 P.3d 845 (Haw. Ct. App. 2002)
Idaho IDAHO CODE § 32-717		Initial burden on moving party	X	Weiland v. Ruppel, 75 P.3d 176 (Idaho 2003) Roberts v. Roberts, 64 P.3d 327 (Idaho 2003)
Illinois 750 ILL. COMP. STAT. ANN. § 5/609		Burden on party seeking modification	X	*In re* Marriage of Johnson, 815 N.E.2d 1283 (Ill. App. Ct. 2004)
Indiana IND. CODE. ANN. § 31-17-2.2-1		Shifting Burden	X	Bettencourt v. Ford, 822 N.E.2d 989 (Ind. Ct. App. 2005)
Iowa IOWA CODE ANN. § 598.21D		Burden on party seeking modification		*In re* Marriage of Theilges, 623 N.W.2d 232 (Iowa Ct. App. 2000)
Kansas KAN. STAT. ANN. § 60-1620	30 days		X	*In re* Marriage of Whipp, 962 P.2d 1058 (Kan. 1998)
Kentucky* KY. REV. STAT. ANN. § 403.340		Burden on party seeking modification	X	Fowler v. Sowers, 151 S.W.3d 357 (Ky. Ct. App. 2004)
Louisiana LA. REV. STAT. ANN. § 9.355.1-17	60 days	Burden on moving party Presumption against	X	Peacock v. Peacock, 903 So. 2d 506 (La. Ct. App. 2005)
Maine ME. REV. STAT. ANN. TIT. 19-A, §§ 1653 (14) & 1657	30 days	Burden on moving party	X	Fraser v. Boyer, 722 A.2d 354 (Me. 1998)
Maryland MD. CODE ANN., Family Law § 9-106	45 days	Burden on non-moving party		Braun v. Headley, 750 A.2d 624 (Md. Ct. Spec. App. 2000)

STATE	Notice	Presumption For/Against or Burdens	Best Interests of Child Paramount	Recent or Significant Case
Massachusetts MASS. GEN. LAWS ANN. Ch. 208, § 30		"upon cause shown" custodial parent may relocate	X	D.C. v. J.S., 790 N.E.2d 686 (Mass. App. Ct. 2003)
Michigan MICH. COMP. LAWS ANN. § 722.31		Burden on moving party if objected to	X	Grew v. Knox, 694 N.W.2d 772 (Mich. Ct. App. 2005)
Minnesota* MINN. STAT. ANN. § 518.18(d)		Presumption for		*In re* Marriage of Geiger, 470 N.W.2d 704 (Minn. Ct. App. 1991) Auge v. Auge, 665 N.E.2d 145 (Minn. 1983)
Mississippi MISS. CODE ANN. § 93-5-23		Burden on party seeking modification	X	Lambert v. Lambert, 872 So. 2d 679 (Miss. Ct. App. 2004)
Missouri MO. REV. STAT. § 452.377	60 days	Burden on moving party	X	Baxley v. Jarred, 91 S.W.3d 192 (Mo. Ct. App. 2002)
Montana MONT. CODE ANN. § 40-4-217	30 days	Burden on party opposing relocation	X	*In re* Marriage of Robison, 53 P.3d 1279 (Mont. 2002)
Nebraska		Shifting burden	X	Wild v. Wild, 696 N.W.2d 886 (Neb. 2005)
Nevada NEV. REV. STAT. § 125C.200		Shifting burden	X	Potter v. Potter, 119 P.3d 1246 (Nev. 2005)
New Hampshire* N.H. REV. STAT. ANN. § 461-A:12	60 days	Shifting burden	X	*In re* Pfeuffer, 837 A.2d 311 (N.H. 2003)
New Jersey N.J. STAT. ANN. §9:2-2		Shifting burden		Baures v. Lewis, 770 A.2d 214 (N.J. 2001)
New Mexico* N.M. STAT. ANN. §40-4-9.1		Equal burden	X	Jaramillo v. Jaramillo, 823 P.2d 299 (N.M. 1992)

APPENDIX (continued)

STATE	Notice	Presumption For/Against or Burdens	Best Interests of Child Paramount	Recent or Significant Case
New York* McKinney's DRL § 240, C240:25			X	Vega v. Pollack, 800 N.Y.S.2d 442 (App. Div. 2005) Tropea v. Tropea, 665 N.E.2d 146 (N.Y. 1996)
North Carolina N.C. GEN. STAT. ANN. § 50-13.2			X	Evans v. Evans, 530 S.E.2d 576 (N.C. 2000)
North Dakota N.D. CENT. CODE ANN. § 14-09-07		Burden on moving party	X	Schmidt v. Bakke, 691 N.W.2d 239 (SD 2005)
Ohio OHIO REV. CODE § 3109.051	Required but no time specified	Initial burden on moving party	X	Rodkey v. Rodkey, 2006 WL 2441720 (Ohio App.)
Oklahoma OKLA. STAT. ANN. Tit. 43 § 1		For		Casey v. Casey, 58 P.3d 763 (Okla. 2003)
Oregon OR. REV. STAT. ANN. § 107.159			X	*In re* Marriage of Colson & Piel, 51 P.3d 607 (Or. Ct. App. 2002)
Pennsylvania 23 PA CONS. STAT. ANN. § 5308		Shifting burden	X	Billhime v. Billhime, 869 A.2d 1031 (Pa. Super. Ct. 2005); Gruber v. Gruber, 583 A.2d 434 (Pa. Super. Ct. 1990)
Rhode Island R.I. GEN. LAWS ANN. § 15-5-16			X	Dupre v. Dupre, 857 A.2d 242 (R.I. 2004)
South Carolina* S.C. CODE ANN. § 20-3-160	45 days		X	Latimer v. Farmer, 602 S.E.2d 32 (S.C. 2004)
South Dakota S.D. CODIFIED LAWS § 25-5-13; 25-4A-17 - 19	45 days	For	X	Fossum v. Fossum, 545 N.W.2d 828 (S.D. 1996)

STATE	Notice	Presumption For/Against or Burdens	Best Interests of Child Paramount	Recent or Significant Case
Tennessee TENN. CODE ANN. §36-6-108	60 days	Depends on custodial parent's time spent w/ child	X	Kawatra v. Kawatra, 182 S.W.3d 800 (Tenn. 2005)
Texas* TEX. FAM. CODE § 156.101		Burden on moving parent	X	Echols v. Olivarez, 85 S.W.3d 475 (Tex. App. 2002); Bates v. Tesar, 81 S.W.3d 411 (Tex. App. 2002)
Utah UTAH CODE ANN. § 30-3-37	60 days			
Vermont* VT. STAT. ANN. Tit. 15, § 668		Burden on non-custodial party	X	Hawkes v. Spence, 878 A.2d 273 (Vt. 2005) Lacaillade v. Hardaker, 878 A.2d 273 (Vt. 2005)
Virginia VA. CODE ANN. § 20-124.5	30 days			Riggins v. O'Brien, 538 S.E.2d 320 (Va. Ct. App. 2000)
Washington WASH. REV. CODE ANN. § 26.09.520-.560		For	X	Ramirez v. Holland, 93 P.3d 951 (Wash. Ct. App. 2004) *In re* Marriage of Horner, 93 P.3d 124 (Wash. 2004)
West Virginia W. VA. CODE § 48-9-403	60 days	Based on amount of time spent with child	X	Cunningham v. Cunningham, 423 S.E.2d 638 (W. Va. 1992)
Wisconsin WIS. STAT. ANN. § 767.327	60 days	Rebuttable presumption for		Hughes v. Hughes, 588 N.W.2d 823 (Wis. Ct. App. 1998)
Wyoming* WYO. STAT. ANN. § 20-2-204(c)		For	X	Harshberger v. Harshberger, 117 P.3d 1244 (Wyo. 2005)

*Denotes general custody statute
**The author prepared an earlier version of this chart which appeared in *States Differ on Relocation: A Panorama of Expanding Case Law*, 28 (4) FAM. ADVOC. 8 (ABA 2006).

Exploring Three Functions
in Child Custody Evaluation
for the Relocation Case:
Prediction, Investigation,
and Making Recommendations
for a Long-Distance Parenting Plan

William G. Austin
Jonathan W. Gould

William G. Austin, PhD, is a practicing clinical and forensic psychologist in North-west Colorado and the Denver area. He is the author of numerous articles on forensic methodology for conducting child custody evaluations that are research-based with practical applications. He has developed forensic models of risk assessment for child custody evaluation for the two instances of relocation and domestic violence. These models are currently being widely applied by custody evaluators across the country. He has also developed a forensic model for considering collateral sources of information in custody evaluation. He is currently co-chair of the task force that produced the recently published AFCC Model Standards for Custody Evaluation. He lives and practices in Colorado and has a national consulting practice in forensic psychology with a specialization in child custody evaluation. He offers services of evaluation, work product review, general testimony, and case consultation. His services are described at www.child-custody-services.com (E-mail: wgaustinphd@yahoo.com).

Jonathan W. Gould, PhD, is engaged in forensic practice based in Charlotte, North Carolina and is a principal in the national consulting group Child Custody Consultants with Austin. He provides consultation services in child custody and other family and dependency law related cases. He is author of the book, "Conducting Scientifically Crafted Child Custody Evaluations (2nd Edition)" and has authored more than 40 peer-reviewed articles on child custody and related issues (E-mail: jwgould@aol.com).

[Haworth co-indexing entry note]: "Exploring Three Functions in Child Custody Evaluation for the Relocation Case: Prediction, Investigation, and Making Recommendations for a Long-Distance Parenting Plan." Austin, William G., and Jonathan W. Gould. Co-published simultaneously in *Journal of Child Custody* (The Haworth Press, Inc.) Vol. 3, No. 3/4, 2006, pp. 63-108; and: *Relocation Issues in Child Custody Cases* (ed: Philip M. Stahl, and Leslie M. Drozd) The Haworth Press, Inc., 2006, pp. 63-108. Single or multiple copies of this article are available for a fee from The Haworth Document Delivery Service [1-800-HAWORTH, 9:00 a.m. - 5:00 p.m. (EST). E-mail address: docdelivery@haworthpress.com].

SUMMARY. The psycho-legal dilemmas posed by child custody relocation cases are discussed in terms of the four decisional alternatives facing the court and evaluator. Different legal contexts for relocation are reviewed in terms of their implications for the custody evaluation. Complexities involved in the evaluator's function of making predictions for the court are presented. The need to conduct careful investigation on both risk and pragmatic factors is highlighted by case illustrations. The obstacles of crafting of long distance parenting plans that will be in the best interests of the child are presented as governed by the goal of harm mitigation. doi:10.1300/J190v03n03_04 *[Article copies available for a fee from The Haworth Document Delivery Service: 1-800-HAWORTH. E-mail address: <docdelivery@haworthpress.com> Website: <http://www.HaworthPress. com> © 2006 by The Haworth Press, Inc. All rights reserved.]*

KEYWORDS. Relocation, prediction, investigation, parenting plans

In this paper, we examine three important aspects of conducting child custody evaluations for the relocation case. The first aspect is composed of an examination of the function of making predictions for the court in custody cases. We argue that the evaluator's analysis needs to address issues of potential harm for the child for each proposed parenting plan. The need to construct a good fit between the evaluator's predictions and the legal standard is discussed.

Second, the "fact driven" nature of most relocation cases requires the evaluator to use an investigative model (Austin & Kirkpatrick, 2004). Reliably identifying "real life" factors of the proposed relocation allows for a comparison of those factors against salient "predictive factors," some of which are identified in case law or statute. The investigative task requires the evaluator to do a good bit of forensic psychological detective work in order to provide the court with important descriptive behavioral data.

Third, we discuss the importance of the evaluator collecting data and offering recommendations based on those data on suitable alternative parenting plans. These plans should include recommendations for parenting time based on a relocation of one parent with or without the child. Although state appellate decisions often have pointed to the ameliorating effects of "visitation," we have observed many relocation cases when a substantial geographical distance is placed between a child and parent, no "suitable" parenting plan is easily developed. The evaluator may craft a parenting plan that mitigates the degree of harm associated with relocation and limits the fundamental changes that will occur in the child-parent relationship. In these extremely difficult and complex cases, the court is trying to grapple with the issue of which type of loss or harm is less painful and less negative in its long-term effects on the child. Data provided by the evaluator can help the court to determine if its definition of the threshold of harm for relocation is met resulting in a decision to allow the relocation or if the threshold of predicted harm is exceeded, resulting in a decision to deny the relocation of the child.

OVERVIEW OF THE LEGAL CONTEXT

Relocation cases continue to present some of the most difficult parenting disputes to custody evaluators and the courts because of the potential for emotional hardship on the parents and developmental harm to the child (Austin, 2000a; 2000b). In one appellate decision, the judge wrote: "Many factors must be considered and weighed by the trial judge, whose responsibility in this type of proceeding is generally difficult and quite frequently most delicate in nature" (*Tanttila v. Tanttila*, 1963). When there is a scenario of (a) two highly involved parents, (b) one of those parents alleges no flexibility and "just has to move," (c) there is a young child, and (d) the other parent alleges that s/he cannot also move, then the court faces the prospect of a "lose-lose-lose" outcome, no matter what the chosen disposition. In such situations, the court's decision may not be geared so much to promote the best interests of the child but to mitigate the degree of harm to the child associated with the natural consequences of the decision. It may often be there is no "good" or "right" decision; the trier of fact will be searching for the least harmful and painful alternative that will allow the child to stay on a normal developmental course.

Evaluators can be most helpful to the courts in producing data-based predictions on the degree of harm associated with different alternative parenting plans and can be helpful in recommending strategies for harm reduction to be included in a parenting plan (Austin, 2000c).

Relocation Scenarios

There are four alternative outcomes affecting residential placement when a parent wants to relocate with that child a considerable geographical distance away from the current home community. The first alternative is when the child is allowed by the Court to move with the relocating parent and the other parent does not relocate. A second alternative is when the court disallows the relocation request and the parent aspiring to relocate does not move and stays in the home community, thus preserving the status quo. A third alternative is when the court disallows the relocation and the relocating parent moves without the child, resulting in primary custody being transferred to the non-moving parent. A final alternative is when the relocation is allowed and the other parent follows the relocating parent and child to the new community. Some states do not allow courts, in alternative two, to issue conditional orders to preserve the status quo (CO, NC) while appellate courts in other states endorse the practice (NY).

Alternative three, a parent relocating without the child, may seem like it would rarely occur, but relocation of nonresidential parents is not uncommon, a fact pointed to by advocates of legal presumptions for allowing residential parents to relocate (Wallerstein & Tanke, 1996; Bruch & Bowermaster, 1996; Bowermaster, 1992-93). Consider the case of the "father who couldn't sit still." At the time of the marital separation, father relocated from his five and seven year old children to a different part of Colorado about three hours away. Mother conscientiously cooperated with the long drive for every other weekend parenting time, even though temporary orders stipulated visitation would be at "mother's discretion." Five months later, father relocated again, this time to Texas. He informed the mother that "the law says I can have the kids for the entire the summer."

When a residential parent's petition to relocate is denied by the court, conventional wisdom is that the residential parent seldom moves without the child. Research suggests that a residential parent who is denied a request to relocate with the child and who decides to move without the child is not as infrequent as previously believed. Braver, Cookston, and Cohen, (2002) surveyed family law practitioners on their estimate of how frequently their clients who wanted to relocate would do so even if the court turned down the relocation request. In what may seem like a counter-intuitive finding, the aggregate estimate was that relocation without the child would occur 37% of the time. Relocation without the child may be the result of the parent determined to pursue his or her own highly valued interests (e.g., educational or vocational interests) or the result of a lack of flexibility regarding the move (e.g., remarriage).

In a recent case we call, "the mother who wanted to stay home," in a surprise move at the time of the marital separation, the mother relocated with the child to her own mother's community two hours away. The father did not immediately oppose the relocation, but asked for primary residential custody in the event the mother did not return to the community. A custody evaluation recommended equal parenting time if the mother returned to the original community and recommended primary custody to the father if she did not return when the boy started preschool in the following fall. A salient factor was the mother's limited ability to support the relationship between the child and father and to facilitate tension-free access to child. The court agreed with the rationale that there were not clear advantages to the child in the new community compared to the home community and the child's relationship with the father would be harmed if relocation was permitted. The mother decided not to return to the original community and the father became the primary residential parent.

More typically, a non-residential parent will relocate without the child. From the perspective of the child, relocation of either parent may create risk. A recent study found negative long-term effects on children of divorced parents with the relocation of *either* parent (Braver, Ellman & Fabricius, 2002). A general explanation for this finding is that like divorce, relocation produces at a temporary lowering of resources available to the child from a variety of sources and relationships, or diminishing of the "social capital" in the child's environment (McLanahan & Sandefur, 1994; Amato & Sobolewski, 2004; Austin, 2005).

Sometimes parents find themselves in "Catch-22" situations concerning relocation. The relocating parent may have very compelling reasons for the move. If the legal climate and the facts of the case do not yield a strong argument for the child relocating with the parent, then the parent may be forced to make choices between his or her own interests and the best interests of the child that may include staying in the home community with the child and foregoing the opportunities that prompted the reasons for the move.

Recent case law has suggested relocation decisions should consider and balance both the interests of the parents and the child (*In re Marriage of Ciesluk*, 2005; *In re Marriage of Spahmer and Gullette*, 2005). There has always been an implicit tension between parent and child interests as well as competing parental interests in relocation cases and law. Forensic lore dictates that relocations are always motivated by a parent's interests that are then cast in a favorable light for the child. *Ireland v. Ireland* (1998) indicates the children's interests in a given case "do not necessarily coincide with those of one or both parents" (p. 680). *In re Marriage of Ciesluk* (2005) makes the dialectical tension among competing interests explicit in its constitutional law analysis, and further, directs courts (and therefore evaluators) to directly consider parental interests and to what extent they are intertwined with the child's. These interests are represented in the "needs and desires" of the parents, which presumably would be reflected (and measured) in the parent's stated reasons for wanting to relocate and for opposing the relocation. Thus, evaluators operating in those states whose case law has articulated this parental interest analysis should indeed attempt to measure this global factor.

Evaluators should also be aware of their case law that direct trial courts to consider indirect benefits to the child associated with relocation (*Goldfarb v. Goldfarb*, 2004; *In re Marriage of Ciesluk*, 2005). Such benefits can be non-economic and ones that promote the relocating parent's sense of well-being (*Goldfarb v. Goldfarb*, 2004). Some states require benefits to the child as well to the as parent to be demonstrated (*Dupré v. Dupré*, 2004) while other states have appellate decisions that have indicated both a need to demonstrate relocation is in the best interests of the child (*Berrebbi v. Clarke*, 2004) and in the best interests of the child and the parent (*Russenberger v. Russenberger*, 1996). Evaluators should gather data, then, on all of the ostensible advantages and disadvantages and on the soundness of the reasons for the relocation.

In another case, we call it the "mother who married the asthmatic husband," the parents had enjoyed equal parenting time with their thirteen year old girl. The child alternated every other week (7 days on/7 days off) between each parent's home for the first two years and then alternated every two weeks (14 days on/14 days off) between each parent's homes for the next two years. When the mother remarried, she requested that she be allowed to relocate from rural Colorado to Boston. She cited in her request to relocate that her new husband had a business in Boston and he had a chronic respiratory illness. Relocation from Boston to Colorado would create financial problems and would likely exacerbate his breathing problems. Mother told the evaluator she would not relocate without the child, saying that she would wait to relocate to Boston until after the daughter graduated from high school. Although it appeared that she was willing to place the needs of her child ahead of her own needs, there were no data to suggest that the relocation would benefit the child.

A recent appellate decision affirmed that clear benefits to the child needed to be shown in order for relocation to be seriously considered. In this case, no clear benefits to the child were identified. The evaluator recommended against relocation and recommended for extended summer parenting time so mother and daughter could go to Boston. The mother promptly announced she was going to relocate without the child. Such a move would likely produce substantial harm as the mother and daughter were quite close. However, evaluation data supported the hypothesis that the mother would likely not actively support the relationship between the daughter and the father if the child relocated with mom. In the event of the mother's relocation without the child, the harm-mitigation intervention that was recommended included the child spending eight weeks during the summer with the mother and for the parents to alternate or split the child's time during other school vacations. The mother could return to Colorado for parenting time as well.

Legal Anticipation of the Relocation Scenarios: The Case of Tennessee

The State of Tennessee tried to anticipate the different relocation contexts or scenarios (*Tennessee Code Annotated, Domestic Relations, 2004*). In determining the viability of a request to relocate out of state, the Tennessee legislature recommended that courts look first at the existing parenting time arrangements. If an equal parenting time arrangement existed, then no presumption in favor of the move would apply and the legal standard used to examine the relocation request would be the best interests of the child. Several best interests factors were to be considered (See Table 1).

If no equal parenting time arrangement existed, then there is a presumption that the residential parent can relocate with the child. To challenge the relocation, the nonresidential parent would need to show the presence of one or more statutorily defined factors that presented risk of harm to the child. If one or more of the factors were found to exist, then the legal standard shifts back to best interests of the child. If, after finding one of the risk factors existed and if the court knew that the residential parent would relocate without the child, then this "fact" can be considered and the proper legal standard would be the best interests of the child.

Relocation Issue at the Time of Dissolution vs. Modification

Case law and the few state statutes that apply to child custody and relocation are primarily designed to address the situation where one par-

TABLE 1

Tennessee's Relocation Statute, T.C.U. § 36-6-108(c)(1-11) Factors to Consider in Relocation
1. Extent to which visitations have been allowed and exercised;
2. Whether the primary residential parent, once out of the jurisdiction, is likely to comply with any new visitation arrangement;
3. The love, affection and emotional ties existing between the parents and child;
4. The disposition of the parents to provide the child with food, clothing, medical care, education, and other necessary care and the degree to which a parent has been the primary caregiver;
5. The importance of continuity in the child's life and the length of time the child has lived in a stable, satisfactory environment;
6. The stability of the family unit of the parents;
7. The mental and physical health of the parents;
8. The home, school, and community record of the child;
9. The reasonable preference of the child if twelve (12) years of age or older;
10. Evidence of physical or emotional abuse to the child, to the other parent or to any other person; and
11. The character and behavior of any other person who resides in or frequents the home of a parent and such person's interactions with the child.

ent wants to move away with the child, the other parent wants to stay in the original community, and a modification of an existing parenting plan is required. In our experience, relocation requests arise as frequently at the time of divorce or implementation of the original or permanent orders as they arise in post-judgment requests. When a request to relocate is filed it may affect which legal standard applies to the court's analysis of the relocation request. When a relocation request is made during the initial divorce proceedings, the legal standard used to evaluate the request is almost always going to be the best interests of the child. Prior to the signing of the original divorce decree, both parents are considered joint custodians of the child even though a primary custodian may have been designated in temporary orders after the marital separation. Typically, temporary orders are not supposed to prejudice the crafting of the permanent orders or be prejudicial, *res judicata*, against parenting time rights or the eventual final determination of the parenting plan (*In re Marriage of Lawson*, 1980).

When a request to relocate is brought before the court after the implementation of the permanent order, then a presumption for relocation may apply (California; New Jersey; Wyoming; *In re Marriage of Burgess*, 1996; *Baures v. Lewis*, 2001; Watt v. Watt, 1999) or against relocation (*Arizona Revised Statutes, Marital and Domestic Relations*, 2004, LaChappelle v. Mitten, 2000); or one may need to show a substantial change in circumstances due to relocation (North Carolina; *Ramirez-Barker v. Barker*, 1992); or one may need to show harm to the child to make a substantial modification (UMDA standard). Colorado seems to have a unique statute in the treatment of relocation as one form of substantial modification of a parenting plan because relocation is carved out as an exception to the standard of needing to show physical endangerment or emotional impairment (*Colorado Revised Statutes, Dissolution of Marriage–Parental Responsibilities*, 2001), while Tennessee has an elaborate statutory scheme for designating relocation as a unique circumstance in child custody issues (*Tennessee Code Annotated, Domestic Relations* 2004). In these statutory schemes, when a modification will result in a substantial change in parenting time, then the movant parent must show harm to the child, e.g., physical endangerment or risk of emotional impairment, but if the issues concern relocation, then it is a best interests of the child standard.

The Supreme Court of Colorado fashioned novel relocation law on the issue of the timing when relocation becomes a legal issue. *In re Marriage of Spahmer and Gullette* (2005) announced when relocation occurs at the time of dissolution, then court must assume the parents will be living in the location they intend to and statutory factors for relocation in the context of modification should not be considered (e.g., reasons for the move, extended family, advantages/disadvantages, etc.). Further, the court may not issue conditional orders (i.e., the relocating parent could continue as the custodial parent if s/he did not relocate). To do so would unconstitutionally impede the relocating parent's right to travel. Thus, at the time of dissolution, when relocation is on the table, the court must award primary custody to one parent or the other, as if relocation has already occurred. The evaluator, however, has to gather data on the likely effects on the child associated with adjustment to both parents' residences, just as in any custody evaluation, but in this case the effects of relocation need to be estimated.

Relocation Created by a Modification of Primary Custody

An atypical relocation scenario may occur after an institution of a permanent custody order and after one parent moves to another state and the relocated, nonresidential parent seeks a change in the primary custody. In this scenario, a permanent custody order may have been designed to incorporate interstate parenting time arrangements in which the child visits with the nonresidential parent after his/her relocation to another state or after the residential parent and child relocates away from the home community and away from nonresidential parent. After some period of time, the nonresidential parent files a motion to modify the original permanent order, asking for a change in custody which would result in the child relocating away from the residential parent to begin living with the other parent.

In a recent case that we will call "the mother who drank too much," the mother of a ten-year-old boy had been the residential parent since the child was two and a half years old. With the child in the car, the mother was arrested for a DUI traffic offense. Her blood alcohol content was very high (BAC = .28). When she arrived at the local jail to serve her 10-day jail sentence, her BAC was again over the legal limit (BAC = .22). Based upon concerns about the mother's alcohol use, the father filed for a change in custody. The father had relocated from Colorado to Florida when the child was a toddler. His parenting time for eight years had consisted of two long weekends in the son's home community in Colorado and for the past four summers the boy had visited the father in Florida for a week. The father regularly called the boy to talk about daily activities, but the amount of involvement in the boy's life over the years had been quite limited. At the same time that the father motioned the court for a relocation and change in custody, the boy who continued to live with his mother, displayed a healthy and positive developmental growth.

Relocation cases often present the evaluator and the court with situations in which the primary focus is to mitigate harm or to choose which type of harm will be less difficult for the child to handle, e.g., a diminished relationship with the nonresidential parent and loss of resources found in the home community versus a potential diminution of the relationship with the residential and relocating parent. In a Colorado case (*In re the Marriage of Steving*, 1999) in which the mother had relocated to New York, the court found the mother had been alienating the child from the other parent, but the degree of harm estimated to be associated with a change in custody and with a disruption of the child's attachment to the mother outweighed the harm caused by the alienation processes. In this case, the court was attempting to balance two types of harms: harm from relocation resulting in disrupted attachments to the mother and harm from the mother's alleged alienating the child against the father.

In the case of "the mother who drank too much," in which it was concluded that she had an alcohol dependence disorder, the court was faced with the risk of harm to the child associated with the mother's alcohol consumption versus a known high probability of harm associated with a change in primary custody to a father who had been minimally involved in the life of his child. The evaluator recommended the court consider not ordering the modification. Instead, the evaluator recommended that the child remain with the mother who would be ordered to attend an alcohol treatment program, including monitored Antabuse therapy. These steps reduced the risk of harm to the child resulting from the mother's alcohol disorder. The court disagreed and sent the child to Florida to live with the father demonstrating the point that only the trier of fact can determine the threshold of harm needed either for relocation and/or modification and a change in primary custody. The boy would need to adjust to a change in the primary residence and a new community.

Legal Standards for Relocation Law

There is wide diversity in states' legal standards for relocation. In the 1990s, state case law decisions began to assert legal standards based upon the best interests of the child with stipulations that certain factors should be considered, such as practical advantages to the child, educational opportunities, and presence of extended family (*Gruber v. Gruber*, 1990; *Tropea v. Tropea*, 1996). These case law decisions represented a movement away from standards that codified an explicit presumption against a custodial parent moving away from the other parent with the child (*New Jersey Statutes Annotated, Marriages and Married Persons*, 2004; see, Terry et al., 2000), while allowing for the presumption against a custodial parent moving with the child to be overcome without too much difficulty (*D'Onofrio v. D'Onofrio*, 1976). The factors drawn from case law were meant to be indirectly beneficial to the child through direct benefits to the custodial parent.

In the mid-1990s, a trend emerged to assert a legal presumption that a residential parent could relocate with the child unless the other parent could show detriment to the child associated with the move. This trend began with the influential case of *In re Marriage of Burgess* (1996) in

California and several states (CO; WA; NJ) followed suit (*In re Marriage of Francis*, 1998; *In re Marriage of Littlefield*, 1997; *Baures v. Lewis*, 2001). The decisions about relocation represented in these cases generally required a showing of clear detriment to the child to overcome the presumption in favor of moving away (*In re Marriage of Burgess*, 1996) and sometimes after the relocating parent demonstrating a *prima facie* case that the move was sensible (*In re Marriage of Francis*, 1996).

A few states passed statutes specifically to deal with the issue of relocation and in one instance, in 2001, to change the legal standard from a presumption if favor of relocation to a best interests of the child standard with consideration of certain factors [*Colorado Revised Statutes, Dissolution of Marriage–Parental Responsibilities*, 2004; see also, *Tennessee Code Annotated*, 2004]. At least two states continue to have presumptions against relocation (*Arizona Revised Statutes*, 2004; *LaChappelle v. Mitten*, 2000). It was deemed a "compelling state interest" in Minnesota. Thus, the state legal standards can be grouped into four groups: (1) Best Interests of the Child; (2) Best Interests of the Child with specific factors to consider (among all relevant ones); (3) Presumption in favor of Relocation by a residential parent; and (4) Presumption against relocation of the child with the residential parent. There still exists a wide disparity in the standards used to judge the appropriateness of a request to relocate. Several states' relocation law appear to be in a continuing state of flux, often resulting in debate over the proper legal standard to use in relocation analyses. Some of these debates over the proper legal standard to use in relocation analyses have become highly politicized and polarized (e.g., California; *see In re Marriage of LaMusga*, 2004 and accompanying amicae briefs filed by mental health practitioners and social science researchers. Also, Colorado where the Supreme Court recently issued two decisions that greatly altered how relocation can be approached after the legislature nullified the court's early precedent). Two states recently asserted best interests standards after reviewing the existing case law and legal standards across the country (PA and RI; see, *Goldfarb v. Goldfarb*, 2004; *Dupré v. Dupré*, 2004). Several states have put forth constitutional law analyses that contrast a parent's right to travel against a parent's right to have access to his or her child to "care and control." The results of these constitutional law analyses have been equally disparate with Wyoming having a presumption to relocate, Minnesota a presumption against relocation, and Colorado and New Mexico courts stating the two parent rights needed to balanced and juxtaposed with the needs of the child.

THE PROCESS OF PREDICTION
IN CHILD CUSTODY EVALUATIONS

Future Orientation of Custody Cases

In forensic psychology, evaluators are routinely called on to make predictions for the court: Will a criminal offender reoffend in the future? Will an involuntarily committed psychiatric patient commit a violent act if released from the hospital? Will parents cause harm to their child if returned to their care, in a dependency and neglect proceeding? Will an elderly, demented person watch out for her best interests if a guardian is not appointed? Will a student act in a violent manner if allowed to return to school, in a school violence risk and threat assessment case?

The family law context also requires the evaluator and the court to make behavioral forecasts about children, in terms of what parenting arrangements will be in the best interests of the child. The fundamental task of the decision maker and of the custody evaluator is to predict how a child will respond and adapt to alternative environmental circumstances associated with differential custodial and access arrangements. In relocation cases, the challenges of predicting how well a child will adapt to the new situation generally will be more difficult because of the obstacles created by geographic separation to maintaining the level of involvement by the other parent in the child's life. The differential predictions will be even more varied due to increased alternatives to consider compared to a "local" parenting plan with the parents both living in the same area.

Elsewhere, Austin (2000b) has discussed how part of the role of the custody evaluator is to make predictions in the form of recommendations about the long-term developmental outcomes for the child. The evaluator offers alternative residential placement suggestions and makes behavioral predictions and forecasts about how well the child will develop and will adjust to each of these placement suggestions.

Social Policy Considerations

The legal standard for custody determination is understandably placed in the positive language of best interests because of social policy concerns for the long-term welfare of the child. It may be that the court's custody decision making more frequently turns on factors related to its perception of the potential harm to the child. A working strategic hypothesis among legal practitioners seems to be that "detriment," rather than best interests, is what persuades decision makers when it steps into its *parens patriae* role, and directs its foremost concern toward protecting the child from harm.

The task to designate a residential parent when one parent seeks to relocate and the other parent seeks to remain in the original community becomes exceptionally difficult when there are two highly involved and competent parents. No matter what choice is made by the court, the child loses some of the developmental advantages that existed when s/ he lived in an environment in which both parents remained active and involved in the child's daily life. When issues of harm are demonstrated to be associated with one parent, e.g., substance abuse, then the resolution of the uncertainty associated with the decision may be less difficult. A similar degree of uncertainty exists when issues of harm are present with both parents.

Best Interests or Harm?

It is proposed that the legal concepts of "best interests" and "least detrimental alternative" are complementary with respect to child custody determinations and child residential placement. Transferring these concepts to the task of behavioral forecasting means both positive and negative developmental outcomes will be considered and weighted in the legal calculus of custody determinations. The child's predicted developmental outcomes (or adjustment following relocation) become the dependent variables in the evaluator's task of behavioral forecasting.

The relationship between the legal concepts of best interests and least detriment recently has been integrated in legal analysis in Colorado. The appellate court [*In re the Marriage of Martin* (2002)] made a ruling that the concept of Least Detrimental Alternative was subsumed under the Best Interests of the Child, as a legal concept because of the linkage provided by the psycho-legal concept of Psychological Parent (as described by Goldstein, Freud and Solnit, 1973). Within this legal context, the behavioral forecasting associated with divorce and custody can be viewed as a prediction of harm to the child.

Historically, the concept of "least detrimental alternative" is associated with the pioneering and controversial work of Goldstein et al. (1973) on residential placement in adoption and divorce. Goldstein et al. proposed that divorce and custody effects are inherently harmful to the child and that placement decisions are most accurately conceptualized as finding arrangements that result in the least detriment to the child. In the context of a custody evaluation, *it is proposed that least detriment is the conceptual obverse or mirror image of best interests and that examination of the least detriment to the child may be the more salient area for the decision maker to examine. Best Interests of the Child and Least Detriment both are a function of the net predicted developmental outcomes associated with the short and long-term effects of divorce on the child or the short and long term effects of changes in parenting plans resulting from situations such as relocation.*

The literature examining the effects of divorce on children's adjustment has uncovered negative outcomes associated with divorce (Wallerstein & Kelly, 1980; Hetherington & Kelly, 2002; Hetherington, 1999) though the negative effects generally are mild and the base rates are low (Emery, 1998). These data suggest that divorce is a negative life transition event that places children at risk for adjustment problems and developmental harm (Kelly & Emery, 2003). The experience of relocation stands as another negative life transition event that can be experienced by children as even more stressful than the divorce itself (Wallerstein & Tanke, 1996). A hypothesis follows: when divorce and relocation are co-occurring events for the child, the risk of harm is greater (Austin, 2005).

Relocation law presents a conspicuous example of how custody decision makers sometimes need to directly address the degree of predicted harm associated with a change in the child's environmental circumstances. In the controlling case in the State of North Carolina [*Ramirez-Barker v. Ramirez* (1992)], the court recognized that a certain amount of harm is expected when a parent relocates with a child after divorce. In determining whether to allow a parent to move with a child, the court needs to know how the harm to the child resulting from the relocation would be counter-balanced by advantages resulting from the relocation.

There appears to be a national trend by state high court decisions characterized by their use of the language of "harm" that focuses attention on the potential detriment caused by a relocation of a child away from one of his/her parents. Landmark cases such as *Burgess, Baures v. Lewis,* and *Francis* provide harm analyses. It is our position that these decisions reflect a misunderstanding of the logic and the science associated with a detriment standard. That is, the *Burgess* and *Francis* courts appear to assume relocation with a residential parent will be in the child's best interests and that the nonresidential parent must show there is sufficient harm associated with relocation to deny the child from moving.

The available data addressing relocation in general suggests there is a base rate of predictable harm to the child who relocates with his intact family. When the relocation occurs after divorce and involves only one parent, the available research from different studies using distinct methodologies suggests that the child in a family of divorce is at greater risk for harm because of the reduced resources available to the child once s/he moves away from one of his/her parents and associated social and emotional supports (McLanahan & Sandefur, 1994). That is, the research on relocation shows there is a risk of significant harm associated with relocation for children of divorce (McLanahan & Sandefur, 1994; Tucker, Marx & Long, 1998; Hetherington & Kelly, 2002; Braver et al., 2002).

Courts have approached relocation with the assumption that normal best interests factors, found in statute and case law, apply to relocation. These factors can viewed as independent variables in predicting the child's adjustment to the changed circumstances that follow from relocation. There is considerable controversy on the importance of one variable–the nonresidential parent-child relationship. Specifically, this controversy has revealed itself in the high profile California relocation cases, (*In re Marriage of Burgess*, 1996; *In re Marriage of LaMusga*, 2004; see, for elaboration Warshak et al., 2003; Wallerstein et al., 2003; Shear et al., 2003) where the surface issue ostensibly is the relative importance of preserving consistent parent-child physical contact with the residential parent.

Continuity in maintaining child-parent relationships has long been held out as the primary protective factor in the child's adjustment to divorce (Kelly, 1994; Hetherington, Bridges & Insabella, 1998; Kelly & Emery, 2003). The debate within the context of relocation has centered on whether this protective function primarily emanates from emotional security in a high quality relationship with one custodial parent or with high quality relationships with both parents. Perhaps not surprisingly, the group of mental health and legal professionals who has supported a presumption in favor of a residential parent relocating has largely reported research based on older data sets describing more sex role specific parenting roles. In this research, the division of parenting responsibilities in the study samples often reflected family roles at the time in which fathers played a secondary parenting role. A bias in the data gathering was that these studies almost always used the self report of mothers addressing both their level of parental involvement and the level of parental involvement of the fathers (Wallerstein et al., 2003; Wallerstein & Tanke, 1996).

The group of mental health professionals and social science researchers supporting a best interests standard and who also oppose legal presumptions as an approach to relocation (Warshak et al., 2003) have based their advocacy on more current research. Quality longitudinal studies, such as Hetherington's forty year representative sample study of families (Hetherington & Kelly, 2002) and Amato's large sample representative survey studies (Amato & Sobolewski, 2001) support the generalization that children's overall, long-term adjustment to divorce is greater when there is the opportunity for meaningful relationships with both parents. Even Wallerstein's small, selective clinical sample of divorced families supports this conclusion (Wallerstein & Kelly, 1980). Stahl (2004) observes how this tenacious debate represents a healthy development for the field of child custody evaluation and how it "reflects an effort to have new research and shifting understanding inform major Court decisions" (p. 15).

The controversy over children's adjustment to divorce is about the potency of independent variables in predicting child outcomes *following divorce* and is only indirectly about relocation, itself, as findings from the divorce effects literature are being extrapolated to the psycho-legal context of relocation (Wallerstein & Tanke, 1996; Warshak, 2000). Even if one accepts the logic of empirical extrapolation to a subset of divorced children (e.g., relocating divorced children), there is the troublesome problem of applying conclusions based on averages drawn from aggregate data to the individual case of the relocating parent and child. Proponents of legal presumptions for relocation often rely on these group averages that are drawn from a broad array of studies (Wallerstein et al., 2003). However, these studies generally produce inconsistent findings likely due to the variability in samples, differences in methodologies and in historical context from which the data were gathered. In their summary of current literature, Kelly and Emery (2003) opine that disruption to the child's relationship with either parent places the child at risk for adjustment difficulties. They suggest that quality relationships with both parents act as the most powerful protective factors for the child.

While there is merit in relying on aggregate research findings to guide social policy, the United States Supreme Court has cautioned about over-reliance on such data in other forensic contexts. The determination of the right of a mentally ill individual to make treatment decisions requires information from individual, case specific evaluations and not information from group research (*Youngberg v. Romeo*, 1982). Legal commentators have noted the challenge for judges in family law cases is to be sensitive to "the uniqueness of each case and the harm that can result for children from uninformed rulings" (Kleinman, 2004, p. 3).

Case law that has established a rule for using a legal presumption to facilitate relocation (*In re Marriage of Burgess*, 1996; *In re Marriage of Francis*, 1996) also has emphasized the determination of custody issues requiring an "individualistic determination" for each case. This point is emphasized by Hetherington (Hetherington & Kelly, 2002) who indicated her large data set on families of divorce is most informative when the variability among the variables, or the "within-group" variance, rather than the group averages is examined. With this caveat in mind in trying to grapple with the relocation controversy that exists at the social policy level, it is the evaluator's challenge to sort out the data for the individual family and to make predictions for the court on the least harm or best psychological interests of the children, while showing awareness of the relevant research.

Risk × Stakes Model

The court's focus on determining potential harm to the child is a form of risk prediction that we refer to as "risk decision making." In the child custody context, the *risk decision maker* is in the position of predicting outcomes for the child, ranging from predicting outcomes for short term adjustment to predicting outcomes for longer-term development. Instead of using intuitive judgment and common sense alone, the trier of fact has available information presented through live court testimony and/or presented through a written forensic mental health evaluation that summarizes the anticipated effects of different risk factors that the child may face if placed in different custody and access arrangements.

The first step for the risk decision maker is to scrutinize the child's alternative residential and parental access options to reduce the risk of harm. The next step is for the risk decision maker to assess the likelihood of how different residential arrangements will help the child reach his/her maximum developmental potential. The step for the risk decision maker is a prediction, or what Simon (1957) calls the "rational choice in the face of uncertainty" (p. 203).

Austin previously presented an analysis of harm prediction in the relocation context (2000a; 2000b), based upon an approach found in the violence risk assessment literature (Webster et al., 1994; Grisso & Appelbaum, 1992). According to Austin, the decision maker is in the best position to make rational decisions and to reduce uncertainty for the child when s/he is informed about the probability (i.e., risk) and the likely consequences (i.e., stakes) for the child that are associated with each of the alternative residential arrangements.

The four relocation scenarios discussed above can be assigned a Risk × Stakes behavioral prediction matrix by the evaluator and each risk scenario can be translated into a separate legal calculus by the court. In non-relocation cases when at the time of the original orders there are two involved and competent parents, the court is faced with low risk-low stakes decision making alternatives. In relocation cases in which both parents were active and involved prior to the divorce, the court is often faced with high risk-high harm alternatives. Whether the relocating parent is going to move with or without the child, the child is at risk because of the reduction in resources available to the child as a result of his or her movement away from one previously active and involved parent.

Fitting the Evaluator's Predictions to the Legal Standard

The evaluator's predictions need to be developed to address the relevant state legal standard for relocation. The specific prongs included in each state's legal standards for relocation become the psycho-legal conceptual umbrella that guides the evaluation. In a state with specifically defined factors drawn from statute or from case law that are used by judges to guide their decision making, the evaluator needs to reliably assess the psychological aspects of each relocation prong and to determine its predictive value. Many legal standards include a best interests rule with discretion to the court to consider all relevant factors. Drawing on research and clinical experience, the evaluator needs to investigate other important factors endemic to the case. In states with case law/statutory factors to consider (i.e., extended family), the evaluator needs to gather data on each factor that is a potential independent variable.

In states with a presumption in favor of relocation, the court needs to find substantial harm or detriment to deny a request for a parent to relocation. For the evaluator to recommend against relocation, there would need to be data from which the evaluator predicts with confidence that the child's adjustment to the relocation would be substantially negative.

The concept of "threshold of harm" and the determination of what defines a "threshold of harm" is a legal concept that is within the province of the court (Austin, 2000b). The evaluator can, however, fully inform the court about the nature and quality of risks to the child and may help the court to understand factors that contribute to developing reliable decision making criteria. When providing oral testimony or a written report, evaluators are encouraged to use the language of probability of risk and the language of severity of likely outcomes for the child. In a best interests standard state, the evaluator needs to make predictions based on the relevant factors and on the practical matters important to implementing a new parenting plan, or other alternative decisions.

Relocation Risk Assessment

Austin has previously presented a forensic psychology model for conducting a child custody evaluation for the relocation case (2000a). This relocation risk assessment model described a research-based and hierarchical model to help the evaluator assemble factors relevant to predicting the degree of risk for potential harm to the child associated with relocation, or the other alternative decisions. These factors included age of the child, geographical distance, degree of involvement by the non-relocating parent, degree of interparental conflict including history of domestic violence, individual resources of the child, degree of psychological stability of the relocating parent, and ability of the relocating parent to support the relationship between the child and the other parent. At the time the risk assessment model was first published, there was very little direct research on the effects of relocation on children of divorce. The divorce effects literature was reviewed and major findings extrapolated to the potential effects of relocation (Emery, 1998; Hetherington et al., 1998). The risk assessment model was also designed as a heuristic to help decision makers process information on what factors might be associated with positive or negative outcomes for the child in the four placement options discussed above. The risk assessment model also identified protective factors that held potential to moderate potential negative effects due to relocation (see Table 2).

In offering predictions to the court, the evaluator needs to be mindful of the possibility of making *prediction errors*. One must consider the possibility of over-prediction of harm due to the decisional alternatives (i.e., false positive) or under-prediction of harm (i.e., false negative). In the case of "the mother who drank too much" discussed above, the court did not follow the evaluator's recommendations, presumably thinking he had made a false negative prediction. The court appeared to reason that the mother's alcohol treatment plan was insufficient to safeguard the safety of the child. Or, the judge may have reasoned, even if intuitively, that while the risk/probability of relapse was as a low as it could be for the alcohol disorder, the stakes were too high. So, in a low risk, high stakes scenario, the court ordered a modification of primary cus-

TABLE 2

Austin's (2000a) Relocation Risk Factors
1. age of the child;
2. geographical distance of the proposed move;
3. degree of involvement by the non-relocating parent;
4. degree of interparental conflict including history of domestic violence;
5. individual psychological resources of the child/individual temperament;
6. degree of psychological stability of the relocating parent/coping skills/life management skills;
7. ability of the relocating parent to support the relationship between the child and the other parent.

tody that produced a relocation of the child. For a sophisticated treatment of the issue of prediction errors in a forensic mental health context, see Horner and Guyer (1991).

THE INVESTIGATIVE COMPONENT IN RELOCATION PARENTING EVALUATIONS: PROVIDING DESCRIPTIVE DATA ON FACTORS, REASONS, AND LOGISTICS

Many contemporary relocation cases and statutes have identified specific factors to be considered in relocation disputes. Part of the conceptual umbrella for the evaluator is to examine these and other specific factors and issues that relate to the relative advantages and disadvantages associated with relocation. These cases require, then, a psychological cost/benefit analysis as well as risk assessment.

Relocation cases are always "fact driven," a point made in numerous appellate cases (*In re Marriage of Ciesluk*, 2005). To uncover the needed data on risk, consequence, and relative advantages, the evaluator often must dig deeply into the unique contextual features of the post-divorce family. The evaluator often needs to do research on key issues (i.e., the quality of the child's new educational program) or go well beyond the surface data on others (i.e., the psychological stability of the relocating parent's new spouse). Data needs to be gathered on the practical, economic realities (transportation costs; can the family afford to pay for air travel?). Factual information on the relocating parent's rea-

TABLE 3

Examples of Investigative Factors to Assess in Relocation
8.   the quality of the child's new educational program;
9.   the psychological stability of the relocating parent's new spouse;
10.   resources available to the family likely to assist in paying for air travel;
11.   checking the parent's reasons for moving;
12.   the reasons the non-relocating parent is opposing the move;
13.   tax returns;
14.   college transcripts;
15.   employment history.

sons for moving need to be checked (i.e., is the parent really going to graduate school? Really have the job offer?).

The importance of the investigative component in all custody evaluations has been described (Austin & Kirkpatrick, 2004), but it seems even more important in relocation cases where key pieces of information may make or break the parent's explanation for why the relocation should be permitted, or to show if the relocating parent has met the "threshold for relocation" (*Baures v. Lewis*, 2001). In implementing the investigative and practical component, the evaluator also must mindful of the state legal standard and precedents. For example, in some states data needs to be gathered to show specific benefits to the child associated with the relocation, but not in other states. The types of data gathered through investigation are described in Table 3.

Most custody evaluators gather descriptive data on issues that lie outside of research-based factors and perhaps involve data gathering of the type for which the evaluator has no special training or particular expertise to analyze. The data, however, are easily gathered and important for fully informing the court and to help fill in the mortar that cements the issues of the evaluation together. Examples would be gross income from tax returns, availability of daycare in the new community, cost of living, crime index in the communities, etc. In a relocation case, the evaluator may need to examine tax returns to see if the family can financially handle the logistics of the parenting time schedule. S/he may need to examine college transcripts to see if the relocating parent really is a viable candidate for the graduate school.

In relocation cases, it is important to verify or disconfirm the validity of oral reports or stated reasons for the move provided by a primary party to the litigation. Heilbrun, Warren and Picarello (2003) and Austin and Kirkpatrick (2004) suggest the evaluator should take note of the analogy to investigative journalism and try to find at least two corroborating sources for oral information or one definitive objective piece of information (i.e., a document or public record) to verify or disconfirm a verbal report by a primary party. Reliance on collateral sources to obtain convergent validation of hypotheses may be even more important in relocation cases because of the critical nature of essential facts on the relocation issues.

The Nurse Who Wasn't

In a recent case, the mother wanted to relocate with the seven year old daughter three hours away from the father so she could attend nursing school. She indicated she had an L.P.N degree and a state license and that she wanted to advance her career by obtaining a four year nursing degree. Her two sons, each from a previous marriage, lived in the new community. The court awarded the mother temporary primary custody of the daughter and awarded the father substantial parenting time with the daughter. A call to her former employer at an assisted living center uncovered that mom was not a nurse; research on the state data base confirmed she was not a licensed nurse. A review of a past custody evaluation on a different child from this mother showed an historical pattern of the mother frequently lying, committing antisocial acts, and having several involvements with local law enforcement. As a result of these investigative steps yielding information about the mother's trustworthiness, the evaluator recommended that the court deny the mother's request to relocate. The court accepted the evaluator's recommendations and awarded primary custody of the daughter to the father.

The importance of verifying reasons and practical benefits for a move lie at the heart of relocation cases. State high court decisions have encouraged analyses of the reasons for the move. Analyses of reasons for the move allow the court to determine if the relocation is sensible and if there are advantages to the child. It is common forensic lore that the putative reasons for a move often do not materialize. That is, the initial reason to relocate may be motivated by an engagement to a new romantic partner that eventually falls apart; the job opportunity of a lifetime that motivated the decision to relocate falls through; the educational program that would have provided a long sought after degree does not admit the parent to the desired graduate program.

The Mother Who Wanted to Be a Nurse

In this case, the court designated the mother as primary custodial parent and awarded the father every other weekend parenting time. At the time of the parenting plan, the father had relocated from a rural area in Colorado to Denver to receive training to become an automobile mechanic. He exercised his parenting plan regularly, driving four hours one-way. The court's parenting plan anticipated that the father would return to the home community after 18 months and his parenting time would be increased. Upon his return to the home community, the parenting plan was extended to a long, every other weekend schedule that included one weekday evening per week. This parenting schedule continued for a couple of years. The mother then wanted to relocate to Denver where her parents had moved. She also wanted to attend nursing school. She had been working as a certified nursing aide for several years and had been attending community college. She indicated she had a 3.8 GPA and that she had dropped out of a couple of math classes. Despite several requests for production of her college records, the mother never produced a college transcript. Further investigation revealed that she had not applied to a nursing program in the new community. Additionally, it was uncovered that there was a new R.N nursing program in the home community. Based upon these facts, the evaluator did not recommend relocation. Mother subsequently obtained her old job at the local hospital and found that the hospital had a plan to pay for the nursing school tuition in exchange for a commitment of working at the hospital as a nurse for several years after they became licensed nurses.

The Mother Who Did Become a Nurse

In an evaluation, at the time of original orders, the mother wanted to relocate from Colorado to Kentucky with her three sons, ages 9 and identical 7 year-old twins. One of her stated reasons was to go to nursing school (she had B.S. degree in biology) so she could provide a better economic situation for the children. Temporary orders set up an equal parenting time arrangement. Investigation revealed she had not applied to any nursing program. The father did not oppose the mother relocating so she could pursue her career, but he wanted her first to consider options that were geographically closer. Relocation was not recommended and the case settled. The mother subsequently moved to Fort Collins, went to the university and became a nurse. As a result of the mother's in-state school attendance, the parents worked out a more workable parenting plan allowing more equal access of the children to both parents who could remain consistently involved with the children. If the mother had demonstrated in the evaluation that she had been accepted to the Colorado State University nursing program, then the relocation would have been recommended. The relocation recommendation would have been based upon specific information that reflected cogent reasons for the mother's move with implications for expanded economic benefits to the children.

In two of these case examples, the relocation issue surfaced at the time of the construction of the original parenting plan; the other was modification case. The evaluations addressed relocation and the overall needs of the children in a parenting plan looking at both risk factors and practical advantages/disadvantages.

Discriminating Use of Collateral Sources

In all custody evaluations, it is important to make use of information obtained from third party sources to assess the credibility of verbal reports by the parties and to collect key data on salient factors (American Psychological Association, 1994; Association of Family and Conciliation Courts, 1995; 2006; Austin, 2002; Austin & Kirkpatrick, 2004; Heilbrun et al., 2003; Kirkland, 2002). Data from third party interviews and collateral record review can be key in a relocation case.

In the case of the "mother who became a nurse," it was asserted by mom that dad had not been very involved with childrearing and, because of his minimal involvement in childcare, she should be allowed to move. The mother described the father as a peripheral figure in the process of parenting. She was prepared for a parenting time schedule to include most of the summer for dad in this interstate situation. In the past, the parents had been the managers of a large ranch in rural Colorado. Both parents agreed their former employers would be neutral third parties who had known and observed the family for many years. The employer reported how involved the dad had been–"the boys were always with him; he was very involved."

The value of information obtained from neutral third parties cannot be underestimated as a means to confirm or disconfirm rival alternative hypotheses. In this case, information about the degree of parental involvement was crucial in assessing the potential risk to the children associated with an interstate relocation.

In another case that we called the "military bride," the mother remarried a man who was in the military and he received a four-year duty assignment in Georgia. She wanted to relocate with the seven year-old daughter. The father, who was living in eastern Wyoming, opposed the mother's relocation because the child now would be much farther away from him. When the child was less than two years old, the biological father relocated from Colorado to eastern Wyoming. There was little contact with the child from the age 6 months to 3 years old. Once the father remarried, he decided to become more involved with the child. A parenting plan was set up that called for two weekends per month in which the mother drove four hours one-way to meet father for exchanges. When the child entered kindergarten, the parenting plan called for 8 weeks of summer parenting time with dad. During the second year of extended summer parenting time, the court directed the child to spend 10 weeks with her father. The father insisted that he had been a highly involved father, with frequent calls to the school. Beyond the minimum parenting time consisting of summer and holiday visits, the father and step-mom insisted that they saw the child 3 or 4 extra days per month. They also said that they frequently called the child and spoke with her on the phone.

The mother had cogent reasons for the move. There were no signs of vindictive motives. She had been a responsible "gatekeeper" for the child's access to the father over the years. Data showed she had a facilitated both physical and informational access.

Interviews with teachers and other third parties showed the father had never called the teachers, had never attended a parent-teacher conference, and had been to the child's home community only once in five years. The investigative "red flag" was the father's misrepresentation of his extra contact with the child. Although he maintained that he spent an extra three or four days each month with the child, no data supported the father's contention that the child spent additional time with the father.

A suitable, alternative parenting time plan was developed that provided the father with almost the same amount of parenting time as had been in place prior to the mother's move to Georgia. The irony of this case lay in the father's opposition to the mother's relocation six years earlier, when the father had relocated away from the child six years earlier.

Going Beyond the Information Given in a Second Evaluation

Sometimes highly salient pieces of information carry much weight with the court. This may occur when there are missing data in an initial evaluation. In a case, mother and father had one child, a six year old boy. The mother relocated from Colorado to Oregon with her two daughters from a previous marriage. After the initial evaluation, the court awarded temporary primary custody to the father of the couple's six year old boy. The first evaluator concluded that the father was more committed to parenting. In the second evaluation, new interview data revealed that while being supervised by his father, the boy had discovered a loaded handgun and discharged it, causing burns to his face. The second evaluator had suspicions about the boy's development, with specific concerns focused on developmental delays. Testing revealed that the child had an IQ score of 68 and suffered from attention deficit hyperactivity disorder. The mother was a special education teacher and was better able to address the child's developmental needs. Although the first evaluators reported that the father's IQ was 83, no attention was paid to the father's ability to help ameliorate his boy's intellectual and attentional deficits. After reviewing the data, the second evaluator opined that the father was likely not positioned to be as efficient as the mother in attending to the child's needs concerning education and social development. The data from the second evaluation was useful to the court in determining that a more appropriate placement for this child was with the mother and, as a result, the court allowed the relocation.

ADDITIONAL FACTORS TO CONSIDER IN RELOCATION ANALYSES

In this section, we discuss several additional factors that may be useful to consider in conducting a comprehensive relocation analysis. Table 4 lists the factors that we discuss in this section.

Extended Family and Social Support

Many state statutes and case law recognize extended family and social support as important factors in support of relocation. The value of extended family and social support is mentioned in prominent cases (*Gruber v. Gruber*, 1990) and in some current relocation statutes (Colorado). *In re Marriage of Tropea (1994)*, the New York high court noted the support from the maternal grandparents buttressed the mother's argument for the benefit of the move to the children. They often are viewed as sources of child care and generally adding to the resources of the relocating parent's family unit. In New Jersey's *Baures v. Lewis* (2001), support from mother's parents in Pennsylvania was seen as im-

TABLE 4

Additional Factors to Assess in Relocation Analyses
16.   Extended family involvement
17.   Social support networks
18.   Educational opportunities for the parent
19.   Educational opportunities for the child
20.   Community comparisons
21.   Parental involvement, past and present

portant support so mother could return to the workforce and a main reason the relocation was allowed.

The research addressing the benefits of extended family and social support to the children in a divorce-developmental context is unclear and there are few studies that are directly applicable. McLanahan and Sandefur (1994), in a national survey data set, when divorced, single mothers and children lived with grandparents the children actually showed worse adjustment. Although the concept of "social support" appears to be well examined in the psychological literature as found when we conducted a search of the APA database that yielded 11,187 citations under the topic of "social support," few of these studies examined social support and relocation after divorce. A much smaller number of citations were located under a search of the term "extended family" (329 citations) and we found almost no studies directly on the topic of benefits of extended family for children of divorce, and none on relocation.

It is not uncommon for legislative and judicial branches of government to list factors in domestic relations matters that do not have any scientific empirical support, but seem to make common sense. Another example would be legislative provisions on the need to consider child preferences in parenting evaluations. There exists little direct research on the issue. Most evaluators, using "clinical experience" as their knowledge base, would probably agree that support from extended family should be a positive factor in a child's adjustment and as a result, more access to extended family in the new community might be a viable benefit from relocation. Interestingly, a recent review of Canadian appellate and trial court relocation decisions (under a best interests plus factors standard) found extended family was not given much weight by decision makers (Thompson, 2004). When relocating back to the family of origin was the main reason for relocation, only 30% of the cases were approved.

Gathering information about extended family involvement calls for evaluators to provide descriptive data about historical involvement and about current involvement. While some critics of child custody evaluations are concerned about "overreaching" by evaluators in offering forensic recommendations (Melton, Petrila, Pythress, & Slobogin 1997), these same critics suggest that a beneficial role for evaluators is to provide the court with behavioral descriptions on a variety of issues.

In the case of the "mother who became a nurse," the mother asserted a reason for the move was to reap benefits from her contact and interactions with extended family in Kentucky. Investigations of the historical and current extended family contacts with the mother revealed that her extended family support was very weak. Her parents were both deceased. The only family in the immediate area in the new community was a great uncle of the boys. When the oldest boy, age 9, was asked about the great uncle, he said, "I can't remember what he looks like."

Perhaps the most common extended family circumstances involve grandparents and the resources and support they provide, either directly or indirectly, to the movant and to the child around the time of divorce or at the time of a subsequent relocation. General questions used to examine the degree and nature of grandparental involvement include (1) whether the grandparents will help the relocating parent and children adjust better to the stress surrounding relocation, (2) whether the grandparents will provide continuing support and can increase the availability of resources to the child, and (3) whether the grandparents will provide direct child care.

A mother returning to the community of her family of origin is a common relocation scenario (Weissman, 1994). A few studies demonstrate the benefits to children in general and to children of divorce, in particular, from contact with grandparents (Lussier, Deater-Deckard, Dunn, & Davies, 2002). Grandparent contact likely is the most common source of the asserted "extended family" benefit in relocation cases and likely is viewed as an "intuitive benefit" in the eyes of the court. Sound data gathering and investigation will uncover the degree of support and the resource availability that will come from increased grandparent involvement. Proper investigation can also determine any possibly negative influence brought by extended family involvement.

In the case of *In re Marriage of Tropea* (1996), the New York high court removed the "exceptional circumstances" rule for relocation in favor of "best interests with factors" standard. The mother's relocation was allowed so she could follow her parents to a new community where they would provide support, where they would provide child care, and where the mother could be better able to find employment.

In the case of "the mother who married the asthmatic husband," the benefit from extended family would be the involvement of the new step-father's two adult children. The step-father's daughter, who had a new baby from a never married relationship, was living in the residence. The adolescent daughter indicated she needed to move with her mother so she would be able to assist in taking care of the baby who had "torticolis." Thus, instead of reaping support, the mother and daughter would be entering a new family unit where they anticipated they would need to assist in the care of an infant with special developmental needs. The extended family that would be left behind included the child's father, with whom there had been an equal time parenting arrangement in place for four years and with whom the child had a positive relationship; an older sister with a new baby; and an aunt who lived next door to the child's father with whom the teenager was quite close.

In the case of "the mother who wanted to stay home" and who refused to move back to the home community to share equal parenting time with the father, the court found the mother and the grandmother "were homebodies and had no friends" so the child would be deprived of normal socialization experiences. The court found, based on the descriptive data in the evaluator's oral testimony and report, that the new community did not offer healthy extended family support.

In another case, the father relocated four hours away for employment purposes. There had been an equal parenting time arrangement for several years. The parents lived in adjoining duplex units. The ten year old boy had a closer relationship with the father than with the mother and he had expressed a clear preference to relocate with the father. The court ruled that the high level of involvement of the maternal grandmother in the life of the child was an important consideration in not allowing the child to relocate to the father's new residence.

In a recent Colorado case, *In re Marriage of Ciesluk* (2004), the trial court did not find the residential parent's argument compelling for relocation, even though the mother had a new job offer and would have the involvement in her child's life of her father and brother in Arizona. The court felt the harm to the father-child relationship outweighed the benefits of increased involvement with extended family that were seen by the court as only indirectly benefiting the child. The Court of Appeals agreed, but the Supreme Court disagreed and cited extended family as one factor that made the mother's request to move sensible.

Educational Opportunities

Relocating for the purpose of obtaining better educational opportunities is a factor identified in case law and statute in numerous states concerning relocation (*Gruber v. Gruber*, 1990; *Colorado Revised Statutes*, 2004; *Tennessee Code Annotated*, 2004). While there are educational consultants who will assist lawyers when this issue comes to the forefront of disputed parenting cases, there does not appear to be a scientific or systematic method for determining the advantages to the child associated with a global comparison of school programs, except in the extreme cases. Nonetheless, it will be helpful to the court to provide descriptive data on the child's educational achievement, including test scores; the school system profile on programs, student-teacher ratios, and average test scores on standardized tests, because the issue of educational opportunities may be argued in court. It will be helpful to provide information on the child's current and past academic and social adjustment to school. How well the child has adjusted to classmates and teachers, both historically and in the current context, are potentially important data, useful in predicting future adaptation to a new environment with relocation. The child's true adjustment and benefit from a particular educational environment ultimately will depend on his or her "goodness of fit" with the school milieu, teachers, and peers. Except in the extreme situations, the quality of the school is usually not a highly determinative factor in relocation, though when the educational achievement of the opposing school systems are highly discrepant, educational opportunities may become a significant factor. If a child had a special developmental need, then the appropriateness of the specific program and the available educational resources would need to be investigated. The argument on the potential comparative advantages associated with a school program or school district would seem to depend on gathering very specific data on a student's needs and the resources available in the respective school programs. If a child has a special educational need, then examination of the specific special educational programs available to children may be tangible issues to research. There was a tangible issue with a special needs child in the New Jersey relocation case, *Baures v. Lewis* (2001). Unfortunately, the state high court seemed to have misinterpreted the data described by the evaluator about the autistic child or it did not appreciate the child was receiving appropriate services in the home community.

Community Comparisons

It is not uncommon for parents to assert relative advantages associated with a community or geographical area as a reason to argue for or against relocation. Such issues as cost of living, crime rate, cultural opportunities may be asserted; urban vs. rural is a frequent question for debate. As with the factor of educational opportunity, it is a very difficult task to make global community comparisons except in the extreme case. The evaluator still may want to provide the court with information about community comparisons based on descriptive data since it may be argued in court. In a case, we'll call it "California Dreaming," the mother wanted to relocate from Steamboat Springs, CO to Santa Barbara, CA. The mother asserted she wanted to get away from the high cost of living in the home community in Colorado and there would be a general better cultural situation, including a low crime rate, access to the ocean, etc. The descriptive data showed the new community was one of very few communities in the country that actually had a higher cost of living than the home community; there was a violent crime index of zero in the home community; and the recreational and aesthetic benefits of the ocean vs. the Rocky Mountains and winter sports opportunities were seen as a stand-off. In this case, the child was about one year old. The main issue was the need to have a parenting plan that facilitated contact between the very young child and both parents. The quality of the community was important to the parent, not the toddler, and both communities afforded opportunities for a high quality of life. The mother was also proposing to relocate away from her extended family that provided extensive support including child care.

Evaluators often encounter value assertions that cannot be resolved. Specific resources that are available to the child will more often come up with older children when there is relocation. Older children may have developed specific interests that are better served in one community compared to another community. It probably would be more often the case that the older child does not want to leave ongoing activities in his/her current community and the child's preference for and interest in his/her ongoing activities will reflect on what the two communities have to offer. For example, the child does not want to leave the volley ball team program at the current school or there may be religious programs in which s/he is intimately involved. Sometimes, the new community has more appealing aspects to a preferred activity for the child such as the daughter who dances ballet and has reaped as much as possible from the smaller, current community. It will probably be the case for older children that the potential benefits of new community with activities for the child will inevitably need to be juxtaposed with losses of peer relationships, community involvement, and established interpersonal/ social connections associated with those activities in the home community. The difficulties adolescents have in fitting in with new peer connections are well established by research (South, Haynie & Boss, 2005).

Parental Involvement

Parental involvement is an omnipresent issue in relocation cases. It defines to a great extent the adjudged degree of loss for the child and resultant harm. Perceived negative changes in the noncustodial parent-child relationship will often be the foundation for denial of relocation. Disruption to the child-noncustodial parent relationship may trump possible concrete advantages to the relocating parent in a best interests state (*Ramirez v. Ramirez-Barker*, 2004) or disruption may be the basis for muting a presumption for relocation by showing potential detriment to the child in a presumption state (In re *Marriage of Burgess*, 1996; *In re Marriage of LaMusga*, 2004; *Baures v. Lewis*, 2001). The child's relationship with both parents and the relative value placed on the child's relationship with the non-moving parent is one of the factors that lie at the heart of the relocation social policy debate (Wallerstein et al., 2003; Warshak et al., 2003).

Parent involvement is one of the key factors in the relocation risk assessment model. The degree of past involvement by a parent, most often the father, will be a focus of attention and debate, sometimes with the relocating parent wanting to minimize the other parent's past involvement in parental responsibilities and the other parent's perceived availability to the child. If the relocating parent shows a relatively low level of past involvement by the other parent, then a showing of lowered involvement may buttresses the argument for relocation based on the degree of perceived loss for the child and the predicted level of harm to the child-non-moving parent relationship. In the case of "the military bride" above, the child's new parenting time schedule with relocation would closely match the plan that was currently in place for an existing interstate parenting arrangement. In contrast, in "the mother who became a nurse" example, credible data did not support her assertion. Historically, the father had been substantially involved and currently he was involved to a similar degree as the mother. Conversely, the non-relocating parent may be motivated to over-emphasize the degree of his or her past involvement as was the case in the "military bride" case, where the father wanted the evaluator to believe he had been a "full service" parent despite his long-distance parenting arrangement.

Descriptive data on parental involvement are important for the court. Consider a hypothetical case where the parents never married and the father has been provided no opportunity to become involved with the child, despite his wishes. In the "California Dreaming" case above, the mother did not tell the father when she went into labor, left for a three week trip to California to stay with a former boyfriend when the child was a week old, and insisted on supervised parenting time for the father in her parents' home during the first year. She then wanted to relocate with the child out-of-state. Data showed the father was highly motivated to be involved and as a "full service" parent to his son. The mother had consistently interfered with the father's attempts to gain access to the child. When the father's parents traveled several times from back East to see the child the mother was uncooperative. This case illustrates the need for the evaluator to gather data both on past involvement by both parents and on the level of genuine motivation to be involved with the child. Motivation can be defined in behavioral terms by specific attempts to be involved and actions. That is, motivation may be operationally defined as assessing what has the parent done since separation to continue and to foster the parent-child relationship; to lend support to the child; to foster the relationship between the child and other parent; and to assume parental responsibilities.

From a social policy perspective, the issue of past parental involvement can lead to a politico-legal controversy and can clash with scientific research. The "Approximation Rule" proposed by the American Law Institute (i.e., ALI), is ripe for application to the issue of relocation. This rule (Kelly & Ward, 2002) proposes that at the time of original orders the parenting time plan following divorce should be based on the pattern of parental responsibilities before the divorce. The problem with this generic proposal is that it does not take account of the post-divorce realities of family reorganization that divorce necessitates and invites a type of behavioral family ledger-keeping on the degree of nitty-gritty parenting behaviors engaged in by each parent (Riggs, 2005). Role responsibilities and definitions are inevitably shifted and changed after the marital break-up. Research shows a high percentage of fathers become more involved with basic childrearing duties and with the children generally, following divorce (Coley, 2001), so the pre-divorce level of involvement is not a good predictor of post-divorce involvement (Hetherington et al., 1998). This is probably a tri-modal distribution with a group of parents (usually fathers) who continue their high level of involvement; a group who greatly increase their level; and a group who either continue their limited level or decrease what input into parenting they had show in the past, especially if they remarry and have another child (Seltzer, 1991). If the ALI rule was adopted in a state, it is easy to see it would evolve to application to the relocation context, based on a more frequent designation of one parent as a "primary parent." The result might be a *de facto* presumption for relocation, based on pre-divorce patterns of parenting. While extrapolation across national legal boundaries is problematic, Thompson's (2004) Canadian study found trial judges are greatly influenced by the perception of a primary caregiver role: ". . . if the custodial mother can attract the label of "primary caregiver," she will be allowed to move almost always, about 90% of the time. Only very badly behaved "primary caregivers" are denied the right to move" (p. 405). (For a discussion of applying the ALI rule to the relocation context, see, *Dupré v. Dupré*, 2004.)

One of the evaluator's contributions for the court, then, is to collect reliable data on the issue of past and current levels of behavioral involvement by both parents and their respective motivations for future involvement. In the case of proposed relocation, the revised parenting plan needs to reflect the current quality of the child-parent relationships and the opportunity for a meaningful relationship in the future. When there are two highly involved parents, then if the relocating parent eventually moves, with or without the child, there needs to be a harm-mitigation focus in the parenting plan (Austin, 2000c).

In a case called "the Maui-bound mom," the mother who had her child out of wedlock, had been a primary caretaker since the birth of her now ten year old daughter. Father had not been consistently involved. He was available very early in the child's life for some child care duties while mother worked as a horse ranch manager. Father had alcohol abuse problems and served 18 months in jail for alcohol-related traffic offenses. Then, for about five years he had parenting time of about one weekend a month as the parents lived an hour away from each other along an interstate mountain corridor. Father attended few of the many activities in which the child was involved, including school, sports, and horses. His attendance was inconsistent, promising to show up and being a no show. In the father's mind, he perceived himself as a reasonably involved dad. Mother was the child's main economic support and father was far behind in his child support. Once he married, he became more consistent in his contact with the child, increasing his parenting time to every other weekend. He did not involve himself in other aspects of the child's life such as teacher conferences. When the mother's job was eliminated by sale of the ranch, she requested permission to relocate with the child to Hawaii where she had lived for many years prior to having the child. She had a job offer. She had become engaged to a former fiancé and she had an established network of friends for social support. She indicated she would not relocate without the child. A co-evaluator conducted an assessment of the fiancé, the new potential living environment, and the schools in the Hawaii community. Relocation was recommended with the father to have extensive summer parenting time and some holiday time. Transportation costs were handled by the child's trust from the deceased paternal grandmother. The mother had demonstrated that she had been a responsible gatekeeper in her role as residential mother. She had promoted the relationship between the child and father over the years despite the father's lack of consistent involvement. Father and his new spouse, in the context of the litigation, were highly derogatory of the mother and were provocative in their actions towards her.

In the "California Dreaming" case, data were collected to show the father was highly motivated to be involved and wanted to eventually be an equal time parent. He had been very consistent in his attempts to exercise parenting time. He had refused to become caught up in the mother's provocative behaviors. He had established a secure attachment relationship with his son. The child's very young age placed him in the high risk category for harm due to relocation (Kelly & Lamb, 2003).

The evaluator can respond to the fact driven nature in relocation cases on this most salient factor of parental involvement by providing the court with complete descriptive data on historical parenting behaviors, on the distribution of parenting responsibilities and care taking behaviors, on parenting involvement and responsibilities since the time of marital separation, and on the perceived level of motivation concerning future parenting.

CRAFTING A SUITABLE ALTERNATIVE PARENTING PLAN

What Is a Suitable Alternative Plan?

In states where there is not a strong presumption in favor of relocation, generally a best interests analysis is appropriate. Case law is replete with references on the necessity to construct a suitable alternative parenting plan when relocation is at issue. One court opined that "[T]he court must consider the availability of realistic, substitute visitation arrangements which will adequately foster an ongoing relationship between the child and the non-custodial parent" (*Gruber v. Gruber*, 1990, p. 439). Even in states that have moved to a presumption in favor of residential parent relocation, the court's concern about the child's relationship with the non-moving parent is apparent. Another court wrote, "whether, under the facts of the individual case, a realistic and reasonable visitation schedule can be reached if the move is allowed" (*Baures v. Lewis*, 2001, p. 226). A problem exists for evaluators because there are few, if any, formal definitions or a good example of what constitutes a "suitable" plan. We suggest that a "suitable" plan should support and maintain the existing quality and integrity of the child-parent relationship and the plan should also contain provisions intended to facilitate the continuation and growth of this relationship. The support and nurturing of the child's relationship with the non-moving parent becomes a formidable task when there is imposed a substantial geographical distance between the non-moving parent and child. The stated goal in the representative state high court decisions noted above, realistically, may be unobtainable in most relocation scenarios because the unavoidable effect of long distance relocation is to fundamentally alter the qualitative nature of the child-nonresidential parent relationship.

State high courts seem to now accept the reality that some degree of harm to the child-nonresidential parent relationship accompanies any relocation when that parent has been significantly involved with the child. Decisions point out that if all one needed to show was some degree of this type of relationship harm, then no contested relocation case would be approved (*In re Marriage of Edlund and Hales*, cited in *In re Marriage of LaMusga*, 2004; Goldfarb v. Goldfarb, 2004).

Effects of Relocation on the Nonresidential Parent-Child Relationship

The practical and logistical realities of long-distance parenting create automatic changes in the ability of the nonresidential parent to play an effectual part in the daily life of the child. The child will inevitably fall outside the dynamic "sphere of influence" of that parent. While courts often view extended summer parenting time and other school vacation time as "suitable visitation," there inevitably occurs a qualitative shift in the nature of the parent-child relationship that will be exponentially greater with younger children. This may be viewed as an inverse risk calculus: the younger the child, the greater potential harm to the parent-child relationship.

Relocation alters the distribution of how the daily, nitty-gritty responsibilities of parenthood are provided–the baths and bedtime book reading for the very young; meal preparation, parent-teacher conferences, attending activities for the school age children; monitoring choice of friends, guiding through adolescent issues, and daily encouragement with academic motivation for teenagers. The several statutes that designate 100 miles as the magic number to trigger statutory relocation provisions seem to reflect an intuitive sense that distance can create these types of practical preclusions to the same degree of parental involvement.

Kelly and Lamb (2003) summarized the developmental research relevant to the issue of relocation for very young children. The overall effect can be expected to fundamentally alter the attachment relationship between the child and nonresidential parent unless both parents decide to relocate to the same new community. In light of the knowledge gleaned from attachment theory (Ainsworth, Blehar, Waters, & Wall, 1978), and the young child's limited sense of time and lack of a sense of object permanence concerning the left-behind parent (Kelly & Lamb, 2003) there is probably a scientific and empirical basis for a *de facto* presumption against relocation in the instance of two involved parents and a very young child. When children pass through toddler age and approach school-age and object permanence and language development progresses, then there is more flexibility for considering a lessening of the risk of harm, but the child's sense of time and functional obstacles to parental involvement by the distant parent remain fairly daunting (Kelly & Lamb, 2003). When children advance through the elementary school years they are cognitively more prepared to deal with a long distance relationship with a parent and they can better respond to the logistics of a parenting time schedule it becomes more feasible to mitigate the effects of the changes to the relationship. Telephone contact is more viable. Extended summer parenting time becomes more of an option.

In the case above that we called "California Dreaming," the mother wanted to relocate with her one year old son that would have had the effect of ending the attachment between the child and father. The mother thought a two week summer vacation in California would be sufficient parenting time for dad. In the case of the "Maui-bound-momma," the child was ten years old, mom had been a primary caregiver, and extensive summer parenting time with dad was proposed. The child had a high level of individual resources for her age so an alternative parenting arrangement was possible, and one that would allow dad to become a full service dad in the summer, an experience he had never before enjoyed with his daughter.

Shear (1996), in perhaps of a bit of hyperbole, suggested the following effect of relocation:

> To sustain any kind of relationship with a parent who lives more than twenty minutes away, the rest of the child's life and activities must be fragmented and compromised to some degree . . . parents and children cannot sustain close relationships unless the parent is involved in all aspects of the child's life and care. A long-distance parent is, at best, a mentor, something like an aunt or uncle. (p. 441)

In the case of "the mother who wanted to stay home," the court decided a distance of two hours was too much to sustain a relationship with both parents when the mother was viewed as a hostile gatekeeper. After the court issued a conditional decree, e.g., there would be equal parenting time and decision making if the mother returned to the home community, the mother decided to stay home with her mother. The court had anticipated the possibility and a parenting time for mom was implemented with three out of four weekends with mom who chose to remain relocated without the child. The evaluator and court both felt shared parenting time was developmentally appropriate and fit the facts of the case. With the mother's choice, a least detrimental alternative parenting plan was implemented, while less than ideal, would allow for the child to have meaningful relationships with both parents. The mother lived close enough to attend special activities of the child in the home community, go to parent-teacher conferences, etc.

Legal Context and Making Developmentally Suitable Modifications to a Parenting Plan

We earlier indicated the relocation issue often arises at the time of original orders. In such a context the determination of a developmentally-suitable parenting plan is needed by the court. This was the case for both the "mom who wanted to stay home" and "California Dreaming" where there were very young children. In most states, this would occur in a legal context of a best interests of the child standard. When there is a modification of an existing parenting plan with a primary custodial parent, then the legal context might be a standard of a presumption in favor of relocation, if there was a designated residential parent.

Different legal standards probably produce different "thresholds" for determining when relocation is permitted. There may be a resultant difference in how much potential risk of harm to the child is tolerated. To wit, what is defined as a "suitable" modification to the parenting plan will be viewed differently. In New Jersey, a court might be inclined to view extended summer time and other contacts as suitable when there has been high involvement by the non-relocating parent.

Logistics and Flexibility: Implications for the Custody Evaluator

The evaluator may assist the court by providing descriptive data on the practical and logistical aspects surrounding a proposed relocation. The evaluator should always examine if the non-relocating parent has flexibility to also relocate to the new community when the relocating parent has sensible reasons, little flexibility not to move, and there are advantages to the child. Recently, one of us (WGA) was asked in a workshop if he thought the non-relocating parent has a "duty" also to move. His response to this "legal" question was that relocation cases were inevitably complicated and that evaluators and decision makers should look for creative and practical solutions.

In a recent case, the mother of a ten year old girl wanted to relocate from Durango, CO to Indiana where the extended family of both parents lived. The mother was the residential parent, but the parents had worked out a de facto equal parenting time plan over the years. The father was highly involved in activities such as the child's soccer coach, among other father-child involvements. Mom had remarried and both she and her new husband had marketable job skills to find employment. Dad was a laborer with little practical investment in the home community. Dad opposed the relocation, but the daughter talked him into also relocating prior to trial.

The evaluator may assist the court by gathering data on the reasons for the proposed move, the reasons for the other parent opposing the relocation, and the flexibility with both parents on the relocation issue. In the event a relocation of parent and child will occur, when developing a parenting plan, the evaluator should describe for the court that anticipated logistical and practical issues to be faced by the child and faced by the parents. Descriptive data on transportation and associated cost and time issues should be provided (i.e., can the parents get time off of work; lost wages; cost of staying in the new community for parenting time; airfare cost; etc.).

Practice Tips for Crafting Parenting Time Plans

1. Consider the child's developmental age and recommend more frequent and shorter parenting time contacts with younger children, when feasible. School age and older children can benefit from extended summer and other school vacation times with the nonresidential parent. With very young and younger school-age children, always consider making specific recommendations about changing parenting time schedules as the child matures. That is, at age five the child may benefit from two three week summer times with the other parent, separated by three weeks. At age eight, the child may be ready for six continuous weeks.

2. Encourage and formalize opportunities for the nonresidential parent to have parenting time in the child's new community.

3. Address the issue of transportation costs descriptively for the court, not proscriptively, as this is an issue for the court to address. Address the issue of mode of transportation. Whether a child can travel by air, unaccompanied by a parent, is a common point of contention and there is no professional consensus on the issue. For auto travel the issue of a meeting point between parent residences or alternating transportation responsibilities will need to be addressed. Parents usually work this issue out.

4. Inform the Court about parenting time guidelines for long-distance parenting arrangements specific to the developmental age (Arizona Supreme Court, 2002) while emphasizing the unique aspects of the case and the children's needs (see Kelly, 2005).

5. Make recommendations for liberal virtual parenting time access arrangements that are age-appropriate (Gottfried, 2002) while being mindful about the issue of intrusiveness by the nonresidential parent. Communication modalities of telephone (land line and cell phone), internet e-mail, web-cam, and audio and video electronic recordings should be available within reason. When there is poor communication and conflict, phone contact between parent and child should be specific and structured with younger school-age children. It is expected older school age children (i.e., twelve and older) will largely regulate phone contact themselves and work out satisfactory communication with the parent. There will be exceptions so phone contact occasionally may need to be scheduled with older children.

6. The factor of a child's preference is a UMDA best interests factor and included in almost every state statute. It demands particular scrutiny in relocation cases. Older children may be more resistant to relocation due to their involvement in peer activities and friendships. It may be unwise to uproot a senior in high school, for example, who needs continuity in her academic program. An athletic commitment may be a student's highest priority, in other instances. It may be more likely that the issue of splitting siblings will arise in relocation cases because of different developmental needs and wishes of the children (Rotman, Tomkins, Schwartz et al., 2000).

7. When there is conflict and poor communication between parents in a relocation context, consideration should be given to the appointment of a parenting coordinator or whatever type of facilitator or conflict reduction role is appropriate for the jurisdiction.

CONCLUSION

Children of divorce face both uncertainty and risk of harm when facing prospects of relocation (McLanahan & Sandefur, 1994), as they do following divorce. Some children face divorce and relocation in close temporal proximity. In this article, we have attempted to unravel some of the complexities involved in conducting a child custody relocation evaluation. Such cases inherently are complex. We discussed the psycho-legal context that has great fluidity between the states (*Dupré v. Dupré*, 2004) and the need for the evaluator to be very familiar with the legal standard for the jurisdiction. Relocation usually requires the evaluator to measure a greater diversity of factors, many of which are dictated by law. We discussed the need for the evaluator to be mindful of the predictions that need to be made for the court concerning the four decisional alternatives in relocation and to be mindful of possible prediction errors. We discussed how relocation is best viewed in terms of mitigating harm for the child and therefore an ultimate issue opinion probably should not be expressed by the evaluator. The evaluator's task is to inform the court so there is an understanding of the degree of risk and potential consequences for the child associated with the decisional alternatives. This will help the trier of fact, in the inherent role of risk decision maker, to act to reduce the uncertainty for the child.

In this article, we presented again the relocation risk assessment model (Austin, 2000a; 2000b). We integrated a discussion of the investigative component of child custody evaluation (Austin & Kirkpatrick, 2004) which is generally more expansive and detailed in relocation cases because of the need to present the court with substantial descriptive data on a number of practical issues that are bound to surface in the relocation context.

Finally, we discussed issues involved with crafting long distance parenting plans. Research from child development and divorce effects are used to examine how to consider the central variable of the child-nonresidential parent relationship. Careful investigation helps better inform the court on this core issue. Throughout the article we tried to illustrate the conceptual and methodological issues with case material to help evaluators get a better feel for how to approach and think through the relocation evaluation, or the art side of the evaluative endeavor (Gould & Stahl, 2000).

REFERENCES

Ainsworth, M.D.S., Blehar, M., Waters, S., & Wall, S. (1978). *Patterns of attachment.* Hillsdale, NJ: Lawrence Erlbaum.

Amato, P.R., & Sobolewski, J.M. (2001). The effects of divorce and marital discord on adult children's psychological well being. *American Sociological Review, 66,* 900-921.

Amato, P. R., & Sobolewski, J. M. (2004). The effects of divorce on fathers and children. In M. E. Lamb (Ed.), *The role of the father in child development* (pp. 341-367). New York: Wiley.

Arizona Supreme Court (2002). *Model parenting time plans for parent/child access.* Phoenix, AZ: Author.

Association of Family and Conciliation Courts (1995). *Model standards for child custody evaluations.* Madison, WI: Author.

Association of Family and Conciliation Courts (2006). *Model standards of practice for child custody evaluations.* Madison, WI: Author.

Arizona Revised Statutes (2004). Marital and Domestic Relations, Rights of noncustodial parent; parenting time; exception; enforcement; access to records; suspension of parenting time; relocation of child § 25-408(C-J). http://www.azleg.state.az.us.

Arizona Supreme Court (2002). *Model parenting time plans for parent/child access.* Phoenix, AZ: Author.

Austin, W. G. (2000a). A forensic psychology model of risk assessment for child custody relocation law. *Family and Conciliation Courts Review, 38,* 186-201.

Austin, W. G. (2000b). Relocation law and the threshold of harm: Integrating legal and behavioral perspectives. *Family Law Quarterly, 34,* 63-82.

Austin, W. G. (2000c). Risk reduction interventions for the child custody relocation case. *Journal of Divorce and Remarriage, 33,* 65-72.

Austin, W. G. (2002). Guidelines for Utilizing Collateral Sources of Information in Child Custody Evaluations. *Family Court Review, 40,* 177-184.

Austin, W. G. (2005). The child and family investigator's evaluation of the relocation case. In R. M. Smith (Ed.), *The role of the child and family investigator and the child's legal representative in Colorado* (pp. C9-1–C9-28). Denver: Colorado Bar Association.

Austin, W.G., & Kirkpatrick, H. D. (2004). The investigation component in forensic mental health evaluations: Considerations in the case of parenting time evaluations. *Journal of Child Custody, 1,* 23-43.

Baures v. Lewis, 770 A2d. 214 (N.J. 2001).

Berrebbi v. Clarke, 2004 WL 177064 (Fla.App. 2 Dist).

Bowermaster, J. M. (1992-93). Sympathizing with Solomon: Choosing between parents in a mobile society. *University of Louisville Journal of Family Law, 31,* 791-884.

Braver, S. L., Cookston, J. T., & Cohen, B. R. (2002). Experiences of family law attorneys regarding current issues in family law. *Family Relations, 51,* 325-334.

Braver, S. L., Ellman, I. M., & Fabricius, W. V. (2003). Relocation of children after divorce and children's best interests: New evidence and legal considerations. *Journal of Family Psychology, 17,* 206-219.

Bruch, C. S., & Bowermaster, J. M. (1996). The relocation of children and custodial parents: Public policy, past and present. *Family Law Quarterly, 30,* 245-265.

Burgess, In re the Marriage of, 913 P.2d 473 (Cal. 1996).

Ciesluk, In re the Marriage of, No. 03CA2047, 2004 WL 1119473, 2004 WL 1117900 (Colo.App. May, 2004).

Ciesluk, In re Marriage of, 113 P.3d 135 (Colo. 2005). Available at www. courts.state.co.us/suptctcaseannctsindex.htm.

Coley, R. L. (2001). (In)visible men: Emerging research on low-income, unmarried, and minority fathers. *American Psychologist, 56,* 743-753.

Colorado Revised Statutes, Dissolution of Marriage–Parental Responsibilities, § 14-10-129. http//www.coleg.co.us.

D'Onofrio v. D'Onofrio, 365 A.2d 716 (App.Div. 1976).

Dupré v. Dupré, 857 A.2d 242 (R.I. 2004).

Edlund and Hales, In re Marriage of, 66 Cal.App.4th 1454

Emery, R. E. (1998). *Marriage, divorce, and children's adjustment, sec. ed.* Thousand Oaks, CA: Sage.

Francis, In re the Marriage of, 919 P.2d 776 (Colo. 1996).

Goldfarb v. Goldfarb, Superior Ct., 861 A.2d 340 (Pa.Super 2004).

Goldstein, J., Freud, A., & Solnit, A. J. (1973). Beyond the best interests of the child. New York: The Free Press.

Gottfried, S. (2002). Virtual visitation: The wave of the future in communication between children and non-custodial parents in relocation cases. *Family Law Quarterly, 36,* 475-485.

Gould, J. W. & Stahl, P. (2000). The art and science of child custody evaluations. *Family and Conciliation Courts Review, 38,* 392-414.

Grisso, T., & Appelbaum, P. (1992). Is it unethical to offer predictions of future violence? *Law and Human Behavior, 16,* 621-633.

Gruber v. Gruber, 583 A.2d 434 (Pa.Super. 1990).

Heilbrun, K., Warren, J., & Picarello, K. (2003). Third party information in forensic assessment. In A. Goldstein (Ed.), *Handbook of Psychology: Forensic Psychology* (Vol. 11). Hoboken, N.J.: Wiley.

Hetherington, E. M. (1999). Should we stay together for the sake of the children? In E. M. Hetherington (Ed.), *Coping with divorce, single parenting, and remarriage: A risk and resiliency perspective* (pp. 93-116). Mahwah, NJ: Erlbaum.

Hetherington, E.M., Bridges, M., & Insabella, G.M. (1998). What matters? What does not? Five perspectives on the association between marital transitions and children's adjustment. *American Psychologist, 53,* 167-184.

Hetherington, E. M., & Kelly, J. (2002). *Divorce reconsidered: For better or for worse.* New York: Norton.

Horner, T. M., & Guyer, M. J. (1991). Prediction, prevention, and clinical expertise in child custody cases in which allegations of child sexual abuse have been made: I. Predictable rates of diagnostic error in relation to various clinical decisionmaking strategies. *Family Law Quarterly, 25,* 217-252.

Ireland v. Ireland, 717 A.2d 676 (Conn. 1998).

Kelly, J. B. (1994). The best interests of the child: A concept in search of meaning. *Family and Conciliation Courts Review, 35,* 377-386.

Kelly, J. B. (2005). Developing beneficial parenting plan models for children following separation and divorce. *Journal of American Academy of Matrimonial Lawyers, 19 (2),* 101-118.

Kelly, J. B., & Emery, R. E. (2003). Children's adjustment following divorce: Risk and resilience perspectives. *Family Relations, 52,* 352-362.

Kelly, J. B., & Lamb, M. E. (2003). Developmental issues in relocation cases involving young children: When, whether, and how? *Journal of Family Psychology, 17,* 193-205.

Kelly, R. F., & Ward, S. L. (2002). Allocating custodial responsibilities at divorce: Social science research and American Law Institute's approximation rule. *Family Court Review, 40,* 350-370.

Kirkland, K. (2002). The epistemology of child custody evaluations. *Family Court Review, 40,* 177-184.

Kleinman, T. G. (2004). An open letter to a young lawyer as she enters the World of Oz: A critical look at the child custody system. *Journal of Child Custody: Research, issues and practices, 1,* 1-7.

LaChappelle v. Mitten, 607 N.W.2d 151 (Minn. Ct.App. 2000).

LaMusga, In re the Marriage of, 88 P. 3d 81 (Cal. 2004).

Lawson, In re Marriage of, 608 P.2d 378 (Colo.App. 1980).

Littlefield, In re the Marriage of, 940 P.2d 1362 (Wash. 1997).

Lussier, G., Deater-Deckard, K., Dunn, J., & Davies, L. (2002). Support across generations: Children's closeness to grandparents following parental divorce and remarriage. *Journal of Family Psychology, 16,* 363-376.

Martin, In re the Marriage of 42 P.3d 75 (Colo.App. 2002).

McLanahan, S., & Sandefur, G. (1994). *Growing up with a single parent: What hurts, what helps.* Cambridge, MA: Harvard University Press.

Melton, G. B., Petrila, J., Pythress, N. G., & Slobogin, C. (1997). *Psychological evaluations for the courts, sec. ed.* New York: Guilford.

New Jersey Statutes Annotated, Marriages and Married Persons (2004). § 9:2-2, http://www.njleg.state.nj.us

Ramirez-Baker v. Baker, 418 S.E.2d 675 (N.C. App. 1992).

Riggs, S. A. (2005). Is the Approximation Rule in the child's best interests? A critique from the perspective of attachment theory. *Family Court Review, 43,* 481-493.

Rotman, A. S.Tomkins, R., Schwartz, L. L., & Samuels, M. D. (2000). Reconciling parents' and children's interests in relocation: In whose best interests? *Family and Conciliation Courts Review, 38,* 341-367.

Russenberger v. Russenberger, 669 So.2d 1044 (Fla. 1996).

Seltzer, J. A. (1991). Relationships between fathers and children who live apart: The father's role after separation. *Journal of Marriage and the Family, 53,* 79-101.

Shear, L. A. (1996). Life stories, doctrines, and decision making: Three high courts confront the move-away dilemma. *Family and Conciliation Courts Review, 34,* 439-458.

Simon, H. A. (1957). *Models of men.* Oxford, England: Wiley.

Spahmer v. Gullette, 113 P.3d 158 (Colo. 2005). Available at www.courts.state.co.us/supctcaseannctsindex.htm.

Stahl, P. (2004). A 20-year personal perspective on child custody evaluations. *Journal of Child Custody: Research, issues, and practices, 1*, 9-15.

Steving, In re the Marriage of, 980 P.2d 540 (Colo. App. 1999).

Tanttila v. Tanttila, 382 P.2d 798 (Colo. App. 1963).

Tennessee Code Annotated (2004). Domestic relations; child custody and visitation; parent relocation, § 36-6-108, http://www.tnleg.state.tn.us

Terry, E. J., Goodale, K. K., Phelan, P. C., & Womack, J. L. (2000). Relocation: Moving forward or moving backwards? *Texas Tech Law Review, 31*, 983-1040.

Thompson, D. A. (2004). Movin' on. Family *Court Review, 42*, 398-410.

Tropea v. Tropea, 665 N.E.2d 145 (1996).

Tucker, C. J., Marx, J., & Long, L. (1998). "Moving on": Residential mobility and children's school lives. *Sociology of Education, 71*, 111-129.

Wallerstein, J., & Kelly, J.B. (1980). Surviving the breakup. New York: Basic Books.

Wallerstein, J.S., & Tanke, T.J. (1996). To move or not to move: Psychological and legal considerations in the relocation of children following divorce. *Family Law Quarterly, 30*, 305-332.

Wallerstein, J. S. et al. (2003). Brief of amici curiae supporting affirmance of the court of appeals decision, In re the Marriage of (Navarro) LaMusga, Supreme Court of California, Case No. S107355.

Warshak, R. (2000). Social science and children's best interests in relocation cases: Burgess revisited. *Family Law Quarterly, 34*, 83-114.

Warshak, R. A. et al. (2003). Amici curiae brief of, on behalf of the LaMusga children, Supreme Court of California, Case No. S107355.

Watt v. Watt, 971 P.2d 608 (Wyo. 1999).

Webster, C. D., Harris, G. T., Rice, M. E., et al. (1994). *The violence prediction scheme*. Centre of Criminology, University of Toronto: Toronto.

Weissman, H.N. (1994). Psychotherapeutic and psycho legal considerations: When a custodial parent seeks to move away. *American Journal of Family Therapy, 22*, 176-181.

Youngberg v. Romeo, 457 U.S. 307 (1982).

doi:10.1300/J190v03n03_04

Avoiding Bias in Relocation Cases

Philip M. Stahl

SUMMARY. Bias is a risk in all family law matters, for judges, custody evaluators, mediators, and attorneys. This paper is focused on particular risks as they relate to relocation matters. A description of various types of risk is followed by ways to reduce or minimize the risk of bias in these cases. Ultimately, this author will suggest a protocol that evaluators and judges can use when reaching conclusions about whether or not to allow a parent who wishes to relocate to be able to take the child with him/her. doi:10.1300/J190v03n03_05 *[Article copies available for a fee from The Haworth Document Delivery Service: 1-800-HAWORTH. E-mail address: <docdelivery@haworthpress.com> Website: <http://www.HaworthPress.com> © 2006 by The Haworth Press, Inc. All rights reserved.]*

Philip M. Stahl, PhD, is a psychologist in private practice. He conducts child custody evaluations and provides consultation and expert witness testimony. He is a provider of continuing education for psychologists and other mental health providers, and attorneys and Family Law Specialists in California. He has conducted trainings throughout the United States and internationally for child custody evaluators and others working with high-conflict families of divorce. He has presented workshops for judges throughout the country and is on the faculty of National Judicial College and the National Council of Juvenile and Family Court Judges. Along with his teaching, Dr. Stahl has written extensively on various issues in high-conflict divorce and custody evaluations. He is the author of *Conducting Child Custody Evaluations: A Comprehensive Guide* (Sage, 1994), *Complex Issues in Custody Evaluations* (Sage, 1999), and *Parenting After Divorce* (Impact Publishers, 2000). The California Supreme Court cited his custody evaluation in its recent landmark decision modifying eight years of relocation case law following Burgess (In re Marriage of LaMusga (2004) 32 Cal.4th 1072, 12 Cal.Rptr.3d 356, 88 P.3d 81).

Address correspondence to: (E-mail: pstahl@earthlink.net).

[Haworth co-indexing entry note]: "Avoiding Bias in Relocation Cases." Stahl, Philip M. Co-published simultaneously in *Journal of Child Custody* (The Haworth Press, Inc.) Vol. 3, No. 3/4, 2006, pp. 109-124; and: *Relocation Issues in Child Custody Cases* (ed: Philip M. Stahl, and Leslie M. Drozd) The Haworth Press, Inc., 2006, pp. 109-124. Single or multiple copies of this article are available for a fee from The Haworth Document Delivery Service [1-800-HAWORTH, 9:00 a.m. - 5:00 p.m. (EST). E-mail address: docdelivery@haworthpress.com].

KEYWORDS. Bias, relocation, child custody evaluations, move-away

Judges, attorneys, family mediators, and child custody evaluators often consider relocation cases among the more difficult and challenging. Many reasons are hypothesized, including: (1) The possibility that they are more difficult to settle since there is rarely a middle ground; (2) Often there is no solution that is optimal for the child; (3) Many jurisdictions have presumptions, which might hurt one class of people (e.g., presumptions in favor of the move may hurt the non-moving party and presumptions against the move may hurt the party requesting the right to move); (4) Jurisdictions sometimes have little guidance in how to decide the case using either case law or statutory law; (5) There is little research guiding custody evaluators and decision-makers in these matters: Fabricious, W and Braver, S, this volume, Braver, S., Elman, I., and Fabricious, W., 2003; Gindes, M. 1998; and Shear, L. 1996; and (6) The fear that a parent's request to relocate with his/her child may increase polarization and conflict between divorced parents who might otherwise be co-parenting reasonably well.

In the aggregate, these concerns present unique and difficult challenges to lawmakers and policy makers. These challenges contribute to the emotional and difficult decision-making in individual cases. In conversations with custody evaluators and judges from across the country, this author has heard many people have a tendency to view relocation decisions in a biased way. According to the Cambridge Dictionaries Online (2005) bias is defined as "a tendency to support or oppose a particular person or thing in an unfair way by allowing personal opinions to influence your judgment." For purposes of this article, bias is defined as any personal or professional reason that contributes to that person's thinking about relocation leaning in one direction or another most of the time, regardless of the facts of a particular case. Many times, I have heard either evaluators or judges say that parents should not move with their child except under extraordinary circumstances. Such a belief runs a risk of creating an "against the move bias" in every case. I have heard others who believe that a custodial parent should be allowed to move wherever and whenever s/he wants, believing that if a move is good for the custodial parent, it will automatically benefit the children. Such a belief runs the risk of creating a "for the move bias" in every case. In this author's opinion, it is critical for evaluators and judges to resist such biases in relocation cases and to look carefully at each case before deciding what is in that child's best interests.

Custody evaluators are encouraged by practice standards, guidelines, and in some jurisdictions Rules of Court to control for bias. For example, the Association of Family and Conciliation Courts (AFCC), in its Model Standards of Practice for Child Custody Evaluation (1994) states, "[T]he evaluator shall provide information on any inherent bias(es) . . . that he or she holds, prior to the commencement of any evaluation." Similarly, the American Psychological Association (APA), in its Guidelines for Child Custody Evaluations in Divorce Proceedings (1994) states, "The psychologist is aware of personal and societal biases and engages in nondiscriminatory practice. . . . The psychologist recognizes and strives to overcome any such biases or withdraws from the evaluation." The 2005 California Rules of Court, Rule 5.220 states, "In performing an evaluation, the child custody evaluator must . . . (m)aintain objectivity, provide and gather balanced information for both parties, and control for bias." In all of their work, psychologists are expected to control for bias and avoid misleading statements when making public statements or testifying in court (APA, 2002).

Similarly, family law mediators and judges have expectations of avoiding personal bias in their work (AFCC, 2000). For example, the Model Code of Judicial Conduct (ABA, 2004) states, "A judge shall perform judicial duties without bias or prejudice."

Shortcuts in decision-making, called heuristics, may affect the ways in which people reach conclusions (Gigerenzer, G., Todd, P., and ABC Research Group, 1999). Biases are examples of such heuristics. While there has been some literature on bias in other areas of family law (e.g., overnights with young children, the psychological parent, and attachment issues), there has been no articles or research addressing the issue of bias directly in relocation cases.

This author's examination of the amicus briefs (see e.g., Warshak, R., 2003; Shear, L., 2003; Wallerstein, J., 2003) submitted to the California Supreme Court prior to their decision in the Marriage of LaMusga (California Supreme Court, 2004) reveals a tendency on all sides to present information that supported the position or outcome that each author wanted, often revealing a pro-move/pro-mother, against-move/pro-father bias. This was particularly troublesome when research findings were highlighted to suggest a particular outcome while ignoring or minimizing research findings that might suggest a different point of view. A careful reading of these three amicus briefs in particular, which psychologists or a lawyer authored, used much of the same research data to reach opposite conclusions about the meaning of those data or how those data should be applied in relocation matters. There is so little research that directly relates to relocation in divorce that we are often left with interpreting other research and making inferences about how this research might apply in relocation cases. However, by highlighting one set of data over another, e.g., that children's adjustment to divorce is linked to the well-being and psychological functioning of the primary parent (the brief authored primarily by Wallerstein) or that children's adjustment in divorce is linked to having both parents actively engaged in a wide range of their children's life and experiences (the briefs primarily authored by Warshak and Shear), it is easy to make an argument that is either "for the move" or "against the move" in the majority of cases.

While none of the briefs oversimplified things to that extent, it is this author's opinion that all of those briefs highlighted research data that supported the relocation position of those authors. While it is not unusual for experts to take advocacy positions in legislative lobbying or amicus briefs to the court, it is critical that, in individual cases, experts and decision-makers need to control for their personal biases by looking at the facts of each particular case and making the tough recommendation or decision about how to apply the law in that family's jurisdiction and all of the psychological research with the family dynamics when making a recommendation or decision.

BIASES RELEVANT TO RELOCATION CASES

Gutheil (2004) lists several types of bias that may affect expert's work as a way of helping to avoid the impact of those sources of bias. While all sources of bias are relevant in any family law or forensic matter, this author will focus on some potential sources of bias and the risk that each has in deciding a particular relocation case.

Gender Bias

Gender bias is one of the more classic biases in family law, as custody evaluators, family mediators, and judges are frequently accused of gender bias and of treating women or men differently in the system. Politically, there are mother's rights advocates and father's rights advocates who, by their very nature, take advocacy positions on a variety of issues. This author believes that the research which focuses on "the psychological parent" (see e.g., Goldstein, Freud, and Solnit, 1984) tends to support and favor mothers over fathers. Other observers interpret the growing research data on fathers and their involvement with children (see e.g., Lamb, Sternberg, and Thompson, 1997) as supporting a father's rights bias. It is critical for judges and custody evaluators to avoid gender bias in their work.

Cultural Bias

This refers to the potential that a judge or custody evaluator will make decisions based on aspects of the culture of one or both of the parties being served. One way this may surface in relocation cases is when one of the parents wants to move children to a country that has very different cultural experiences or to a country that has not adopted the Hague Convention on the Civil Aspects Of International Child Abduction. While the cultural issues may be important, especially in a long-distance relocation, it is only one factor and might not be the only relevant issue to be considered. This author has seen a situation in which an evaluator highlighted the distance to a South American country and the need for the child to adjust to a new culture as being more important than all of the other issues in a particular case, including the child's special education needs and the relative attachment differences, when making a recommendation against the move.

Using Research to Support One's Bias

There is a risk that custody evaluators, judges, and those who write amicus briefs and lobby politicians will use research to support a pre-conceived opinion (Ramsey, S., 2006). Many custody evaluators generically describe that "research suggests" a particular thing when formulating opinions and recommendations at the conclusion of an evaluation, without providing citations to the research being mentioned. This author has seen evaluators refer to the need for both parents being actively involved in the child's life experiences and using this as the reason for rejecting a parent's request to move with a child, even though that research might not apply to the particular facts of the case because the other parent had spent very little time with the child over the previous few years. Another example would be when an evaluator cites the primary parent theory as a reason for supporting a move, in spite of the flimsy rationale for the move and the active involvement of the other parent on a regular and consistent basis during the child's life. In addition, none of this research might apply when a parent's job is relocated and the parents have shared custody and the parenting for years. In such a case, the decision will need to be based on an analysis of advantages of mother-custody in one location or father-custody in the other location rather than a recitation of such research. The risk is that an expert might cite only the research that supports the position with which the expert agrees. This could lead to some type of "pro-mother in favor of the move" or "pro-father against the move" position in a particular reloca-tion case. This author believes that it is important to cite any research used in reaching conclusions to reduce the risk of a bias interfering with those conclusions.

Primacy or Recency Bias

Primacy bias refers to the tendency to rely on the first pieces of infor-mation that an evaluator hears, whereas recency bias refers to the evalu-ator relying on the last pieces of information that an evaluator hears (Gutheil, 2004). While these potential biases are typically associated with bias risk in all custody evaluations, they are a significant risk in re-location cases. For example, if the evaluator hears early in the evalua-tion from one parent that the other parent who wants to move with the child has often interfered with access two things might occur. First, the evaluator is at risk of interpreting everything s/he hears through the fil-ter of this allegation and anchoring all data toward that filter. Second, the evaluator is at risk of giving that piece of data significantly more weight than all of the rest of the data. A similar risk occurs when an evaluator hears from a collateral witness toward the end of an evalua-tion that the parent who does not want the child to move has not at-tended any parent-teacher conferences. While all of this might be important data, the risk of bias occurs when the evaluator stops gather-ing additional data because s/he believes that this last piece of data puts the proverbial nail in the coffin. If the evaluator anchors data to what is heard first or stops gathering data prematurely when more data might lead to a different conclusion, such potential biases can lead to a conclusion that is not in the child's best interests.

Confirmatory Bias

Like the bias associated with primacy or recency effects, confirma-tory bias is the tendency for a custody evaluator or a judge to look for certain data or evidence that supports a particular position and then try and fit all of the other data into that position. Hence, the evaluator or judge is looking for data to support the position that the evaluator or judge holds or believes. This is a significant risk in relocation cases if the evaluator or judge believes that moves are either generally a good thing or generally a bad thing. Confirmatory bias interferes with the evaluator's or judge's ability to look for data or evidence that does not support the conclusion reached. In order to reduce the risk of confirmatory bias, the evaluator or judge must consider multiple hypotheses and continue gathering all relevant data before reaching any conclusions on the case. In fact, California Rule of Court 5.220 is clear that child custody evaluators must include all data that supports their conclusions, as well as data that don't support their conclusions in any reports or testimony to the court.

Using Psychological Test Data to Support One's Bias

Like these other biases, psychologists who are prone to view relocation cases a certain way are at risk for interpreting psychological test data to support a particular position rather than using it to generate hypotheses. While there is risk for the misapplication of psychological test data in any child custody evaluation, it is this author's opinion that there is great risk of this misapplication of test data to support a particular conclusion in a relocation case. For example, if a parent who wants to move tests as defensive and presents herself in a favorable light on an MMPI-2, as many custody litigants do (Bathurst, Gottfried, and Gottfried, 1997), a psychologist who is reluctant to recommend in favor of a move might use that data, and that data alone, to suggest that she cannot be trusted to support the child's relationship with the other parent after she moves. Similarly, a psychologist might suggest that a parent who scores as narcissistic on the MCMI-III and Rorschach might not be sufficiently child-focused to be the primary parent and recommend that the other parent be able to move with the child. The problem with both of these situations is that psychological tests, just like any one data source, should only be used to generate hypotheses about people's personality traits and should never be used to generate recommendations (Gould, 1998 and Stahl, 1999). Thus, the risk with psychological test data is that the evaluator will subjectively select those test data which will support the bias that the evaluator holds.

"Truth Lies in Somewhere in the Middle" Bias

This author believes that there are other potential sources of bias that are not mentioned elsewhere in the literature. One example is what this author calls "truth lies somewhere in the middle" bias. Many evaluators and judges, in particular those who are at risk for burnout because they have worked in the system for so long, are at risk for exhibiting this bias. There is a tendency to perceive that each member of a couple in conflict has equal contribution to that conflict. While that situation is common in many high conflict situations, there are other instances in which one parent drives most of the conflict and the other parent tends to be more reactive to that conflict. This "truth lies somewhere in the middle" bias prevents evaluators and judges from recognizing the unique contributions of each parent to the conflict. However, these unique contributions to the conflict are likely to be an important and relevant factor to consider in a given case, and in particular in a relocation case. Assigning equal blame to both parents is a mistake when the responsibility for different components of the conflict are more likely caused by one parent rather than the other parent. In relocation cases, in particular, this author has seen numerous instances in which evaluators who judge the conflict to be equally driven by both parents avoid recognizing the unique contributions of each parent and how it may be differentially harmful to the child. When that occurs, it is easy for an evaluator to be swayed by his/her pro-move or against-the-move bias rather than by the complete data, including data relevant to each parent's contribution to the conflict.

"Atilla the Hun Doesn't Marry Mother Theresa" Bias

Another potential bias that is not described elsewhere is what this author calls "Atilla the Hun doesn't marry Mother Theresa" bias (Rotman, 2000). Many experienced evaluators and judges have long recognized that in most families, parents are often relatively equal in parenting ability. Like the "truth lies somewhere in the middle" bias, this bias presupposes that a healthy parent is not likely to marry a less functional parent. While that frequently may be the case, it is not necessarily the case. When looking at a family individually, there are many instances in which one parent or the other is clearly psychologically healthier than the other, has a healthier attachment with the child, and/or has a parenting style that is more consistent with a particular child's temperament and needs. While all custody evaluations and decisions demand clarity on the strengths and weaknesses of all parents, the risk of assuming that parents are equal when they are not is particularly troublesome in relocation cases. This might lead to an assumption that shared custody and not moving is in a child's best interests when the data would support that the child is more attached to the moving parent or that residing with one parent is healthier for the child even in a different location away from the other parent.

"For the Move" or "Against the Move" Bias

All of this leads to this author's concern that many evaluators and judges have a bias that moves are either a good thing or a bad thing for children. Those who tend to be pro-move take the position that a custodial parent who wishes to move should generally be allowed to move as long as the custodial parent has a legitimate reason for moving and is not attempting to interfere with the access rights of the other parent. Evaluators and judges might bring a unitary approach and conclude that this parent can move with the child-once they determine that one or the other parent is "the psychological parent" or primary custodial parent and once they determine that there is a legitimate reason for moving or that there is no evidence of interference with the other parent's access. Jurisdictionally, there are many states in which case law or statutory law supports such a presumption in favor of moving, but there is no evidence in the literature to suggest that psychologists should have such a presumptive belief in relocation cases.

Similarly, there are many custody evaluators and judges who perceive that it is a parent's responsibility to stay near the other parent in order to preserve the child's access to the other parent and the involvement of both parents in her life. This author believes that, while there is research data to support the belief that children benefit with both parents' active involvement in their lives (Kelly and Emery, 2003), extrapolating that data to support a presumption against moves confounds the issue. Clearly, there are many circumstances in which a move is both legitimate and justified, whether for academic, economic, or other personal/family reasons. In those cases, a parent is going to move, with or without the child. It is incumbent on evaluators and judges not to confuse the preference and value for shared co-parenting that exists in some of the research and some statutory laws with a presumption that moves will harm children. Rather than having a presumption against the move, it is this author's view that evaluators and judges must consider and weigh the relative risks and benefits of having the child move with one parent vs. having the child not move and remain primarily with the other parent. Those observers who encourage "conditional change of custody orders" to try and prevent some parents from moving (e.g., Braver et. al., 2003 and Fabricious and Braver, this volume) run the risk of using an "against the move" bias as a way to keep both parents in the same geographic location.

REDUCING THE RISK OF BIAS

One of the ways to reduce the risk that bias might affect a person's conclusions is to clearly recognize that biases exist and that we are all at risk of being affected by our biases. Once we consider this fact, evaluators and judges can examine their conclusions and decisions and look for trends or evidence of such bias. This author has talked with evaluators who have stated that they have rarely recommended in favor of a move. Similarly, this author has talked with judges who have stated that they rarely make an order in favor of a move and other judges who rarely make an order denying a move. If these judges and evaluators do not examine the reasons for this propensity they can never determine if they are based on an "against the move" or "for the move" bias or if they are related to the facts of a specific case. Whenever a person concludes that s/he is acting largely in a particular way, s/he must consider that this is bias driven. If bias is found in one's decisions, the evaluator or judge should examine both the sources of that bias and look for ways to reduce it.

One way to reduce the risk of such bias is to participate in peer consultation. Discuss your challenging cases (and most relocations are challenging) with several peers, especially those who you know to be equally or more experienced in these matters. This author suggests that evaluators and judges use that consultation to challenge your thinking, so it is helpful to choose colleagues who might not always see things the same way as you. Encourage your colleague to play devil's advocate with you to force you to make a less biased analysis.

Along the same lines, play devil's advocate with yourself. Challenge your reasoning. Ask yourself if you've considered all of your data or if you've showed evidence of confirmatory, recency, primacy, or anchoring bias. Then, show such thinking in your report or your order. If you've used multiple methods to gather data or evidence (which is expected of judges and evaluators) and maintained multiple hypotheses at each stage of the case, and if you've considered and integrated all data before reaching conclusions, you'll be at less risk of having a bias affect the outcome of a particular case.

Another excellent way to reduce the risk of bias is to take, and teach, continuing education courses in all areas of assessment and family law.

Evaluators and family law judges need to stay up to date on all of the relevant research in the areas of family law, including relocation, domestic violence, issues of abuse, child development and attachment theory, alienation, the effects of divorce and high conflict on children, and ways to ameliorate the negative effects of divorce. In so doing, they can reduce the likelihood that biases like the ones mentioned above will contribute to their conclusions.

A SUGGESTED PROTOCOL FOR RELOCATION CASES

For purposes of relocation, it is impossible to meet all relevant goals to helping children and their families. It is often difficult to mediate relocation issues, though some families can use mediation successfully in a relocation dispute. Many parents who successfully co parent are unable to remain free of conflict when a parent announces plans to relocate. It is impossible for two parents to continue sharing day-to-day parenting when one of them lives a considerable distance from his/her child. This requires judges and evaluators to develop a different analysis when working with a family where relocation is the issue. All too often, no one wins when either parent wishes to relocate, and the parenting options are more limited when parents are geographically far apart. To reduce the risk of letting bias interfere, it is critical to approach a relocation case differently than all others. The rest of this paper will focus on a suggested way to address the issues, either in your evaluation or in your order.

Tippins and Wittmann (2005) suggested that custody evaluators avoid making recommendations on the ultimate issue. While this author does not agree with their position in general (Stahl, 2005), I agree that one way to avoid bias in many relocation cases is to follow their suggestion. Rather than making custodial recommendations, Tippins and Wittman suggest that evaluators should provide relevant family data and an analysis of that data to help the court understand important family dynamics in relation to the psycho-legal question. Both the psychological literature (Austin, W., 2001 and 2006; Elrod, L., 2006; Kelly and Lamb, 2003; and Stahl, 1999) and statutory or case law in many states describe many factors that are relevant in relocation cases. One example of a comprehensive list of such factors is found in the California Supreme Court decision in the marriage of LaMusga (California Supreme Court, 2003). These factors include:

1. The children's interest in stability and continuity of the custodial arrangement.
2. The distance of the move.
3. The age of the children.
4. The children's relationships with both parents.
5. The relationship between the parents, including but not limited to:
   a. Their ability to communicate and cooperate effectively.
   b. Their willingness to put the interests of the children above their individual interests.
6. The wishes of the children if they are mature enough for such an inquiry to be appropriate.
7. The reasons for the proposed move.
8. The extent to which the parents are currently sharing custody.

It is this author's opinion that a comprehensive custody evaluation will list relevant factors that can be found in the literature or in your respective state law and provide an analysis of your understanding of each of these factors. After completing this part of the analysis, it is important to consider an analysis of the advantages and disadvantages of primary mother-custody in one location, primary father-custody in another locations, and shared-custody for the family. As described by Austin (2000 and 2006), this risk-benefit analysis needs to consider all of the relevant factors and not confound the desire for both parents to be actively involved in the child's life with the tough decision needed in a relocation case. Rarely is a relocation case simple enough that all of the benefits fall with one parent and all of the risks fall with the other parent. If that situation exists, the decision will be an easy one and I believe the evaluator in such circumstances can make a recommendation. However, in the vast majority of cases, there will be benefits to be derived from moving with one parent and benefits to be derived from remaining in the current location with the other parent. In an evaluation report, all of these benefits (and any risks) should be described so that the reader can fully understand the comprehensive analysis and the interaction of family data with the legal issues and be confident in a job well done. Similarly, if a judge places such an analysis in his/her statement of decision, keeping focused on the interaction of the family data and the legal mandate, an appellate court will have confidence in a job well done. Of course, there is always a risk that the evaluator will skew which data gets presented because of one's bias, so it is important to include data that supports one's conclusions as well as data that does not support one's conclusions.

As Stahl (1999) previously described, it is best if an evaluator outlines the specific questions that need to be understood in a particular relocation case. With the recent listing of various relevant factors (see e.g., Austin, 2000; Kelly and Lamb, 2003; Marriage of LaMusga, 2004), this author suggests providing a relevant listing of those factors and the responses to those factors. Considering all of the factors addressed in these articles and case law, a variety of factors seems relevant for all relocation cases. An example of the relevant questions and factors follows (for a 10 year old boy):

1. A move typically leads to greater instability and change. How can we expect Steve to deal with these changes in his life?
2. Is the move representative of stability or a pattern of instability on the part of the moving parent?
3. Are there concerns about the mental health of the moving parent and whether or not the moving parent will facilitate a positive relationship between Steve and the other parent over time?
4. Are there concerns about the mental health of the non-moving parent that might mitigate against a change of custody if one would otherwise be warranted?
5. Does Steve have any special needs, siblings, activities or friends that will be affected by the move?
6. What has been the actual custodial arrangements, how have they been working, and what are the problems?
7. Is there some type of detriment to Steve in moving?
8. Does Steve have an interest in stability and continuity of the custodial arrangement?
9. How does the distance of the move affect the recommendation?
10. How does Steve's age affect the recommendation?
11. Describe Steve's relationships with both parents.
12. What is the relationship between the parents, including but not limited to their ability to communicate and cooperate effectively?
13. How willing are they to put Steve's interests above their individual interests?
14. What are Steve's wishes and is he mature enough for such an inquiry to be appropriate?
15. What are the reasons for the proposed move?
16. To what extent are the parents currently sharing custody?

For a child custody evaluation, addressing the specific responses to these questions and overall family data can help lead to an unbiased conclusion as long as all relevant data is presented. At times, the psychological data line up in a way that suggests moving, or not moving, is clearly in the child's best interests. In those circumstances, a specific recommendation is warranted. However, in most circumstances, the evaluator may not have sufficient data to make a specific recommendation about the move and instead should be careful to outline the relative risks and benefits of living with mother in one location vs. living with father in another location. Additionally, in many jurisdictions, it is inappropriate to make a specific recommendation to the court since the relocation is a specific legal issue that is within the purview of the judge.

Under those circumstances, I would encourage custody evaluators to provide 3 sets of recommendations, one if the judge allows the moving parent to take the child with him/her, one if the judge does not allow the moving parent to take the child but the parent moves anyway, and one if the moving parent abandons his/her request to move or both parents end up moving so that both parents are in the same geographic area. By doing so, the evaluator reduces even further the risk that his/her biases might contribute to the recommendations being made while providing the court with the necessary information from which to make a decision.

CONCLUSIONS

In this author's opinion, bias is a phenomenon that cannot be removed; it can only be managed and controlled for. The steps to managing bias are found in identifying it, acknowledging it, self-checking for the impact of bias in our work, and having an approach that reduces the risk of bias interfering with sound conclusions. Relocation cases, by their very nature, are difficult for all practitioners. These cases are often complex and have no "best" answer. By recognizing the risk of bias, by utilizing various methods for gathering data, and ultimately by addressing the factors relevant to relocation cases before reaching our conclusions, custody evaluators and judges will reduce the risk of being influenced by one's bias. Additional research would help us in our understanding of how relocation affects children and families, and hopefully reduce bias as well. Ultimately, we must be very careful in all relocation cases and check against bias, otherwise decision-making will be short-changed and over-simplified.

REFERENCES

American Bar Association (2004). Model Code of Judicial Conduct. Available online at *www.abanet.org/cpr/mcjc/canon_3.html* (Last accessed on May 30, 2005).

American Psychological Association (1994). Guidelines for Child Custody Evaluations in Divorce Proceedings. *American Psychologist.* 49, 7, 677-680.

American Psychological Association (2002). Ethical Principles of Psychologists and Codes of Conduct. *American Psychologist.* 57, 12, 1060-1073 and available online at *www.apa.org/ethics/code2002.html* (Last accessed on May 30, 2005).

Association of Family & Conciliation Courts (1994). Model Standards of Practice forChild Custody Evaluations. *Family Court Review.* 32, 4, 504-513 and available online at *www.afccnet.org/resources/resources_model_child.asp* (Last accessed on May 30, 2005). Note that the AFCC Model Standards of Practice for Child Custody Evaluations were revised effective at the AFCC Board meeting on May 31, 2006 but were not published at the time this article went to press. The new Model Standards, which similarly address the issue of bias, can be accessed at the AFCC web site, www.afccnet.org.

Association of Family and Conciliation Courts (2000). Model Standards of Practice for Family and Divorce Mediation. *Family Court Review.* 39, 1, 121-134 and available online at *www.afccnet.org/resources/resources_model_mediation.asp* (Last accessed on May 30, 2005).

Austin, W. (2000). A Forensic Psychology Model of Risk Assessment for Child Relocation Law. *Family & Conciliation Courts Review.* 38 (2), 192-207.

Austin, W. (2006). Exploring Three Functions in Child Custody Evaluation for the Relocation Case: Prediction, Investigation, and Making Recommendations for a Long Distance Parenting Plan. *Journal of Child Custody.* (This volume).

Bathurst, K., Gottfried, A., Gottfried, A. (1997). Normative Data for the MMPI-2 in Child Custody Litigation. *Psychological Assessment.* 9 (3), 205-211.

Braver, S., Elman, I., and Fabricious, W. (2003). Relocation of children after divorce and children's best interests: New evidence and legal considerations. *Journal of Family Psychology,* 2003, 17, 2, 206-219.

California Rules of Court, Rule 5.220. Court-Ordered Child Custody Evaluations. Available online at *http://www.courtinfo.ca.gov/rules/titlefive* (Last accessed on May 30, 2005).

California Supreme Court (2004). *In re Marriage of LaMusga.* 32 Cal.4th 1072.

Cambridge Universities Press (2004). Cambridge Dictionaries Online. Available online at *www.dictionary.cambridge.org/* (Last accessed on May 30, 2005).

Elrod, L. (2006). "Moving On"–Searching for Standards for Relocation Cases. *Journal of Child Custody.* (This issue).

Gigerenzer, G., Todd, P., and ABC Research Group (1999). *Simple Heuristics That Make Us Smart.* New York: Oxford University Press.

Gindes, M. (1998). The psychological effects of relocation for children of divorce. *Journal of the American Academy of Matrimonial Lawyers,* 15 (1), 119-148.

Goldstein, J., Freud, A., and Solnit, A. (1984). *Beyond the Best Interests of the Child.* New York: Free Press.

Gould, J. (1998). *Conducting Scientifically Crafted Child Custody Evaluations*. Thousand Oaks, CA: Sage Publications.

Gutheil, T., and Simon, R. (2004). Avoiding Bias in Expert Testimony. *Psychiatric Annals*. 34, 4, 260-270.

Kelly, J., and Emery, R. (2003). Children's Adjustment Following Divorce: Risk and Resilience Perspectives. *Family Relations: Interdisciplinary Journal of Applied Family Studies*, 52, 4, 352-362.

Kelly, J., and Lamb, M. (2003). Developmental Issues in Relocation Cases Involving Young Children: When, Whether, and How?, *Journal of Family Psychology*, 17, 2, 193-205.

Lamb., M., Sternberg, K., and Thompson, R. (1997). The Effects of Divorce and Custody Arrangements on Children's Behavior, Development, and Adjustment. *Family & Conciliation Courts Review*. 35 (4), 393-404.

Ramsey, S. (2006). Personal Communication.

Rotman, A. (2000). Personal Communication.

Shear, L., (1996). Life stories, doctrines, and decision making: Three high courts decide the move-away dilemma. *Family and Conciliation Courts Review*. 34, 439-458.

Shear, L. (Lead Author) (2003). Amicus Brief Submitted to the California Supreme Court in Re: Marriage of LaMusga.

Stahl, P. (1999). *Complex Issues in Child Custody Evaluations*. Thousand Oaks, CA: Sage Publications.

Stahl, P. (2005). The Benefits and Risks of Child Custody Evaluators Making Recommendations to the Court: A Response to Tippins and Wittmann. *Family Court Review*. 43, 2, 260-265.

Tippins, T., and Wittman, J. (2005). Empirical and Ethical Problems with Custody Recommendations: A call for Clinical Humility and Judicial Vigilance. *Family Court Review*. 43, 2, 193-222.

Wallerstein, J. (Lead Author) (2003). Amicus Brief Submitted to the California Supreme Court in Re: Marriage of LaMusga.

Warshak, R. (Lead Author) (2003). Amicus Brief Submitted to the California Supreme Court in Re: Marriage of LaMusga.

doi:10.1300/J190v03n03_05

Relocation Cases:
Analyzing Relevant Evidence

Martha Ann Lott

SUMMARY. This article offers a format for analysis of evidence in re-location cases where both parents are fit to have primary custody of the child. The suggested analysis of evidence in family relocation cases after dissolution of marriage results in a positive and workable resolution of the issues presented to the court. The end point is a workable plan for parenting in the best interest of the child. The format balances the interests of both parents and the child in compliance with state, federal and international law. doi:10.1300/J190v03n03_06 *[Article copies available for a fee from The Haworth Document Delivery Service: 1-800-HAWORTH. E-mail address: <docdelivery@haworthpress.com> Website: <http://www.HaworthPress. com> © 2006 by The Haworth Press, Inc. All rights reserved.]*

Martha Ann Lott became a Judge in January 1991 and has presided over all areas of state trial court jurisdiction at the county court and circuit levels. She has had the opportunity to teach at the County Judges Conference and at the Circuit Judges Conference, and has been on the Faculty of the University of Florida: Levin College of Law, the New Judges College of Florida, the Advanced Judicial College of Florida, and the National Judicial College in Reno, Nevada. Many have seen the significant changes in both the law and the application of the law in the area of family litigation during those years. The author is very pleased to join the discussion of how they can best create the outcomes they intend through this article on Relocation Cases.

Address correspondence to: Judge Lott, The Alachua County Courthouse, Criminal Justice Center, 220 South Main Street, Gainesville, FL 32601 (E-mail: mal@ circuit8.org; identifying the article in the subject line, please).

[Haworth co-indexing entry note]: "Relocation Cases: Analyzing Relevant Evidence." Lott, Martha Ann. Co-published simultaneously in *Journal of Child Custody* (The Haworth Press, Inc.) Vol. 3, No. 3/4, 2006, pp. 125-137; and: *Relocation Issues in Child Custody Cases* (ed: Philip M. Stahl, and Leslie M. Drozd) The Haworth Press, Inc., 2006, pp. 125-137. Single or multiple copies of this article are available for a fee from The Haworth Document Delivery Service [1-800-HAWORTH, 9:00 a.m. - 5:00 p.m. (EST). E-mail address: docdelivery@haworthpress.com].

Available online at http://jcc.haworthpress.com
doi:10.1300/J190v03n03_06

KEYWORDS. Family law, interstate, primary residence, change in custody, best interest of the child, evidence analysis, relocation

In our 21st century mobile society, divorce and relocation are such common events that the courts in every state are frequently challenged with issues in this arena. The dissolution of marriage laws were written a century or more ago and in some states have not been modified in decades except for adoption of the Uniform Child Custody Jurisdiction Enforcement Act (or Uniform Child Custody Enforcement Act) which is largely jurisdictional. During the past two to three decades, mobility has increased exponentially, the rate of divorce has skyrocketed, the roles of men and women in the work force and in the home have changed dramatically, and the rights of children, separate from the rights of the parents, have come to public consciousness. All of these factors increase the number of variables in each dissolution of marriage relocation action, making the job of the judge more complex and more time consuming. How can the evidence be analyzed so that the law applied to the facts results in a positive and workable resolution for a particular family?

Relocation can occur before or after judicial review. A parent can apply to the court for authorization to move or a parent may move with the child without a court order. Then, application might be made to the court to sanction the move or to remedy the impact of the move on the other parent. The first issue for the courts, in any case, is jurisdiction. The determination of jurisdiction in relocation cases is controlled by International, Federal and Uniform State Law, the Hague Convention, the Parental Kidnapping Law, and the UCCJEA (or UCCJA).

Although the law as to jurisdiction is uniform, the legislatures across the country vary in their philosophy regarding parent's and children's rights. The law that judges must apply varies from state to state. On the other hand, the issues raised by families faced with dissolution, custody and relocation do not vary state to state.

The issues judges must decide are not dependant upon location or law. They spring out of human relationships, child development, the complexities of our society as a whole and our time in history. Relocation by a custodial parent may be initiated due to a new job, a desire to move closer to extended family, a new marriage or relationship. Sometimes, it is initiated as a means of interfering with access to the children by the non-custodial parent, to start fresh after a divorce or to pursue something intangible.

The court system is faced with deciding when a move should be supported by the courts and how a move will affect the other members of the family. A move by the custodial parent almost always necessitates a modification of the of the Final Judgement of Dissolution and almost always involves a change to the parenting plan. The smallest changes have to do with the visitation schedule; the largest with primary residence of the child. The orders entered by the judge provide a framework for parenting. A good order in this context is one that increases the likelihood of effective parenting by two fit parents.

While judges are in large part controlled by the law, in the overall picture judges formulate analysis of the facts in the application of that law. In this way, judges can determine how complex and competing factors are considered, and can analyze these factors in a logical manner toward a practical and workable result.

GOVERNING LAW–AS TO JURISDICTION

If relocation has occurred before judicial review, jurisdiction must be resolved first and is controlled by law. In most cases, jurisdiction stays with the divorce court until and unless it is abandoned so that legal action taken before a move or promptly after a move will remain with the court that entered the Final Judgment of Dissolution. Although this article is not about jurisdiction, interstate relocation is so common that reference to the controlling law on jurisdiction is essential to this article. The law is not analyzed in detail, but the essential citations are included so that the issue of jurisdiction can be analyzed in any case that results in reference to this article. Relocation cases are governed by the UCCJEA or UCCJA, the Federal Parental Kidnapping Act, USC Title 28 Part V. 1738A, and the Hague Convention. These laws cover all relocations made in good faith and all relocations where misconduct occurs.

Criminal kidnapping laws may come into play in some factual scenarios but those situations are far removed from the context of this article and the law pertaining to court sanctioned relocation. Statutory reference to or discussion of criminal conduct is not contemplated. Instead, this article is restricted to arguable claims of custody by "fit" parents.

The Federal Parental Kidnapping Act is jurisdictional in nature and directs that states not exercise jurisdiction where another state has lawfully accepted jurisdiction except in emergencies. It also prohibits a state from modifying visitation unless the original state has lost or declined jurisdiction. When custody questions arise involving jurisdictional issues between states, a review of this section of the US Code is advisable.

Review of the Hague Convention of 1980 is essential when handling international custody cases. The Hague Convention does not address applications for, or modifications of, custody. It only controls the international procedure for return of custody and the defenses against return.

Within the United States, disputes are limited by the Parental Kidnapping Act. Jurisdiction is determined by the UCCJA or UCCJEA and then the appropriate state law is applied to the facts.

Much of the law we apply in relocation cases is applicable across all fifty states due to the adoption of the UCCJEA or UCCJA. The UCCJEA is the revised version of the 1968 UCCJA and was created by the Uniform Law Commissioners in 1997. Since that time, the revamped UCCJA known as the UCCJEA has been adopted by forty-two states, the District of Columbia and the Virgin Islands. It will be introduced in three more states in 2006. The UCCJA, which preceded the UCCJEA, was adopted by all fifty states. Both the UCCJA and the UCCJEA were created in an attempt to standardize the rules and proceedings regarding child custody determinations in order to avoid entry of conflicting orders by more than one state. The act limits child custody jurisdiction to one state, and provides enforcement provisions for child custody orders. To streamline interstate child custody disputes and prevent multi-state jurisdiction enforcement issues, the act clarifies two basic areas of jurisdictional disputes. First, it prioritizes which state should have jurisdiction over the dispute. Second, it makes enforcement of child custody orders less complex, thereby accelerating their execution. This is important because, historically, the lack of uniformity between the states delayed the execution of child custody orders. In many cases, the lack of expediency had an adverse impact on the child and/or on the non-custodial parent, because their right to access and/or visitation was stymied by the delay.

APPLYING STATE LAW

In cases of judicial review prior to or after relocation, when jurisdiction has been determined by the UCCJEA or UCCJA, the law of the home state is applied. Judges are often faced with evidence in a trial which appears to have been dumped without organization into the record. A format for analysis of the evidence in consideration of the law makes application of the law a more simple and logical process. Analysis involves individual study of components and can include a sequence for consideration, a priority of consideration, and a plan for consideration. Analysis is a tool judges can use when considering evidence and the applicable law. An analytical approach helps create order or simplify the examination of evidence.

In relocation cases, the evidence presented is from the perspective of what the parents want or need. It is not usually framed from the perspective of the "best interest" of the child. Frequently, the facts needed to find a workable resolution that is positive for the child are left out as the parents present their competing interests. In dissolution, property is divided; children are provided for. It is often up to the judge to insure that the children are not divided like the assets and debts of the marriage. In relocation cases, it is up to the judge to find a workable plan that will allow both parents to continue to be involved with the child whenever possible. Therefore, the analysis ends, not with where the child will primarily reside, but with making that residence work for the family through the parenting plan and other equitable considerations.

In a dissolution of marriage action involving an issue of relocation, or in any action involving relocation of the child, the competing needs and positions of the parents dictate what evidence (and law) is offered to the judge for consideration by the parents and by the lawyers. Children rarely have lawyers. Children generally have no income and children cannot vote. Children are simply small people with no power. Their individual interests have only been sporadically addressed by the court system. Judges can focus attention on the child's issues by choosing to utilize a format for analysis that supports a workable resolution to the problem presented without just issuing an order that "gives" the child to one parent or the other.

Clarifying the most significant facts in the following order in applying the law simplifies the process: (1) determine the developmental stage of each child; (2) determine what the primary needs of each child are; (3) determine what each parent has to offer in order to provide for each child; (4) determine the location where the needs of each child will be best met; (5) determine what the most workable parenting plan will look like; and finally, (6) determine what the equitable considerations are between the parents. In each section discussed below, simplistic examples are used so that the point can be demonstrated without inviting the argument or discussion that would obviously and appropriately apply in complex situations.

DEVELOPMENTAL STAGE

The child must live somewhere. The best placement depends in large part on who this child is as an individual. The developmental stage is the first step in understanding the child as an individual. While the judge considers every other fact, it is also very important to be clear on who this child is. The developmental stage of a child creates totally different opportunities and obstacles that change as the child grows. It is the changing nature of the developmental stage that makes it *the* essential initial determination for the court. What may be completely appropriate for a 5-year-old just starting school may be devastating to a 15-year-old in a special academic program not commonly available. Infants need constant care that requires the primary caretaker to provide stability, consistent contact, and quality care for the child whether the parent is working or not. This includes the ability to make arrangements for child care in the event of illness. Teenagers need preparation for adulthood. This involves supervision, direction, and an environment that allows them to learn safely about the world. Therefore, in order to look at the facts favoring or disfavoring relocation, the court must know the developmental stage of the child so that the court can consider the relevant factors of relocation in relation to the specific needs of the child. Because developmental changes can often be substantial, this consideration gives the court latitude to create a positive outcome. The judge necessarily uses discretion by examining these factors. The judge also accesses the discretionary powers of the court in formulating a plan and an order that consider the individual needs of a specific child. By first looking at the developmental stage of the child, the judge can analyze the evidence in each of the other steps in a logical and methodical manner.

NEEDS

Defining the individual characteristics of the child is the second step in understanding who this child is. The needs of the child are very individualistic and often become more specific and clear as the child ages through each developmental stage. A child may be academically advanced, athletic, musically talented, developmentally delayed, or socially awkward. Moreover, the combination of opportunities and obstacles is unique to each child. When a legal choice must be made between parents seeking primary residential status or custody in two different locations, a clear understanding of the needs of the individual child can make the judge's decision much easier and is likely to result in a much more workable plan for the child. The testimony of individuals who have worked with the child, e.g., teachers, as well as school reports and evaluations will help illuminate the needs of the individual child. Introduction of evidence regarding the specific needs and characteristics of a particular child can either be required by the court through pretrial conferences and orders, or simply encouraged using those same mechanisms.

OFFER

The third step in analyzing the evidence of the case is matching a potential placement to a specific child. This requires understanding the details of each potential placement. After determining the developmental stage of the child and the needs of the individual child, the judge can look at what each parent has to offer individually. This article contemplates that both parents are "fit." However, "fitness" to parent does not address who is the best parent for a particular child in a case involving relocation. The judge must decide which parent is a better match for the needs of this child, at this stage of development, based upon the evidence presented. The personality and temperament of each parent and of the child must come into consideration. To a parent and child who share a love of the outdoors, rural Alaska might be a life enhancing adventure with access to natural wilderness unsurpassed in any other state. A Broadway-bound thespian may be better off not going with the adventuresome parent, but instead staying in Manhattan, even if that means changing the primary residential custodian. Having determined the developmental stage of a child and the individual child's needs, what the relocation would offer the child, versus what a change in custody would offer the child, is the next step in a logical sequence for the judge's consideration. Starting from the point of view of the child's best interest allows the judge to examine what each parent offers the child with a fresh eye. Relocation will mean change in more than one area. The facts may illuminate that relocation will change the child's access to the primary parent, perhaps due to new job responsibilities or other circumstances. If so, what is being offered in the home of the relocating parent may result in much less contact and supervision than what is being offered by the non-relocating parent. In such a scenario, a change in custody or the primary residential designation may be in the child's best interest. It is also important to consider what each parent has to offer in terms of facilitating and supporting the relationship and communication between the child and the other parent. The factual analysis includes looking at what each potential home would look like after the move before deciding on the best placement.

LOCATION

This is the fourth step and the time to ultimately decide where the child will reside. Here, the judge must determine whether relocation of the child is the best decision considering the specific developmental stage of the child, the child's individual needs, and what each parent has to offer in each location. All of these facts must be considered in light of the applicable state law and any presumptions contained therein as to the rights of both parents and the best interest of the child. The judge's process of analyzing the facts and the applicable law should now result in placement of the child that is workable as a solution for the family. If there is more than one child, will the siblings be separated? The court can best address each child's needs by considering the relationship between each parent and each child and the relationship between the siblings. Whether or not siblings should be separated is an important consideration. Because relocation introduces new variables to consideration of custody or primary physical residence and visitation, the conclusion as to whether the siblings should be separated may be different from the conclusion at the point of dissolution. The developmental stage of each child may have changed and the individual needs of each child may have changed. What each parent has to offer in the two locations must be considered in relation to each individual child. For example, if a proposed relocation occurs during a teenager's final year in high school, many families and many courts would favorably consider that teenager's desire to stay in the same school in lieu of relocation if possible. Focusing on the evidence regarding the best interest of the child, rather than the desires of the parent, is what will insure a workable result.

PARENTING PLAN

Development of the parenting plan is the fifth step in the factual analysis. Once the decision on the child's primary residential location has been reached, the parenting plan is a tool that the family will use to make the decision work. A parenting plan is much more than a communication, visitation, and travel schedule, although these are important ingredients. With every child, there are issues of bedtime or curfew, sports or activities, chores or allowance, suitable movies or TV. The plan must address which issues of child rearing and decision making are to be shared, if any. If there is no parenting plan or agreement, there is no procedure for resolving new issues that arise. Without intervention through a court order, divorced parents often implement two different and inconsistent plans. All aspects of interaction relating to the child that can be structured to facilitate child rearing form the parenting plan.

How the parents' interaction with each other is structured is dependent upon many factors. Often, judges back away from involvement in these details because of the complexity of the issues and the difficulty involved in crafting a solution. However, not all cases require an in-depth parenting plan created by the court. In the relatively small number of cases where a specific parenting plan with many specific parameters is warranted, taking the time and expending the energy to work through the details will save the court and the family a substantial amount of court intervention later on. The court can make a huge contribution toward a viable solution by accepting an appropriate plan that the parties have worked out, or ordering something different when necessary.

Most families are amenable to judicial direction. However, court orders that amount to "*you two need to get along*" are not enforceable. On the other hand, many families will follow a system for communication or interaction if one is laid down by the court. Parents who will not initiate communication with the other parent on their own will do so if ordered and will do so on the schedule that is ordered. Parents who will not share the responsibility for transportation for visitation on their own will do so if ordered. Often, a professional can suggest to the court what will be an effective plan for a particular family. Recommendations by a competent professional, when made based on the dynamics of the individuals rather than on an ideal family, should be considered carefully by the court and should be included in the order when the judge is convinced that the recommendation is workable.

The judge must also consider the worst-case scenario of a proposed parenting plan. If all goes wrong, there must be a safety net for the parents and for the child. Safety is created when problems are anticipated and the resolution of the problem is contained within the parenting plan. Lawyers and judges who are adept at drafting contracts will have no difficulty with this concept. Lawyers and judges who are experienced in family law and contracts can also master its application. The questions that reveal a comprehensive safety plan include questions about what the aggrieved party can or should do in the event the other party does not comply with the parenting plan. The safety plan portion should encompass provisions for "makeup" visitation if visitation is blocked, or a provision awarding costs of transportation against the parent who does not comply with the order. Announcing consequences for non-compliance and specifying what the consequences will be encourages the parties to follow the order and to react in a less volatile manner if non-compliance does occur, because they will have more confidence that any failure to comply will result in adverse consequences to the parent who fails to comply.

EQUITABLE CONSIDERATIONS

The equitable considerations are the sixth and final step in the analysis. This step allows the court the opportunity to balance things out as best they can be balanced. When one parent is the beneficiary of the needs of the child and is named as the primary residential parent, how can other factors be distributed to make the outcome between the parents as equitable as possible? Equity has to do with fairness, not necessarily equality, and may be expressed in a variety of ways. In *Hass v. Hass*, 74 Ark. App. 49, 44 S.W.3d 773 (2001), the custodial parent moved 300 miles away for the purpose of career advancement. The non-custodial parent had fewer resources to effectuate continued visitation, but the custodial parent was willing to facilitate the child's visitation, even to the extent of employing charter air service as transportation for the child. In *Trent v. Trent*, 111 Nev 309, 890 P2d 1309 (1995), the trial court used its discretion to modify the order to minimize the child's loss of contact and visitation with the non-custodial parent by increasing visitation during vacations from school and allocating transportation expenses to the custodial parent. Once the court has determined that it is in the child's best interest to relocate, the best interest of the child and the non-custodial parent's right to access can all be protected by a ruling utilizing the visitation portion of the order.

In *Cooper v. Cooper*, 99 N.J. 42, 491 A.2d 606 (1984), the court found, ". . . [the] custodial parent's freedom to move is qualified by the special obligation of custody, by the state's interest in protecting the best interests of the child and by competing interest in the non-custodial parent." The law may well affect the weight to be given each element but the weight given by statute does not dictate to the court the format for analyzing the evidence. Even within the differing statutes, the format for analysis is helpful. Because the weight to be given each element is discretionary, without such a format for analysis, judges are often unclear as to how to organize the evidence so that the law can be applied effectively.

For instance, Illinois law clearly states that the best interest of the child is the deciding factor. In California, a custodial parent's right to remove a child is presumed, absent evidence that would stop a move. In New York, the presumption is almost the opposite. In *Tropea v. Tropea*, 87 N.Y. 2d 727, 642 N.Y.S. 2d 575, 665 N.E. 2d 145 (1996), the Court of Appeals replaced the exceptional circumstances standard and focused on the best interest of the child. The court then considered many factors to determine whether to permit the move. Additionally, the court stated that each case was to be determined on its own merits and that the goal was to "minimize the parents discomfort and maximize the child's prospect of a stable, comfortable and happy life." *Id.*

State law sets parameters on what factors the courts are to consider and how they are to weigh those factors. Of course, the laws and the considerations vary from state to state. One difference is the preference for one of the three classes involved. The Court must consider: (1) the custodial parent who has the most responsibility and their need for relocation; (2) the non-custodial parent and their right to access to the child free from interference; and (3) the child and his or her right to be raised by a fit parent in a suitable environment. There are no laws that state that a child should be allowed to mature to his or her maximum potential, but we do have laws directing that the judge rule in the child's best interest.

Even with the differing statutes, the analysis is helpful. Because the weight to be given to each element is discretionary, judges are often unclear as to what they should do. The analysis makes that assignment of weight more logical and less arbitrary and assists in a thoughtful and workable resolution.

CONCLUSION

The court system faces numerous constraints procedurally, legally, and ethically. Sometimes the focus is too much on what cannot be done and consequently we blind ourselves to the power that exists in the court system which can lead to a positive resolution in the lives of those involved.

In the end, judges make decisions that impact lives and because of that, have tremendous power. Judges can require that certain concerns and issues be addressed through evidence and can create the opportunity for professionals and parents to focus on the best interest of the child. By inquiring about the specific facts that impact an individual child's life using case management and pretrial orders, through orders appointing experts, and through in court inquiry, judges can direct the preparation for trial as well as the trial itself toward a positive and workable resolution.

To reach a workable resolution in relocation cases, judges look at complex evidence in relation to competing interests. In considering relocation cases presented to the court, analyzing the evidence in steps leads to a workable resolution. The steps are to: (1) determine the developmental stage of each child; (2) determine what the primary needs of each child are; (3) determine what each parent has to offer to provide for the child; (4) determine the location where the needs of each child will be best met; (5) determine what the parenting plan will look like optimally and what is the worst case scenario that might develop with that plan; and finally, (6) determine what the equitable considerations are between the parents. In our modern society we move around. We change our relationships. We are free to make these changes but we must take responsibility for our children. The orientation of the court in considering relocation can make the best interest of the child the priority, not to the exclusion of the parent's right to relocate, but in balance to their claim for custody, primary physical residence, and visitation. This allows for the personal freedom of the adults but moderates it so that their freedom is not exercised at the expense of the child. Society can mandate that parents take responsibility to provide for their children and the courts can enforce the law in a manner that ensures it. The balance of all three interests in a workable plan is the challenge for the courts in our millennium society.

REFERENCES

Cooper v. Cooper, 99 N.J. 42, 491 A.2d 606 (1984).

Hass v. Hass, 74 Ark. App. 49, 44 S.W.3d 773 (2001).

International Child Abduction Remedies Act, the Hague Convention, 42 U.S.C., Chapter 121, 11601 through 11608 (2005).

Parental Kidnapping Prevention Act, 28 U.S.C. Part V. § 1738A (2005).

Trent v. Trent, 111 Nev. 309, 890 P2d 1309 (1995).

Tropea v. Tropea, 87 N.Y. 2d 727, 642 N.Y.S.2d 575, 665 N.E. 2d 145 (1996).
UCCJA, Unif. Child Custody Juris. Act (1968).
UCCJEA, Unif. Child Custody Juris. Enf. Act (1997).

doi:10.1300/J190v03n03_06

The Problem with Presumptions–
A Review and Commentary

Lyn R. Greenberg

Dianna J. Gould-Saltman

Hon. Robert Schnider

Lyn R. Greenberg, PhD, specializes in work with children and families involved with the courts. She performs child custody evaluations, evaluations of alleged abuse, forensic consultation, expert witness services, parent coordination/special master services, and specialized treatment for court-involved children and families. She has written and presented both locally and nationally on forensic psychology, professional ethics, child custody evaluation, valid interviews of children, and court-related treatment. Dr. Greenberg currently serves as Chair of Continuing Education, and co-chair of the Family Forensic Interest Group for the Division of Family Psychology of the American Psychological Association. She is a Member of the (Southern) Children's Issues Committee of the CA State Bar Association (E-mail: lrgreenberghd@earthlink.net).

Dianna J. Gould-Saltman, Esq., attorney at law, is a principal in the Los Angeles firm of Gould-Saltman Law Offices, LLP, specializing in mediation and litigation of family law issues. A certified family law specialist (The State Bar of California, Board of Legal Specialization) and a fellow of the American Academy of Matrimonial Lawyers, Ms. Gould-Saltman received her B.A. in psychology from the University of California, Irvine and her Juris Doctor from Southwestern University School of Law. She has written about family law, ethics and gender bias issues and has presented across the U.S. and Canada. She currently serves as co-vice Chair of the American Bar Association Family Law Section Ethics Committee. She has been named a "Super Lawyer" in each edition of Los Angeles Magazine's special edition and has been named by them as one of the top 50 women lawyers in Southern California (E-mail: dgsaltman@aol.com).

Judge Robert Schnider received his AB degree from UC, Berkeley in 1967 and his JD degree from Boalt Hall, UC, Berkeley in 1970. He was a partner in the law firm of Schnider & Schnider from 1971 until his election as a Commissioner of the Superior Court in 1981. In 2002 he was appointed a Judge of that court. In practice he was a Certified Family Law Specialist. Since 1981 he has been assigned to the Family Law Department of the Los Angeles Superior Court at the Central Civil (Mosk) Courthouse handling a variety of family law assignments including ex parte/domestic violence, DA enforcement and general trial matters. Currently he serves as presiding judge of the Family Law Department. He has lectured and taught extensively to both lawyers and judicial officers and has received several awards including the Judicial Officer of the Year Award in 1997 from the Family Law section of the State Bar of California and the Outstanding Jurist Award in the year 2000 from the Los Angeles County Bar Association (E-mail: RSchnide@LASuperiorCourt.org).

[Haworth co-indexing entry note]: "The Problem with Presumptions–A Review and Commentary." Greenberg, Lyn R., Dianna J. Gould-Saltman, and Robert Schnider. Co-published simultaneously in *Journal of Child Custody* (The Haworth Press, Inc.) Vol. 3, No. 3/4, 2006, pp. 139-172; and: *Relocation Issues in Child Custody Cases* (ed: Philip M. Stahl, and Leslie M. Drozd) The Haworth Press, Inc., 2006, pp. 139-172. Single or multiple copies of this article are available for a fee from The Haworth Document Delivery Service [1-800-HAWORTH, 9:00 a.m. - 5:00 p.m. (EST). E-mail address: docdelivery@haworthpress.com].

SUMMARY. Decisions in child custody cases involve a myriad of factors, including the application of state statutes, case law and the specific facts of a case. In recent years, presumptions regarding child custody have become an increasingly frequent part of the decision-making process. Upon the finding of a threshold fact, these presumptions, in effect, create "secondary facts" which the judicial officer is required to use, in lieu of actual evidence, once the threshold fact is established. Barriers to overcome the presumption are often high, and judicial officers may vary as to the standards they apply in determining whether the evidence required to overcome the presumption has been met. In this commentary the authors describe various types of presumptions and arguments usually advanced to support them, then provide a critical analysis of the problems that occur when this type of reasoning is applied to decisions in child custody cases. While some examples of presumptions are discussed and examined in light of relevant research, the authors' focus is more conceptual, examining the issue of detailed presumptions as a mechanism for decision-making in child custody cases. We suggest that, while much debate focuses on the wisdom of specific custody presumptions, less attention has been focused on the general appropriateness of presumptions as an approach to decision-making about the lives of children and families. doi:10.1300/J190v03n03_07 *[Article copies available for a fee from The Haworth Document Delivery Service: 1-800-HAWORTH. E-mail address: <docdelivery@haworthpress.com> Website: <http://www.HaworthPress. com> © 2006 by The Haworth Press, Inc. All rights reserved.]*

KEYWORDS. Presumptions, child custody, custody decisions, evidence

Nothing matches the appeal of simple solutions to complex problems. When the answer to the question is, "yes" or "no," it's much easier (and faster) to make a decision. This is the beauty of a presumption. It allows a court, rather than going through the painstaking task of taking testimony or reviewing evidence, to simply ask, "Does X exist in this case? If so, the result is Q. If not, we must delve deeper."

Such formulae are particularly attractive when court resources are overstretched, an overcrowded calendar creates extensive delay, and the family does not have the resources necessary for a thorough child custody evaluation or a full presentation of the evidence. Proponents of such presumptions often argue that these mechanisms reduce demands on the court and the time required to adjudicate issues, and provide common expectations of the likely outcome of a case that will reduce litigation in contested family law cases. (Bartlett, 2002). In an area of law where there has historically been a high degree of turn-over, a directive, more formulaic approach can be attractive both to judicial officers with minimal experience in family law, and to litigants who are fearful of inexperienced judicial officers using their own personal experiences of raising children in the exercise of their discretion in making child custody orders.

In this commentary, we offer a brief description of the types of presumptions and arguments usually advanced to support them, then provide a critical analysis of the problems that occur when this type of reasoning is applied to decisions in child custody cases. While most of the articles in this volume focus specifically on the issue of relocation, we focus more broadly on the issue of detailed presumptions as a mechanism for decision-making in child custody cases. We suggest that, while much debate focuses on the wisdom of specific custody presumptions, less attention has been focused on the general appropriateness of presumptions as an approach to decision-making about the lives of children and families. Moreover, the application of presumption-based decision-making models to relocation cases may involve the less-than-obvious application of other presumptions, including those regarding each parent's prior involvement with the child and presumptions about a child's age-related capacity to express meaningful preferences.

DEFINING TERMS:
STANDARDS, GUIDELINES,
PARAMETERS AND PRESUMPTIONS

Both legislatures and case precedents establish general parameters for decision-making in child custody cases. "Guidelines" and "Rules of Law" describe general polices that courts must consider in making custody determinations. For example, California law expresses the general policy that children should have "frequent and continuing contact" with both parents after a separation or divorce, except where such contact would endanger or would not be in the best interests of the child.[1] Other laws, based on similar policy considerations, establish a presumption of parenthood in a man who has fulfilled the functions of a child's father and "openly holds out the child as his natural child," even if he is not the biological father of the child.[2]

"Standards" and "Statutory Factors" set out more specific issues that courts must consider in making custody determinations for children. Many states have adopted some form of "best interest of the child" standard for decision-making in child custody cases, although the definitions and criteria for determining "best interest" vary among jurisdictions (Bartlett, 2002; Krauss & Sales, 2000). Several states, including California, have set out specific factors to be considered by child custody evaluators and the courts in determining the best parenting plans for children.[3]

Presumptions may be established to augment these standards, further a general expression of public policy, or address a perceived problem in the handling of child custody cases. Presumptions require courts to assume a certain fact if another, prerequisite fact has been established. For example, if a court finds that one parent has committed violence against the other, the court may be required to assume that the aggressor should not have custody of the children. A custody presumption may require a court to weigh one factor more heavily than another. A presumption may impose a greater burden on one parent to produce more evidence than otherwise would be required. It may require one parent to meet a higher standard of proof than otherwise would be required. Depending on the issue involved, such presumptions may or may not be consistent with psychological research findings about children's development and adjustment.

DEVELOPMENT OF THE PROBLEM

Presumptions are not new as an approach to decision-making in family courts, and they have long been reflective of values and prejudices in society. As Bartlett (2002) describes, fathers received automatic preference throughout much of history, while mothers began to receive automatic preference in the 1940s, a pattern that persisted for at least twenty years. Until the landmark 1972 decision, Stanley v. Illinois [405 U.S. 645, 657], unwed fathers in Illinois were presumed to be unfit upon the death of the mother, such that the children were automatically placed in the foster care system. Few current scholars or practitioners would defend any of these presumptions a representing current research or adequate analysis of children's needs.

As we learned more about the complexity of children and families, more states moved toward some form of the "best interests of the child" standard, as noted above. Jurisdictions vary as to the specificity of their standards and the factors used, but many include such elements as the children's safety, some assessment of the child's feelings/wishes and relationship with each parent, and the likelihood that each parent will support the child's relationship with the other parent. This standard maximizes judicial discretion in looking at the individual situation of each child and families.

Some proposals for presumptions have been based on perceived problems in the application of the "best interests" standard. Several authors (e.g., Krauss & Sales, 2000; Bartlett, 2002; Emery, Otto, & O'Donohoe, 2005) cite the ambiguity of the standard, inconsistencies in its application, ambiguity, and the requirement that judges weigh factors that are outside their area of expertise. A number of authors (Krauss & Sales, 2000; Shuman & Sales, 1998, 1999) have also raised concerns about the validity of some evidence presented by the mental health professionals upon whom judicial officers rely to assist with such decisions. These authors have also expressed concern about judicial officers' ability to assess the quality of services provided by mental health professionals. Concern about children's exposure to parental conflict have also led some authors to suggest a return to more formulaic, determinative rules for determining parenting plans after parental separation.

For example, the American Law Institute (ALI) proposed a formula for child custody decisions that would require post-separation parental responsibility to be allocated according to the proportion of time that each parent spent caring for the child when the family was intact [American Law Institute, Principles of the Law of Family Dissolution: Analysis and Recommendations, Chapter 2 (2002)]. The ALI Principles also support a presumptive right of the custodial parent to move. While the ALI principles allow for adjustment based on the "firm and reasonable" preference of a child or a "gross" disparity in the quality of parent-child relationships, they primarily focus on "concrete acts and patterns of parenting, rather than subjective or qualitative judgments about parenting, the strength of emotional relationships, and the like" (Bartlett, 2002). The ALI standards do not envision consideration of a host of other variables, such as child temperament, developmental issues, support of peer activities, changes in parenting time or quality based on the post-separation reorganization of the family, or the various dimensions of stability (E. Mavis Hetherington, 1999; E. M. Hetherington & Kelly, 2002). Many of the factors ignored in such presumptive formulae have been found in other studies (e.g., Emery & Kelly, Amato) to be important in children's adjustment. Nevertheless, some authors (Emery, Otto, & O'Donohue, 2005) even suggest that these formulaic presumptions remain intact even if parent is known to have a history of depression or substance abuse, *unless the problem impacts parenting to such a degree that the child would*

*be removed by Child Protective Services if the family were intact (empha-
sis added)* (Emery, Otto, & O'Donohue, 2005).

PRESUMPTIONS AS A PROBLEM-SOLVING TOOL, OR TO CREATE SPECIFIC RESULTS

Some presumptions have been enacted for more specific purposes, such as resolving a perceived problem in the adjudication of child custody cases. For example, California had established policies favoring both children's safety and their continuing relationship with both parents. A perception then developed that some judicial officers were not applying these presumptions as envisioned by the legislature. Specifically, some legislators and advocates felt that judicial officers were placing a higher priority on frequent parent-child contact than on children's safety, or that their view of safety was impacted by their belief in the importance of frequent and continuing contact. California law was then modified to establish the presumption of safety as more important than continuing contact. This modification did not specify a public policy, since frequency of contact and safety are both established public policies, but it directed judges to prioritize the issue of safety over that of continuing contact.

The last several years have seen an increasing trend toward legislative action in response to individual decisions by appellate courts and even trial judges (Schnider, 2002). In some areas, such as cases with allegations of child abuse or domestic violence, legislatures have gone beyond establishing a primary concern for safety to prescribing specific procedures for evaluations or mediation and imposing sharp restrictions on the discretion that can be exercised by trial judges. These presumptions, in effect, create "facts" which the judge is required to use, in lieu of actual evidence, once the prerequisite fact is established. The presumption must be applied whether or not the underlying assumptions are "true," supported by scientific evidence, or consistent with the child's needs. Barriers to overcome the presumption are often high, and judicial officers may vary as to the standards they apply in determining whether the evidence requiring exercise of the presumption has been met.

As the legislature became more involved in giving detailed directions for resolution of custody cases, political forces become increasingly entwined in the process. While many legislators undoubtedly have a sincere desire to protect children, the political process impacts the depth and quality of information they receive about children's needs. This increases the risk that presumptions may be established that are more re-flective of competing political interests than the product of objective deliberation and consideration of social science evidence. For example, as post-*Burgess*[4] relocation cases progressed through the appellate courts in California, the legislature attempted to pre-empt or restrict future court rulings by establishing the *Burgess* decision as the intent of the legislature. This occurred despite mounting social science evidence about stresses caused by relocation, the importance of father involvement in children's lives, and the multitude of individual characteristics and circumstances that may determine how any child will respond. After the *LaMusga*[5] decision was issued by the California Supreme Court, attempts were made to pass legislation that would have exalted the primary custodial parent's presumptive right to move over any individual consideration of children's best interests.[6] Conversely, the California Legislature recently considered legislation that would have established a presumption of 50-50 custody, absent *clear and convincing* evidence that this would be harmful to a child.

Political forces, interest groups, and media coverage of high profile cases have all contributed to legislation that is more reactive, specific in its intent, and restrictive of judicial officers' discretion to consider the circumstances of the individual child and family.

ILLUSORY ADVANTAGES

Proponents have advanced a number of arguments in support of presumptions. In this section, we address some of the primary arguments.

Presumptions Reduce Litigation–Or Do They?

Proponents of detailed presumptions often suggest that they will reduce custody litigation and children's exposure to conflict, by providing "surer, quicker, and more certain results when families break up." (Bartlett, 2002; also see Emery et al., 2005). This argument appears to rest on two premises: (1) that the establishment of a presumption will, in fact, reduce litigation; and (2) that, even if true, this mechanism of decision-making will result in custody arrangements that benefit children. Certainly, it is well established that prolonged exposure to parental conflict is harmful to children (Johnston & Roseby, 1997; J. B. Kelly, 2000; J. B. Kelly and Emery, Robert E., 2003; Roseby & Johnston, 1998), and it stands to reason that prolonged litigation may increase children's exposure to conflict. Nevertheless, other mechanisms, such as mandatory mediation, have proven effective in reducing the amount of child custody litigation, without abandoning children's individual interests in favor of a predetermined formula. (Emery, Laumann-Billings, Waldron, Sbarra, & Dillon, 2001)

We have found no controlled studies demonstrating that determinative custody presumptions (i.e., those that prescribe a particular formula for parenting time) have been effective in reducing child custody litigation. The majority of separating parents arrive at a parenting plan through some form of negotiation. This was also the case before the recent movement toward determinative presumptions. While many parents likely negotiate out of a true desire to reach an amicable resolution, it stands to reason that others agree to settlement out of a conviction that the "deck is stacked against them" by the existence of legal presumptions. It is unknown how many of these settlements provide different outcomes than would have been achieved if an evaluation had been conducted or evidence reviewed.

While pre-determined results may reduce custody litigation, predictable results do not necessarily equate to support of children's best interests. With current social science knowledge, few would argue children's best interests' were met by automatic decisions based on the gender of parent, or on the presumption that children would be better off in foster care than with an unwed father. While we have little research about the period when fathers had preference, more recent research (Sanford L. Braver & Griffin, 2000; Pleck, 1997) certainly illustrates that perceived maternal preference has often led to decreased involvement of fathers and hardship to children.

Even if presumptions were shown to discourage litigation by some parents, we have seen no evidence that they would reduce litigation in the 10-15% of cases with the highest level of conflict. These are the cases that consume a disproportionate amount of court time and resources and likely place the greatest burdens on children. Indeed, it has been our observation that, in high conflict cases, presumptions merely shift the focus of conflict to areas not addressed by the presumption, or to an arena that might influence the court to determine that a specific presumption has been met or overcome. This may lead to inflation of allegations of misconduct by a parent and/or distortion of past history to demonstrate that a particular parent has spent more time with the child. As even Emery et al. (2005) acknowledge, this may also lead to parents jockeying for position by leaving with children, quitting jobs, or fighting to remain in the marital home, even when a short-term separation might be better for everyone involved. This could increase children's exposure to parental conflict, which is precisely the outcome that presumption advocates say they want to avoid. Similarly, presumptions requiring strict 50-50 custody splits between high conflict parents may simply shift the arena of conflict to other issues on which, by statute, parents have been given equal authority. The child may be increasingly impacted, or have important aspects of life suspended, as parents litigate issues such as school placement or after-school activities.

All of this suggests that the impact of presumptions on litigation is much more complex than proponents argue. We know of no studies that have provided a comparison of litigation rates before and after presumptions were established. Our own experience suggests that detailed presumptions may discourage litigation in some cases, but not necessarily to the benefit of the child. In effect, a presumption may prompt settlement due to the existence of the presumption, rather than based on the child's individual needs. In other cases, as described above, the presumption may simply shift the focus or timing of litigation, exposing the child to just as much parental conflict.

Many parents are also better able to accept an evaluator's recommendation or decision of the court, if they believe that the evidence regarding their individual cases has been heard and considered, rather than having decisions made based on generalizations that may not be accurately applied to them (Schepard, 2004, suggests that this even applies to domestic violence offenders). This may, in turn, have an effect on the parties' future ability to co-parent.

Further study would likely be needed to determine the relationships between child custody presumptions, litigation, parental conflict, the ability to accept a custody decision and co-parent for the benefit of the child, and future child adjustment. We do not argue that we know the exact nature of these relationships, or that our own professional experience is an accurate reflection of all custody-contesting parents. On the other hand, since we no data to support the *assumption* that detailed child custody presumptions reduce litigation or children's exposure to parental conflict in a way which benefits children, it is not responsible to require trial judges to ignore many other factors (such as qualitative aspects of parent child relationships) that research suggests *are* important to child adjustment.

In our opinion, this issue illustrates the difference between general parameters for decision-making in child custody cases and specific presumptions that predetermine outcomes. Where general parameters (e.g. safety, continuing parent-child contact, stability, etc.) are established to guide family law decision-making, these issues can be examined in light of the individual circumstances and history of the child and family. As presumptions become more formulaic and determinative, the focus of decision-making is shifted away from the broad-based factors important to child adjustment and onto the specific formulae required by the presumptions. The individual needs of a child can easily get lost in such a process.

"Reigning In" Unreasonable Judges–Or Undermining Good Decision-Making?

Many proponents of child custody presumptions suggest that they are needed to control or prevent inappropriate decisions by judicial officers. These authors suggest that judges have little training in family law or child development, are ill-equipped to evaluate the qualitative aspects of parent-child relationships, and get little useful guidance from the "best interests" standard. They contend that, as a result, judges make their decisions based on personal biases and values, rather than relevant psychological research or parameters set by the legislature. Specifically, it has been argued that judicial officers have been insensitive to the dynamics of domestic violence and child abuse and the impact of these issues on children. (This issue will be discussed in greater detail in a subsequent section.) As a result of their various concerns, proponents of presumptions suggest that judges be limited to fact-based determinations such as "the shares of past care-taking" engaged in by each parent (Bartlett, 2002).

This approach is problematic at best, since pre-separation parenting is not necessarily predictive of post separation parenting. Various factors, including the post-separation need for both parents to work, renegotiation of parental relationships and adjustments in parental "gatekeeping" may impact both the amount and quality of time that parents and children spend together (Emery, 1999; E. M. Hetherington & Kelly, 2003; J. B. Kelly, 2000). Moreover, this proposal also is inconsistent with the research suggesting that the quality of a parent-child relationship is at least as important as the number of hours that parents and children spend together (P. Amato, 2003; P. R. Amato, 1994, Emery & Kelly, 2005). Thus, the proponents of presumptions are arguing that much psychological research be ignored, just to make the decision-making process simpler.

Judicial officers often rely on mental health experts to assist them with decisions in these difficult cases. Elrod (2002) notes that the use of mental health experts in child custody cases increased from approximately ten percent of cases in the 1960s to over 30 percent in the 1990s. While this may partly reflect the increasing complexity of child custody decisions (i.e., the movement from an automatic gender-based presumption to a more complex assessment of both parent-child relationships), it cannot be denied that mental health experts play increasingly prominent and varied roles in child custody cases. Several authors (Bartlett, 2002; L. R. Greenberg, Martindale, Gould, & Gould-Saltman, 2004; Krauss & Sales, 2000; Shuman & Sales, 1998) have expressed concern about the quality of mental health expertise provided to judicial officers, and about the tendency of some mental health professionals to exceed their roles and applicable knowledge in making recommendations to the court. Treating professionals may also escalate the family conflict if they undertake a biased position in the case, abandon professional objectivity, undertake treatment of a child without attempting to engage both parents, or exceed their roles and available knowledge by offering custody recommendations to the Court (Elrod, 2001, 2002; L. R. Greenberg, Gould, Schnider, Gould-Saltman, & Martindale, 2003; L. R. Greenberg, Gould, Jonathan W., Gould-Saltman, Dianna, & Stahl, Philip M., 2001). Concerns have also been expressed about the ability of judges to differentiate between good and poor quality mental health services or expert testimony (Bartlett, 2002; Krauss & Sales, 2000; Shuman, 2002).

Family law judicial officers certainly come with widely varying personal and professional experiences. Judicial officers, like attorneys and mental health professionals, may have personal and professional biases that impact their perceptions of events. Such biases are not limited to these professionals, of course, and may also become evident in legislation that arises in response to high profile cases or political pressure. Wherever it occurs, if a decision-making process involves a high degree of personal bias, one-sided consideration of the research literature, invalid procedures or short-cuts through the family's individual circumstances, it is more likely that the result will be inappropriate decisions for children and families.

Ultimately, we would argue that the cure for poor decision-making, to the degree that it exists, is better decision-making. Where training gaps exist in the preparation of judicial officers or mental health professionals, the best approach to improving results is to enhance ethical and training standards for those who can so profoundly impact the lives of children (Elrod, 2001, 2002; L. R. Greenberg et al., 2004). Also, training of attorneys and judicial officers should include material on how to assess the quality of mental health expertise, as well as effective questioning or cross-examination of experts. Movements toward improved training of judicial officers, the recruitment of a specialized family law judiciary, more effective use of children's attorneys, specialized models of court-related treatment, parent coordination and other intervention services, and judicial case management all provide improved possibilities for management of contested family law cases (Elrod, 2001, 2002; L. R. Greenberg, Gould, Gould-Saltman, & Stahl, 2003; L. R. Greenberg, Gould, Schnider et al., 2003; Levanas, 2005; Levanas, Greenberg, Drozd, & Rosen, 2004; Leverrette, Crowe, Wenglensky, & Dunbar, 1997; Taylor, Greenberg, & Doi Fick, 2004).

Tying the hands of decision-makers merely creates another poor model for decision-making, as it results from generalizations about classes of people, parenting patterns and events, without considering the individual circumstances of children and families. While presumptions may create improved results for some children who have been the subject of poor or uniformed judicial decisions, they also tie the hands of the increasing number of trained and concerned judicial officers making decisions about children and families.

THE PROBLEMS WITH PRESUMPTIONS

In the prior sections, we have critically responded to primary arguments that have been advanced to support detailed presumptions in child custody cases. In this section, we describe some of the problems with using such presumptions as the basis for decision-making about children and families.

Labels Don't Describe Reality–Children and Families Are Complicated

One issue that is characteristic of all child custody presumptions is the attempt to impose relatively simple decision-making rules on complex phenomena. Even those with some sympathy to presumptions (Bartlett, 2002; Emery et al., 2005; Hetherington, 2005) acknowledge that they are based on generalizations, and that past generalizations (e.g., global statements about parenting abilities based on gender or the child's age) did not prove to be accurate, fair or helpful to children. Few scholars, practitioners or legislators currently argue that child custody decisions should be based on the types of generalizations or stereotypes used in the past, yet some are arguing for a renewed use of similar decision-making patterns. The nature of the proposed generalizations may have changed, but they are no more reflective of the complexity of families than has been the case in the past, when generalizations now recognized as inaccurate were used to direct decisions about families.

Recent years have seen an explosion of research regarding the adjustment of both parents and children following parental separation. A review of the professional literature demonstrates the complexity of issues contributing to children's adjustment. Studies with different populations, using different methodologies, may yield strikingly different results. Moreover, where the literature is used in pursuit of a particular agenda rather than for a truly balanced review, findings may be selected, used, or misused to support a particular viewpoint (R. Gelles, Johnston, Pruett, & Kelly, 2005).

Individual children and families may present circumstances that differ from those found in research studies, and thus caution is needed when applying any research results to an individual case. Austin (this issue) further describes some of these concerns.

Outcome research generally demonstrates that children adjust most successfully when they can develop and/or maintain quality relationships with both parents, particularly when they are not placed in the middle of parental conflict (J. B. Kelly, 2005). Long-term exposure to parental conflict may cause significant harm to children, who may need protection or supervised contact when conflict is intractable or a parent is severely impaired. Such families may also require structured plans for parental decision-making, as well as parent education and treatment services for parents and children (P. R. Amato & Gilbreth, 1999; J. B. Kelly, 1998, 2000, 2001; J. B. Kelly and Emery, Robert E., 2003; Roseby & Johnston, 1998). When high conflict families are assigned to 50-50 custody situations without any decision-making structure in place, the result may be long-term, intractable conflict that has a profound effect on children's lives.

Children may be both directly and indirectly impacted by exposure to parental conflict, domestic violence, changes in family structure and the economic consequences of parental separation. Deterioration of parenting quality is common following parental separation, as parents may be more angry, overwhelmed by situational stressors, less able to separate their own emotional needs from children's needs, less affectionate and less effective with discipline and limit setting (Emery, 1999; E. M. Hetherington & Kelly, 2002; J. B. Kelly, 2005). Disruption of activities, routines, parent-child relationships and extended family relationships present risk factors for many children. If the child has a primary custodial parent, the psychological health and parenting practices of that parent may be of paramount importance (E. M. Hetherington & Kelly, 2002). Alternatively, if there are unhealthy aspects of both parent-child relationships, the child's relationship with each parent may buffer the child from unhealthy aspects of the other parent-child relationship (J. B. Kelly, 2005).

More fathers are remaining involved with their children after parental separation than at any other time in our history, and most children benefit from such involvement (J. B. Kelly & Lamb, 2003; J. B. Kelly and Emery, Robert E., 2003). While protracted exposure to parental conflict can have profoundly negative effects on children, children whose parents remain in conflict but avoid involving the children often do as well as children of lower-conflict parents (Buchanan, Maccoby, & Dornbusch, 1996; J. B. Kelly, 2000). Moreover, an increasing variety of program models are available for allowing children to have relationships with both parents while reducing their exposure to conflict (Elrod, 2001; L. R. Greenberg, Gould, Schnider et al., 2003; J. B. Kelly, 2001). Of course, issues such as family resources, emotional disturbance in parents, and other situational factors may determine whether these interventions can be successful for particular families.

The relationships among these variables, and their impact on children, are extraordinarily complex (P. R. Amato & Gilbreth, 1999; Bauserman, 2002; E. Mavis Hetherington, 1999; E. M. Hetherington & Kelly, 2003; J. B. Kelly & Emery, Robert E., 2003; King & Heard, 1999). A true understanding of the issues requires an appreciation of that complexity and balanced consideration of research supporting a variety of perspectives. Advocates of generalized solutions often argue that the research purely supports selected global solutions for children, failing to acknowledge the variations that may make different studies applicable to children in different situations (R. Gelles, Johnston, Pruett, & Kelly, 2005).

The complexity of the research, and the inapplicability of simple solutions, can be demonstrated by an examination of three of the most controversial areas addressed by child custody preferences: domestic violence, relocation and children's preferences.

Domestic Violence

There is widespread agreement that exposure to domestic violence can be harmful to children, presenting risks in terms of both parenting quality and the child's short and long term development. (Ayoub, Deutsch, & Maraganore, 1999; Dawud-Noursi, Lamb, & Sternberg, 1998; Levendosky & Graham-Bermann, 2000; Sternberg, Lamb, & Dawud-Noursi, 1998a). Here, however, much of the unanimity ends.

Some of the early research on domestic violence was conducted by focusing on women and children residing in battered women's shelters. These women were often fleeing severely violent relationships, in which the dynamics of conflicted divorce were often not a factor and the primary focus was on female victims of men exhibiting a pattern of controlling and violent behavior (Austin, 2001; Graham-Bermann, 1998). In subsequent years, definitions of domestic violence have evolved, such that the focus is increasingly on a pattern of coercive conduct by one partner, aimed at controlling the behavior of the other (Greenberg, Drozd, & Gonzalez, 2005).

Application of this research is also complicated by the manner in which domestic violence is defined, both in the research and in the statutes governing child custody decisions. These definitions can be widely variable.[7] In some states, a showing of physical injury or a criminal conviction is necessary, while other states have adopted much broader definitions.[8] While the research broadly supports the proposition that children are harmed and endangered by exposure to violence, stalking, threatening or intrusive/controlling parenting, the associations are less clear between children's distress and some of the other behaviors that some states, and some scholars, now define as domestic violence. Assessment of these issues is also complicated by evidence of the harmful effects on children exposed to high levels of parental conflict (Johnston & Roseby, 1997; Roseby & Johnston, 1997).

Disagreement also exists about the characteristics of violence between parents. For example, while there is general agreement that women are more likely to be seriously injured by men than the reverse, some studies indicate that large numbers of respondents in violent relationships reported incidents that were bi-directional and did not result in serious injury (Kwong, Bartholomew, & Dutton, 1999). Several authors have identified subtypes of domestic violence events, and have emphasized the importance of differential assessment for making appropriate assessments, recommendations for child custody, and treatment recommendations (Johnson & Ferraro, 2000; Johnston & Campbell, 1993). Other authors (Bancroft & Silverman, 2002) strongly dispute that any subtypes exist which may be relevant to risk assessment, custody decisions and treatment planning. This may pose particular concerns when a violent incident is an outgrowth of high conflict dynamics, rather than preceding the separation. The increasing number of domestic violence allegations in custody conflicts (Elrod, 2001) adds to the complexity of the assessment problem.

None of this is intended to deny the serious risks to children from exposure to conflict and violence, nor the importance of prioritizing children's safety over other factors in determining parenting plans. The validity of these concepts varies according to how important terms such as *domestic violence, high conflict* and *safety* are defined, and how closely those definitions, and the circumstances of the case, approximate those used in the research cited to support them. Specifically, research conducted on known victims of physical violence may be relevant when the statutory requirements, or facts of the case are similar to the circumstances of the study. On the other hand, one must use much greater caution in applying such research to an allegation that a coffee cup was destroyed or that one parent feels "harassed" by the other. Moreover, recent research has highlighted a number of factors that may contribute to the impact of family violence on children, including the nature of events experienced, ongoing parental conflict, children's innate resources/resilience, mental health of the parents, external support, systemic stressors, and access to treatment (Austin, 2001; Ayoub et al., 1999; Dawud-Noursi et al., 1998; Sternberg, Lamb, & Dawud-Noursi, 1998b). All of these issues may be relevant to devising the best plan for children and families.

Various authors have proposed complex models for assessing allegations of domestic violence, arriving at custody decisions and devising treatment interventions. These approaches are based on considering a broad range of the research on these issues (Austin, 2001; L. R. Greenberg, Drozd, & Gonzalez, 2005; L. R. Greenberg, Gould, Schnider et al., 2003; Levanas et al., 2004, Dalton & Olesen, 2004). Such complexity is rarely reflected in the position statements of advocacy groups, press accounts of high profile cases, or other highly public political processes. While the research demands a complex, individualized approach, interest groups may demand simple or more sweeping responses. In such a highly charged context, interventions as basic as requiring treatment for victimized parents may be recast as blaming the parent rather than promoting a mentally healthy environment for the child. Given the high stakes involved in protecting a child's safety and the strains on family court resources, simple rules may be particularly appealing to decision-makers but not as effective or helpful to children.

Relocation

As other authors in this collection have noted, relocation is one of the most difficult problems that family courts face. As Elrod (this volume) noted, relocation cases often involve losses for everyone involved. Even in cases where differences have previously been resolved through negotiation, conflict can rapidly escalate when one parent perceives a threat to his/her relationship with the child due to the proposed relocation, and the other perceives a threat to his/her autonomy and ability to travel if the relocation is denied. As in many high conflict cases, children's independent needs can rapidly be overwhelmed by each parent's attempt to pursue his or her own interests.

As Elrod also observed, relocation cases often invoke an irreconcilable conflict between fundamental rights and issues, e.g., the right of a parent to travel, the right of a parent to care for his or her child and, most importantly, children's needs. The perception that requests to relocate are more frequent among custodial mothers has led to disputes about relocation law being expressed against the heated political backdrop of interest group and gender politics. In the process, psychological research has been selectively cited, extrapolated, and attacked with a level of vitriol that is relatively uncommon in the professional psychological literature. As the trend is toward individual assessment of a child's best interests in contested relocation cases, it is useful for all consumers of the research to have a general understanding of the complexity of the issues, and of what we do and do not know about children's adjustment.

It would be difficult, if not impossible, to conduct fully controlled studies of children's adjustment following a contested relocation case. Such a study would raise serious ethical concerns, as it would require that children be randomly assigned to conditions of relocation or non-relocation and matched based on any number of characteristics that may complicate the outcome in any particular case. As in many types of cases involving real families in actual distress, researchers are limited to those methods that can provide information without increasing risks to the families and children being studied. These methods include surveys and questionnaires, comparing outcome measures in naturally occurring comparison groups, applying research from related areas of study, and in-depth case studies. Each of these methods has limitations, and, for this reason, mental health experts must consider (and convey to the Court) the reasons that particular results are or are not applicable to the case at issue. Amato has provided a useful analysis of the different types of research on divorce, and the information that each can contribute to our understanding of children's outcomes (P. Amato, 2003). Unfortu- nately, when the environment discussing these issues becomes politi- cized, advocates may focus on attacking the weaknesses of research supporting opposing viewpoints, rather than assessing the data to find the results that are most relevant to the individual child at issue. Stahl (this volume) provides an extensive discussion of how such biases enter into discussions and consideration of relocation cases.

Austin (this volume) has presented a critical analysis of research and opinion literature on the impact of relocation on children of divorce. As he discusses, the research on relocation is only one special aspect of re- search related to the effects of parental separation on children. Our pur- pose here is not to exhaustively review this research, but rather to highlight core concepts and findings, many drawn from related areas of psychological study and both sides of the relocation debate. Any of these concepts can be selectively cited to support the interests of one ad- vocacy group over the other. To produce the best results for children and families, however, research findings must be discriminatingly applied to the facts of a specific case.

The first and rather obvious concept is that relocation may be stress- ful to both children and adults. Relocation requires children to adjust to new surroundings, adapt to new schools and establish friendships and connections to the community. When the relocation follows parental separation, children may need to adjust to profoundly changed relation- ships with the left-behind parent and extended family, as well as peer networks and other activities in the community of origin. Visitation structures that require the child to spend full summers or vacations in another community may also cause stresses or interrupt peer activities in the new community. Even the proposal to relocate may substantially increase conflict between parents (Elrod, 2002, this volume), as one faces the possibility of profound change in his/her relationship with the child. Of course, these disadvantages may be overcome by improve- ments in economic circumstances or other opportunities, reduced expo- sure to the parental conflict or an abusive parent, support from family members in the new community, and the improved mental health or happiness of the parent who was permitted to relocate with the child and pursue other goals or opportunities.

Relocation also occurs against the backdrop of children's develop- mental stages, capabilities, and the skills they must develop at various ages in order to achieve a healthy adjustment. As Kelly and Lamb (2003) and Austin (this volume) note, relocation may pose particular risks to young children, as they are least able to maintain an image of the distant parent and participate in long-distance communication such as email and telephone contacts. The development of close parent-child relationships takes place across a variety of activities and responsibilities, ranging from intimate care-taking responsibilities to involvement in homework, assisting children with decision-making skills, and providing the developmental experiences that allow children to grow and mature. While Wallerstein (2003) and others have presented case studies (particularly involving older children) in which children have been able to maintain close long-distance relationships with parents, other researchers present data suggesting that relocation risks significant disruption of parent-child relationships and distress to children who are separated from a parent (Stanford L. Braver, Ellman, & Fabricius, 2003; Fabricius, 2003; Fabricius & Braver, this volume).

It is likely that each of these outcomes occurs in some children. A new study also suggests that supportive relationships with grandparents may be important to children's adjustment after divorce, and that children's assessment of these relationships does not always coincide with what their parents think of them (Lussier, Deater-Deckard, Dunn, & Davies, 2002). This factor might weigh either in favor or against a parent's desire to relocate, depending on the quality of the grandparent-grandchild relationships and how those relationships would be affected by the proposed relocation.

As several authors have noted, relocation cases often involve forced choices between alternatives that create risks to children, whether or not the relocation is permitted. As Austin (this volume) and others have noted, decisions in some cases may ultimately have to be directed toward risk mitigation and harm reduction, rather than producing the "best" outcome. The literature suggests that relevant factors include the child's age, the level of parental conflict, available resources for maintaining both parent-child relationships, each parent's willingness to support the other parent-child relationship, the child's activities and peer involvements, and a host of other *individual* variables. Best-interests analyses, rather than generalized presumptions, are more likely to be consistent with complex research findings and the individual needs of children and families.

Children's Preferences

Recent years have seen an increasing trend toward asking courts to consider children's preferences in child custody decisions. Most states include some consideration of children's preferences in their standards for child custody decisions, while a few states have established a rebuttable presumption that children's preferences should be controlling after a certain age.[9] In addition, children's preferences often represent a component in other presumptions, as they are listed among the issues to be considered in determinations about relocation, parenting schedules and other issues. Thus, assumptions about children's statements and decision-making ability may exert a pervasive, and often unrecognized, influence on child custody decisions–including the application of other presumptions.

Like most of the issues discussed in this section, the emphasis on considering children's preferences is based on a commonly accepted premise–i.e., that the thoughts and feelings of children are important and should be considered in reaching decisions about parenting plans. After decades in which children's needs were completely subordinate to the interests of parents, recent years have seen an increasing trend toward valuing and considering the independent needs and concerns of children (Crossman, Powell, Principe, & Ceci, 2002).

Most professionals also accept the fact that not all of children's statements are equally valid, and that poor interviewing can lead to invalid statements and misinterpretation of children's needs. In recent years, there has been an explosion of increasingly sophisticated research and professional literature about valid methods of child interviewing and the appropriate interpretation of children's statements and behavior. While much of this research began around the issues of assessing allegations of child sexual abuse, children's responses have been studied in a wide variety of situations both related and unrelated to allegations of abuse.

Much of the relevant research has been summarized elsewhere (Crossman, Powell, Principe, & Ceci, 2002; Kuehnle, Greenberg, & Gottlieb, 2004; Lamb, Sternberg, & Esplin, 2000; Lamb, Sternberg, Esplin, Hershkowitz et al., 1997; Leichtman & Ceci, 1995; Pezdek, Finger, & Hodge, 1997) and a comprehensive review is beyond the scope of this paper. For the purpose of our commentary here, it is sufficient to note the broad areas of agreement and controversy regarding children's preferences and interview data.

As is evidenced by the summary above, appropriate consideration of children's data involves a delicate balance of careful interviewing by trained professionals, considering multiple interpretations of children's behavior, asking questions that allow the interviewer to gain some knowledge of the *whole* child (rather than just the child's "position" on a contested issue), appreciation of developmental patterns, and an understanding of the family factors that may give rise to reasoned preferences, healthy or unhealthy problem solving, or a child "caving in" to pressure from a needy or angry parent. The literature overwhelmingly argues for a multidimensional approach to listening to children.

Unfortunately, as children's preferences have been incorporated into other presumptions, the responses to children's data have often become politicized and subsumed into larger battles between adult interest groups. Some authors are now using adult-like discussions of children's "rights" to advocate that children be given *control* over major parenting decisions-including decisions about parenting plans, contact with parents and extended family, and involvement in medical treatment or psychotherapy. This contrasts with more midrange approaches (Elrod, 2005; L. R. Greenberg, Gould, Gould-Saltman et al., 2003; L. R. Greenberg, Gould, Schnider et al., 2003; J. B. Kelly, 2000, 2005) recommending that children's information, feelings and perceptions be considered, with weight assigned based on the child's age, abilities, functioning level, coping skills, family dynamics, and a variety of other individual factors. Those who argue for a more nuanced approach to children's data have been accused of being unconcerned about children's feelings, taking children's safety lightly, or "forcing" children into activities, relationships, or treatment against the child's wishes (Walker, Brantley, & Rigsbee, 2004).

Even without the politicized environment, responses to children's data can be emotionally loaded. Responsible adults feel a need to respond to children and, in the case of allegations of violence or abuse, to protect them (Levanas et al., 2004). Children at certain ages (e.g., early adolescents) may also have an emphatic style in expressing their opinions on any subject, which increases the pressure on adults to respond. The judicial officer or mental health professional who does not have (or take) the time to interview the child on issues outside the parental conflict may never learn that the adolescent is equally emphatic on any number of subjects, where a lack of judgment in their opinions may be more apparent. Conversely, some children are able to arrive at effective perceptions or problem solving on issues relevant to their daily lives (e.g., the pros and cons of particular extracurricular activities), but are ill-equipped or emotionally unprepared to express opinions on the major issues in the custody conflict. Such children may become overwhelmed and/or inappropriately emphatic, one-sided and lacking in developmentally expected characteristics when questioned about contested issues in the parental conflict.

Children's expressed preferences may reflect any combination of reasoned opinions or perceptions, unhealthy problem solving, or external influence on the child's perceptions and statements. Careful, balanced, and broad-based interviewing may reveal information that can meaningfully contribute to the evaluator's recommendations or the court's decisions. Conversely, interviewing that exclusively focuses on the adults' contested issues may lead to distorted data and interpretation. The combination of demands on court resources and a highly charged political context may make it difficult to arrive at such a contextual understanding of children's statements. It may also result in overwhelming pressure on children to express "positions" that adults believe are likely to sway the court.

It is useful to place these issues in the context of normal and expected patterns in children's development, as well as typical responses to children's statements in intact and lower-conflict families. A number of authors (including some who have been attacked as not listening to children) have emphasized the importance of children and adolescents having *input* into decisions about their daily routines and parenting plans (Dunn, Davies, O'Connor, & Sturgess, 2001; J. B. Kelly, 2000, 2005). As Kelly (2000, 2005) has pointed out, most children know the difference between having input into decisions and being burdened with the responsibility for adult decisions that they may be unprepared to make, and which may subject them to undue emotional burdens. The first author of this paper commonly conducts informal polls of training participants to assess how many of them usually allow their children to make unfettered decisions about academic programs, major medical decisions, or attending family events. The results of these unscientific explorations, as well as the professional literature, suggest that most parents commonly serve as gatekeepers for considering their children's preferences.

Allowing children to be *involved* in decision-making increases their perception of being heard and considered. Such a process also allows the parent to consider children's reasoned preferences, and provides an opportunity for the parent to engage the child in critical thinking, consideration of alternatives, and effective problem solving (Dunn et al., 2001; Lussier et al., 2002). At the same time, maintenance of final adult authority allows the adult's (usually) more reasoned judgment to prevail, balances children's input with consideration of broader family issues, and helps children to master the coping skills they need to develop successfully.

This process is also consistent with the professional literature, which indicates that most children have better outcomes when they are exposed to authoritative parenting and achieve more successful adjustment when they learn to resolve problems by active engagement with others rather than by simply avoiding a stressful situation (Fields & Prinz, 1997; E. Mavis Hetherington, 1999; E. M. Hetherington & Kelly, 2002). Thus, the child who is having difficulty with a parent may benefit more, both in short and long-term development, by engaging in a therapeutic process designed to address the issues rather than cementing the problems by avoiding contact with the parent (L. R. Greenberg, Gould, Gould-Saltman et al., 2003; L. R. Greenberg, Gould, Schnider et al., 2003; Johnston, Walters, & Friedlander, 2001; J. B. Kelly, 2001, 2002). Even children who have been exposed to violence or abuse may ultimately achieve better adjustment if they have an opportunity to resolve their feelings in a safe and protected environment with the parent involved (Chaffin, Wherry, & Dykman, 1997; L. R. Greenberg et al., 2005; Levanas et al., 2004).

Children's statements and expressed preferences, particularly when stated in emphatic or global terms, may be a tempting "tie breaker" when difficult decisions arise. This is a particular danger in that children's statements, and adults' assumptions regarding them, may carry an unrecognized influence as components of decision-making regarding other child custody presumptions. Certainly, we believe that children's feelings, perceptions and experiences should be strongly considered when decisions are being made about their lives, and the literature suggests that they adjust better when their voices are heard (Crossman et al., 2002; Dunn et al., 2001). Overall, however, both research and common experience argue against global, age-based or "bright line" presumptions about children's statements and expressed preferences. Moreover, available social science argues for scientifically informed interviews and caution in how children's statements are used to support or rebut other presumptions.

Problems with Politicizing Social Science

Social advocacy has long been an effective force in promoting political change. For example, years of denial and minimization about the effects of domestic violence, combined with movements advancing women's rights, led to legislative changes placing a greater emphasis on children's safety. Social science research played a role in those changes. At the same time, as described above, concerns have been raised about the applicability of earlier studies to different populations or expanded definitions of domestic violence. Few would argue for a return to the "bad old days" in which the seriousness of child abuse or domestic violence was denied. As noted above, however, similar concerns can be raised about the social science research in a variety of other areas, used by interest groups all over the political spectrum.

Political debates, as well as journalistic coverage, tend to be painted in broad strokes. Advocates often select those research results–or parts of research results–that they believe most strongly support their positions and desires regarding the legislation or court case, ignoring or minimizing the limitations in a supportive study or the contributions of research supporting a different view (Stahl, this volume).While psychologists have an ethical obligation to articulate the limitations in data they present (American Psychological Association, 2002; Ceci & Hembrooke, 1998; Gould & Stahl, 2000; L. R. Greenberg et al., 2004), attorneys have an obligation to highlight that data most favorable to the client's case. Moreover, unrecognized bias may play a role in how professionals *select* the research they review. While no professional has the time to read everything, objective consideration of the research requires balanced consideration of literature supporting a variety of perspectives. The well-informed attorney (or the attorney assisted by a well-informed expert) may be able to effectively cross-examine an opposing expert who presents a one-sided review of the psychological literature. Such opportunities are less likely to exist in advocacy-driven attempts to rewrite the law.

Many legislators are genuinely concerned about children, and may be impacted by high-profile cases or disturbing results in individual cases. By the very nature of their function, legislatures craft broad, generalized solutions. Moreover, the vocabulary used to describe a bill may hide important facts about its provisions. For example, a recently introduced bill in California was represented by proponents as a "shared parenting" bill, when it in fact would have gone a great deal further–requiring a strong presumption (rebuttable only by clear and convincing evidence) that a 50-50 custody arrangement was best for children. As noted above, while there is considerable research support for the benefits of having both parents constructively involved in children's lives (P. R. Amato & Gilbreth, 1999; J. B. Kelly, 2000), we have seen no scholarly support for a near-blanket presumption that 50-50 custody arrangement is in children's best interests.

It is sometimes suggested that legislation about child-custody presumptions is advanced by mothers'-rights or fathers'-rights groups in response to the perception of legislative gains by parents of the other gender. Some of the legislation is also intended to advance truly noble policy goals, such as protecting children. Even the most well-intentioned policy goal, however, rarely achieves good results if it is advanced by poorly conducted, selectively represented or distorted social science.

Not all research is of equal quality, and refinements in research design have allowed us to gain an increased understanding of the complexity of children's reactions and outcomes. It is also in the nature of science–and social science–that it rarely stands still. In the 1980s, for example, concern about allegations of abused children led to slogans such as "believe the children"–with the attendant implications that those who were concerned about suggestibility didn't listen to children– while other organizations described "victims" of child abuse laws. Both groups had compelling case examples to support their generalized opinions about the believability of children's statements. In the ensuing quarter-century, increasingly sophisticated studies have illustrated the complex strengths and weaknesses of both child and adult memories, as well as the types of interview conditions most likely to yield valid or distorted information. Each of these studies has strengths and weaknesses, and responsible authors articulate the both the applicability and limitations of their results. No study, however, can fully account for the individual differences that a judge can hear when he or she considers evidence.

Unintended Consequences and the Importance of Fairness

Detailed presumptions also impact perceptions of fairness in the judicial system, since decisions are based on generalizations about classes of parents and children rather than individual examination of evidence. It is our opinion that where general parameters or child custody presumptions are established, those presumptions need to address significant issues and be supportable based on a broad-based, thorough and balanced consideration of social science research. Presumptions are, by their very nature, short cuts, which reduce the need–and opportunity to present–actual evidence regarding an individual case. As presumptions multiply and become more restrictive or detailed, the result is reduced discretion for the judicial officer and more restricted opportunities for a parent to present his/her case. It stands to reason that custody decisions that are more formulaic and presumption-driven will leave litigants feeling that their individual circumstances have not been heard or considered. This result may have real consequences, including increased litigation, decreased post-decision involvement by the "losing" parent, and decreased compliance with court orders. The limited social science available suggests that even domestic violence offenders are more likely to comply with court orders if they believe that the process leading to those orders has been reasonably balanced and fair (Schepard, 2004). Thus, it seems reasonable to suspect this dynamic would also operate–perhaps to an even greater degree–in cases that do not involve allegations of violence.

SO WHAT DO WE SUGGEST?

Complexity Is More Difficult, But It Is Also Real

The first step to solving any problem is to recognize and acknowledge its existence. Increasing divorce rates and the escalating caseloads in family courts have created real strains on court resources. High percentages of litigants are unrepresented, and even more are unable to afford the comprehensive evaluations, expert testimony and presentation of evidence that lead to truly individualized decisions. Parent coordination and expert-level treatment may be valuable to many families, but relatively few have the resources to afford them. Conciliation court services are also overstretched, limiting the publicly funded services that can be made available to families.

In this context, formulaic custody presumptions present an appealing, if illusory, solution. Instead of considering qualitative aspects of parenting, the court need only count the hours that a parent has reportedly spent with a child (Bartlett, 2002). Instead of considering the complex impact of a proposed relocation on the child, the Court need only assign the label "primary caretaker" to one parent and the rest of the decisions follow. Instead of considering the subtypes of domestic violence and the varying impact on parent-child relationships, the court need only determine that violence has occurred and assign blame. Instead of determining when conflict is sufficiently high to make 50-50 custody unworkable, the court need only determine if the "clear and convincing" threshold has been met to provide a different parenting plan. By proposing a formulaic outcome, presumptions also present the short-term promise–although quite possibly, *not* the reality–of cost savings in an over-stressed system.

The illusion of a solution is not an actual solution. While presumptions have continued to multiply, judicial caseloads have not decreased. The available evidence suggests that compliance with court orders is actually *more* likely when a parent has had the chance to present evidence (Schepard, 2004) or perceives the Court process as fair. Moreover, research on the impacts of divorce suggest that children are at risk for any number of psychological difficulties that may affect them, their future family relationships, and their functioning in society (Ackil & Zaragoza, 1995; P. Amato, 2003; P. R. Amato, 1994; E. M. Hetherington & Kelly, 2002; J. B. Kelly, 2000, 2002, 2005). The fact that these longer-term outcomes are more difficult to measure doesn't make their costs to society any less real. In our view, the first step to solving these problems is to recognize the fact that detailed child custody presumptions are unlikely to provide effective solutions.

Let Judges Be Judges

The cornerstone of our family law system is an independent judicial officer providing an individualized consideration of evidence regarding children's best interests. While not every judicial officer is equally qualified or interested in family law, many committed judicial officers have accepted or kept family law assignments out of a genuine desire to make a difference in the lives of children. In some jurisdictions, an increased appreciation of the need for training and the importance of family law cases has led to greater interdisciplinary cooperation and more training resources being provided to the family law judiciary (e.g., California Rules of Court, Rule 5.30).

There is no generalized rule that can substitute for the judicial officer's consideration of individual differences and family circumstances. In the words of Justice White,[10]

> Procedure by presumption is always cheaper and easier . . . than individualized determination. But when . . . the procedure forecloses the determinative issues of competence and care, when it explicitly disdains present realities in deference to past formalities, it needlessly risks running roughshod over the important interests of both parent and child.

Presumptions may shift the focus of controversy, but they do not eliminate it. Ultimately, the outcome of many cases will rest in the hands of a judicial officer doing his/her best to apply the law fairly and make decisions that support children's needs. Our informal experience suggests that many judges took the bench out of a sincere desire to serve the law and make a positive difference in people's lives. As noted above, our view is that the best cure for poor outcomes is to provide judges and families with the tools for effective decision-making. This may include access to mental health expertise, resources for judicial case management and, fundamentally, respect for the vital role these judges play in the lives of the children who come before them. To the degree that we restrict judges' ability to consider evidence and make individual decisions, we risk losing the best judicial officers from this vital area of the law.

Make Children a Priority

It is obvious that many of our suggested solutions would require that more resources be made available to the family courts and related services. Unified family courts, parent education, special master/parent coordination, and mental health treatment require expenditure of resources that are not currently available to most family courts. These services, while costly, are likely to offer substantial savings over the massive costs of prolonged family conflict and allowing children's needs to go unmet.

Our rather idealistic suggestion is that true resolution of these problems will require that funding be reallocated to make children a priority. Decisions regarding children's lives must be given a higher priority than disputes over car accidents, property damage, or most other areas of civil law. Judicial resources should be allocated in support of how high the stakes become every time a child's life is before the Court. There is no substitute for considering children's custody thoroughly and deliberately, and we believe our children deserve nothing less.

Ultimately, our society will need to decide if it values children enough to expend the resources necessary to truly protect them. We do not propose to have the solution to every problem. We believe that the best solutions will likely emerge through continued research and interdisciplinary cooperation, applying the different skills of judges, attorneys and mental health professionals to protecting families and assisting them through the crisis of parental separation. As a first step, we believe it essential to recognize that there are no easy, simple, cheap, or short cut solutions that will truly support children's needs. Most children will continue to be best served by arrangements negotiated between their parents, particularly if sufficient supportive services are available to promote parental cooperation. Those minority of severely impaired or high conflict families who remain will place the most vulnerable children in the hands of our judicial system. Ultimately, the cost of providing resources for these children is likely to be far less than the long-term implications of failing to do so.

NOTES

1. California *Family Code*, Section 3020.

2. California *Family Code*, Section 7611.

3. California *Family Code*, Section 3111.

4. The California Supreme Court, in the case, *In re Marriage of Burgess* (1996) 13 Cal.4th 25, 51 Cal.Rptr.2d 444, 913 P.2d 473, held that after a parent has obtained a judgment which awards him or her sole legal custody (in fact) that parent has the right to change the residence of the child (per *Family Code*, Sec. 7501). The only limitation on this right is if the move is in bad faith or will cause detriment to the child.

5. In the case, In *re the Marriage of La Musga* (2004) 32 Cal.4th 1072, 12 Cal.Rptr.3d 356, 88 P.3d 81, the California Supreme Court, while affirming the *Burgess* decision, appeared to make it easier to prove detriment to the child by overruling Court of Appeal decisions limiting the factors trial courts could consider as constituting detriment to the child. The general perception is that *La Musga* will make it easier to successfully oppose the relocation with the child.

6. California Assembly Bill 721.

7. See, ABA Child Custody Pro Bono Project, http://www.abanet.org/legal services/probono/childcustody/domestic_violence_chart1.pdf

8. For example, California *Family Code*, Section 3044 states that "a person has 'perpetrated domestic violence' when he or she is found by the court to have intentionally or recklessly caused or attempted to cause bodily injury, or sexual assault, or to have placed a person in reasonable apprehension of imminent serious bodily injury to that person or to another, or to have engaged in any behavior involving, but not limited to, threatening, striking, harassing, destroying personal property or disturbing the peace of another, for which a court may issue an ex parte order pursuant to Section 6320 to protect the other party seeking custody of the child or to protect the child and the child's siblings."

9. See: ABA Pro Bono Child Custody Project, *http://www.abanet.org/legal services/probono/childcustody.htm* for a comparison of these provisions among jurisdictions.

10. Stanley v. Illinois, 405 U.S. 645 (1972) .

REFERENCES

Ackil, J. K., & Zaragoza, M. S. (1995). Developmental differences in eyewitness suggestibility and memory for source. *Journal of Experimental Child Psychology, 60*(1), 7-83.

Amato, P. (2003). Reconciling Divergent Perspectives: Judith Wallerstein, Quantitative Family Research, and Children of Divorce. *Family Relations, 52*, 332-339.

Amato, P. R. (1994). Life-span adjustment of children to their parents' divorce. *Future of Children, 4*(1), 143-164.

Amato, P. R., & Gilbreth, J. G. (1999). Nonresident fathers and children's well-being: A meta-analysis. *Journal of Marriage & the Family, 61*(3), 557-573.

American Psychological Association. (2002). Ethical Principles of Psychologists and Code of Conduct. *American Psychologist, 57*(12), 1060-1073.

Austin, W. G. (2001). Partner violence and risk assessment in child custody evaluation. *Family Court Review, 39*(4), 483-496.

Ayoub, C. C., Deutsch, R. M., & Maraganore, A. (1999). Emotional distress in children of high-conflict divorce: The impact of marital conflict and violence. *Family & Conciliation Courts Review, 37*(3), 297-314.

Bancroft, L., & Silverman, J. G. (2002). *The Batterer as Parent*. Thousand Oaks: Sage Publications.

Bartlett, K. T. (2002). Preference, Presumption, and Common Sense: From Traditional Custody Doctrines to the American Law Institute's Family Dissolution Project. *Family Law Quarterly, 36*(1), 1-25.

Bauserman, R. (2002). Child adjustment in joint-custody versus sole-custody arrangements: A meta-analytic review. *Journal of Family Psychology, 16*(1), 91-102.

Braver, S. L., Ellman, I. M., & Fabricius, W. V. (2003). Relocation of Children after Divorce and Children's Best Interests: New Evidence and Legal Considerations. *Journal of Family Psychology,* 17(2), June 2003, 206-219.

Braver, S. L., & Griffin, W. A. (2000). Engaging fathers in the post-divorce family. *Marriage & Family Review, 29*(4), 247-267.

Buchanan, C. M., Maccoby, E. E., & Dornbusch, S. M. (1996). Adolescents after divorce. In *Cambridge, MA, US: Harvard University Press (1996) x, 331 pp.*

Ceci, S. J., & Hembrooke, H. (1998). Expert witnesses in child abuse case: What can and should be said in court. In *Washington, DC, US: American Psychological Association* (1998) viii, 299 pp.

Chaffin, M., Wherry, J. N., & Dykman, R. (1997). School age children's coping with sexual abuse: Abuse stresses and symptoms associated with four coping strategies. *Child Abuse & Neglect, 21*(2), 227-240.

Crossman, A., Powell, M. B., Principe, G. F., & Ceci, S. (2002). Child testimony in custody cases: A review. *Journal of Forensic Psychology Practice, 2,* 1-31.

Dawud-Noursi, S., Lamb, M. E., & Sternberg, K. J. (1998). The relations among domestic violence, peer relationships, and academic performance. In M. Lewis & C. Feiring (Eds.), *Families, risk, and competence* (pp. 207-226). Mahwah, NJ: Lawrence Erlbaum Associates, Inc., Publishers.

Dunn, J., Davies, L. C., O'Connor, T. G., & Sturgess, W. (2001). Family lives and friendships: The perspectives of children in step-, single-parent, and nonstep families. *Journal of Family Psychology, 15*(2), 272-287.

Elrod, L. D. (2001). Reforming the System to Protect Children in High Conflict Custody Cases. *2001, 28*(2), 495-551.

Elrod, L. D. (2002). Protecting Children in High Conflict Custody Cases. In R. Brown & L. Morgan (Eds.), *2002 Family Law Update*. New York: Aspen Law and Business.

Elrod, L. D. (2005). Personal communication. In P. D. Lyn R. Greenberg (Ed.). Los Angeles, CA.

Elrod, L. D. (2006). A move in the right direction? Best interests of the child emerging as the standard for relocation cases. *Journal of Child Custody, in press.*

Emery, R. E. (1999). Marriage, divorce, and children's adjustment (2nd ed.). In *Thousand Oaks, CA,* US: Sage Publications, Inc (1999) xii, 164 pp.

Emery, R. E., Laumann-Billings, L., Waldron, M. C., Sbarra, D. A., & Dillon, P. (2001). Child custody mediation and litigation: Custody, contact, and coparenting 12 years after initial dispute resolution. *Journal of Consulting & Clinical Psychology, 69*(2), 323-332.

Emery, R. E., Otto, R.K., O'Donohue, W.T. (2005) A Critical Assessment of Child Custody Evaluations: Limited Science and a Flawed System. *Psychological Science in the Public Interest,* 6 (1), 1-29.

Fabricius, W. V. (2003). Listening to Children of Divorce: New Findings That Diverge From Wallerstein, Lewis, and Blakeslee. *Family Relations: Interdisciplinary Journal of Applied Family Studies, 52*(4), 385-396.

Fabricius, W. V., & Braver, S. H. (2006). Relocation, Parent Conflict, and Domestic Violence: Independent Risk Factors for Children of Divorce. *Journal of Child Custody, 3*(3/4), 7-127.

Fields, L., & Prinz, R. J. (1997). Coping and adjustment during childhood and adolescence. *Clinical Psychology Review, 17*(8), 937-976.

Gelles, R. J., Johnston, J. R., Pruett, K. D., & Kelly, J. B. (2005). *The Politics of Research: The Use, Abuse and Misuse of Social Science Data.* Paper presented at the Association of Family and Conciliation Courts, 42nd Annual Conference, Seattle, Washington.

Gould, J. W., & Stahl, P. M. (2000). The art and science of child custody evaluations: Integrating clinical and forensic mental health models. *Family & Conciliation Courts Review, 38*(3), 392-414.

Graham-Bermann, S. A. (1998). The impact of woman abuse on children's social development: Research and theoretical perspectives. In G. W. Holden & R. Geffner (Eds.), *Children exposed to marital violence: Theory, research, and applied issues.* (pp. 21-54). Washington, DC, US: American Psychological Association.

Greenberg, L. R., Drozd, L. M., & Gonzalez, D. (2005). *Assessment and Management of Cases Involving Domestic Violence.* Paper presented at the Association of Family and Conciliation Courts, California Chapter Conference, Sonoma, CA.

Greenberg, L. R., Gould, J. W., Gould-Saltman, D. J., & Stahl, P. (2003). Is the Child's Therapist Part of the Problem? What Judges, Attorneys and Mental Health Professionals Need to Know about Court-Related Treatment for Children. *Family Law Quarterly, 37*(2), 241-271.

Greenberg, L. R., Gould, J. W., Schnider, R., Gould-Saltman, D. J., & Martindale, D. (2003). Effective intervention with high-conflict families: How judges can promote and recognize competent treatment in family court. *Journal of the Center for Families, Children & the Courts, 4,* 49-66.

Greenberg, L. R., Gould, Jonathan W., Gould-Saltman, Dianna, & Stahl, Philip M. (2001). Is the child's therapist part of the problem? What attorneys, judges, and mental health professionals need to know about court-related treatment for children. *Association of Family & Conciliation Courts of California Newsletter* (Winter), 6-7, 24-29.

Greenberg, L. R., Martindale, D., Gould, J. W., & Gould-Saltman, D. J. (2004). Ethical Issues in Child Custody and Dependency Cases: Enduring Principles and Emerging Challenges. *Journal of Child Custody, 1*(1), 7-30.

Hetherington, E. M., & index Subject, i. (1999). Coping with divorce, single parenting, and remarriage: A risk and resiliency perspective. In *Mahwah, NJ, US: Lawrence Erlbaum Associates, Inc., Publishers (1999) x, 359 pp.*

Hetherington, E. M., & Kelly, J. (2002). *For Better or Worse: Divorce Reconsidered.* New York: W.W. Norton.

Hetherington, E. M., & Kelly, J. (2003). For better or for worse. Divorce reconsidered. *Journal of Child Psychology & Psychiatry & Allied Disciplines, 44*(3), 470-471.

Johnson, M. P., & Ferraro, K. J. (2000). Research on Domestic Violence in the 1990s: Making Distinctions. *Journal of Marriage & the Family, 62*, 948-963.

Johnston, J. R., & Campbell, L. E. (1993). A clinical typology of interparental violence in disputed-custody divorces. *American Journal of Orthopsychiatry, 63*(2), 190-199.

Johnston, J. R., & Roseby, V. (1997). In the name of the child: A developmental approach to understanding and helping children of conflicted and violent divorce. In *New York, NY, US: The Free Press (1997) xiv, 337 pp.*

Johnston, J. R., Walters, M. G., & Friedlander, S. (2001). Therapeutic Work with Alienated Children and their Families. *Family Court Review, 39*(3), 316-333.

Kelly, J. B. (1998). Marital conflict, divorce and children's adjustment. *Child & Adolescent Psychiatric Clinics of North America, 7*(2), 259-271.

Kelly, J. B. (2000). Children's adjustment in conflicted marriage and divorce: A decade review of research. *Journal of the American Academy of Child & Adolescent Psychiatry, 39*(8), 963-973.

Kelly, J. B. (2001). Legal and educational interventions for families in residence and contact disputes. *Australian Journal of Family Law, 15*, 92-113.

Kelly, J. B. (2002). Psychological and legal interventions for parents and children in custody and access disputes: Current research and practice. *Virginia Journal of Social Policy & the Law, 10*, 147-164.

Kelly, J. B. (2005). *Adjustment of Children Following Separation or Divorce: Research Updates and Implications for Practice.* Paper presented at the Association of Family and Conciliation Courts, California Chapter, Sonoma, CA.

Kelly, J. B., & Lamb, M. E. (2003). Developmental issues in relocation cases involving young children: When, whether, and how? *Journal of Family Psychology* (Vol. 17, pp. 193-205). US: American Psychological Assn, US, http:\\www.apa.org.

Kelly, J. B. & Emery, Robert E. (2003). Children's Adjustment Following Divorce: Risk and Resilience Perspectives. *Family Relations, 52*, 352-362.

King, V., & Heard, H. E. (1999). Nonresident Father Visitation, Parental Conflict, and Mother's Satisfaction: What's Best for Child Well-Being? *Journal of Marriage & the Family, 61*(May, 1999), 385-396.

Krauss, D. A., & Sales, B. D. (2000). Legal standards, expertise, and experts in the resolution of contested child custody cases. *Psychology, Public Policy, & Law, 6*(4), 843-879.

Kuehnle, K., Greenberg, L. R., & Gottlieb, M. C. (2004). Incorporating the Principles of scientifically Based Child Interviews Into Family Law Cases. *Journal of Child Custody, 1*(1), 97-114.

Kwong, M. J., Bartholomew, K., & Dutton, D. G. (1999). Gender differences in patterns of relationship violence in Alberta. *Canadian Journal of Behavioural Science, 31*(3), 150-160.

Lamb, M. E., Sternberg, K. J., & Esplin, P. W. (2000). Effects of age and delay on the amount of information provided by alleged sex abuse victims in investigative interviews. *Child Development, 71*(6), 1586-1596.

Lamb, M. E., Sternberg, K. J., Esplin, P. W., Hershkowitz, I. et al. (1997). Assessing the credibility of children's allegations of sexual abuse: A survey of recent research. *Learning & Individual Differences, 9*(2), 175-194.

Leichtman, M. D., & Ceci, S. J. (1995). "The effects of stereotypes and suggestions on preschoolers' reports": Correction. *Developmental Psychology, 31*(5), 758.

Levanas, J. M. (2005). Personal communications. In P. D. Lyn R. Greenberg (Ed.) (email communication). Los Angeles, CA.

Levanas, J. M., Greenberg, L. R., Drozd, L. M., & Rosen, P. (2004, December). *When Allegations of Abuse Arise: Special considerations for minor's counsel.* Presentation at the conference on Minor's counsel in family law, Los Angeles, CA.

Levendosky, A. A., & Graham-Bermann, S. A. (2000). Behavioral observations of parenting in battered women. *Journal of Family Psychology, 14*(1), 80-94.

Leverrette, J., Crowe, T., Wenglensky, R., & Dunbar, J. M. (1997). Judicial Case Management and the Custody and Access Assessment: Melding the Approaches. *Canadian Journal of Psychiatry, 42,* 649-655.

Lussier, G., Deater-Deckard, K., Dunn, J., & Davies, L. (2002). Support across two generations: Children's closeness to grandparents following parental divorce and remarriage. *Journal of Family Psychology* (Vol. 16, pp. 363-376). US: American Psychological Assn, US, http:\\www.apa.org.

Pleck, J. H. (1997). Paternal involvement: Levels, sources, and consequences. In M. E. Lamb (Ed.), *The role of the father in child development (3rd ed.)* (pp. 66-103). New York, NY: John Wiley & Sons, Inc.

Roseby, V., & Johnston, J. R. (1997). High-conflict, violent, and separating families: A group treatment manual for school-age children. In *New York, NY, US: The Free Press (1997) 121 pp.*

Roseby, V., & Johnston, J. R. (1998). Children of Armageddon: Common developmental threats in high-conflict divorcing families. *Child & Adolescent Psychiatric Clinics of North America, 7*(2), 295-309.

Salliday, R. (2004). The State; Last-Minute Legislation Challenged; the governor threatens to veto 'gut and amend' measures. Drastically altering dormant bills is common, but it allows little public scrutiny. *Los Angeles Times,* p. B.6.

Schepard, A. I. (2004). *Children, Divorce and Custody: Interdisciplinary Models for Divorcing Families.* Cambridge, United Kingdom: Cambridge University Press.

Schnider, R. A. (2002). Family Law: The Increasing Involvement of the California Legislature. *Los Angeles Lawyer, March 2002.*

Shuman, D. W. (2002). The Role of Mental Health Experts in Custody Decisions: Science, Psychological Tests, and Clinical Judgment. *Family Law Quarterly, 36*(1), 135-162.

Shuman, D. W., & Sales, B. D. (1998). The admissibility of expert testimony based upon clinical judgment and scientific research. *Psychology, Public Policy, & Law, 4*(4), 226-1252.

Shuman, D. W., & Sales, B. D. (1999). The impact of Daubert and its progeny on the admissibility of behavioral and social science evidence. *Psychology, Public Policy, & Law, 5*(1), 3-15.

Sternberg, K. J., Lamb, M. E., & Dawud-Noursi, S. (1998a). Using multiple informants to understand domestic violence and its effects. In *Holden, George W. (Ed); Geffner, Robert (Ed); et al. Children exposed to marital violence: Theory, research, and applied issues.* (pp. 121-156). Washington, DC.

Sternberg, K. J., Lamb, M. E., & Dawud-Noursi, S. (1998b). Using multiple informants to understand domestic violence and its effects. In G. W. Holden & R. Geffner (Eds.), *Children exposed to marital violence: Theory, research, and applied issues.* (pp. 121-56). Washington, DC, US: American Psychological Association.

Taylor, C. G., Greenberg, L. R., & Doi Fick, L. (2004, December). *Treatment and Management in High Conflict Cases.* Paper presented at the Minor's Counsel in Family Law, Los Angeles, CA.

Walker, L. E. A., Brantley, K. L., & Rigsbee, J. A. (2004). A Critical Analysis of Parental Alienation Syndrome and Its Admissibility in the Family Court. *Journal of Child Custody, 1*(2), 47-74.

doi:10.1300/J190v03n03_07

CONCLUSION

Final Thoughts and Future Direction

Philip M. Stahl

In concluding this volume on relocation, we look to the future with these thoughts:

1. We are part of a mobile society. Families relocate. That is a fact. The question frequently is not "if" but how can it best be done while keeping the child's best interest in mind? How can we best facilitate an environment where a given child has an ongoing relationship with two healthy parents, regardless of where each parent lives?
2. It is important to remember that relocation is a very complex issue. The key to finding the answers in this area of child custody is research. More is needed.
3. Mediation continues to be an important contribution for families of divorce. I hope that mediators find a way to help families resolve their relocation disputes without resorting to evaluators or judges to make decisions for them.
4. Collaborative strategies and collaborative law strategies can also help families prepare for the possibility of a future relocation. It is suggested that all families develop a contingency plan for one par-

[Haworth co-indexing entry note]: "Final Thoughts and Future Direction." Stahl, Philip M. Co-published simultaneously in *Journal of Child Custody* (The Haworth Press, Inc.) Vol. 3, No. 3/4, 2006, pp. 173-174; and: *Relocation Issues in Child Custody Cases* (ed: Philip M. Stahl, and Leslie M. Drozd) The Haworth Press, Inc., 2006, pp. 173-174. Single or multiple copies of this article are available for a fee from The Haworth Document Delivery Service [1-800-HAWORTH, 9:00 a.m. - 5:00 p.m. (EST). E-mail address: docdelivery@haworthpress.com].

Available online at http://jcc.haworthpress.com
© 2006 by The Haworth Press, Inc. All rights reserved.
doi:10.1300/J190v03n03_08

ent's possible relocation when the original Marital Settlement Agreement is developed. At a minimum, I would urge parents to recognize that a potential move might be needed and develop an initial plan for how the parents might resolve any differences that develop as a result of a future move. This could include a statement about using some type of ADR, either mediation or a return to collaboration, if a future move leads to an impasse between the parents. Other parents might agree that stability lies in the children remaining in their community and that the children will not move. In those circumstances, if either parent moves, that parent will have to arrange for his/her access. Given the unlimited scenarios, i.e., distance, age of child, reasons for move, etc., it is hoped that conflict can be reduced if parents agree ahead of time how they might address a parent's request to move during the ongoing minority of the children.

5. Finally, as always, it is my hope that future generations of child custody evaluators, mediators, and judges find new ways to help families resolve their differences, especially when relocation issues surface, and always to do so in a way that minimizes the risk of harm to children.

In conclusion, I want to thank *Journal of Child Custody* editor Leslie Drozd for this opportunity and thank the authors for their excellent contributions. It is my hope and prediction that this volume *will be one that judges, attorneys, child custody evaluators, and mediators turn to for years when the issue of relocation comes up in a given family.*

Index

Page numbers annotated with *n, f,* or *t* indicate notes, figures, or tables.

BOOK ORDER FORM!

Order a copy of this book with this form or online at:
http://www.HaworthPress.com/store/product.asp?sku= 5997

Relocation Issues in Child Custody Cases

—— in softbound at $28.00 ISBN-13: 978-0-7890-3534-9 / ISBN-10: 0-7890-3534-0.
—— in hardbound at $54.00 ISBN-13: 978-0-7890-3533-2 / ISBN-10: 0-7890-3533-2.

COST OF BOOKS ————

POSTAGE & HANDLING ————
US: $4.00 for first book & $1.50
for each additional book
Outside US: $5.00 for first book
& $2.00 for each additional book.

SUBTOTAL ————
In Canada: add 6% GST. ————

STATE TAX ————
CA, IL, IN, MN, NJ, NY, OH, PA & SD residents
please add appropriate local sales tax.

FINAL TOTAL ————
If paying in Canadian funds, convert
using the current exchange rate,
UNESCO coupons welcome.

❑ **BILL ME LATER:**
Bill-me option is good on US/Canada/
Mexico orders only; not good to jobbers,
wholesalers, or subscription agencies.

❑ **Signature** ————————————

❑ **Payment Enclosed: $**————————

❑ **PLEASE CHARGE TO MY CREDIT CARD:**
❑ Visa ❑ MasterCard ❑ AmEx ❑ Discover
❑ Diner's Club ❑ Eurocard ❑ JCB

Account #————————————————

Exp Date————————————————

Signature————————————————
(Prices in US dollars and subject to change without notice.)

PLEASE PRINT ALL INFORMATION OR ATTACH YOUR BUSINESS CARD

Name	
Address	
City	State/Province	Zip/Postal Code
Country	
Tel	Fax
E-Mail	

May we use your e-mail address for confirmations and other types of information? ❑Yes ❑No We appreciate receiving
your e-mail address. Haworth would like to e-mail special discount offers to you, as a preferred customer.
We will never share, rent, or exchange your e-mail address. We regard such actions as an invasion of your privacy.

Order from your **local bookstore** or directly from
The Haworth Press, Inc. 10 Alice Street, Binghamton, New York 13904-1580 • USA
Call our toll-free number (1-800-429-6784) / Outside US/Canada: (607) 722-5857
Fax: 1-800-895-0582 / Outside US/Canada: (607) 771-0012
E-mail your order to us: orders@HaworthPress.com

For orders outside US and Canada, you may wish to order through your local
sales representative, distributor, or bookseller.
For information, see http://HaworthPress.com/distributors

(Discounts are available for individual orders in US and Canada only, not booksellers/distributors.)

Please photocopy this form for your personal use.
www.HaworthPress.com

BOF06